I0082716

THE
ALABAMA HISTORICAL
QUARTERLY

MARIE B. OWEN, Editor

EMMETT KILPATRICK, Co-Editor

Published by the

STATE DEPARTMENT

OF

ARCHIVES AND HISTORY

VOL. 4   NOS. 1 and 2

SPRING AND SUMMER ISSUE
1942

History
of
Coosa County
Alabama

By:
the Rev. George E. Brewer

Southern Historical Press, Inc.
Greenville, South Carolina

This volume was reproduced
from a personal copy located in
the Publishers private library

Please direct all correspondence and book orders to:
SOUTHERN HISTORICAL PRESS, Inc.
PO Box 1267
Greenville, SC   29602-1267

Originally printed: Montgomery, AL 1955
New Material Copyright 2023 by:
          Southern Historical Press, Inc.
ISBN #978-1-63914-138-8
Printed in the United States of America

PREFACE

This history of Coosa County has been reproduced from a revised edition of the *Alabama Historical Quarterly*, published by the State Department of Archives and History Montgomery, Alabama.

Coosa County was created in 1832 from land acquired in the Creek Cession of 1832, and named for the Coosa River which shapes the western boundary of the county. The county seat is Rockford.

In 1900 all court records were destroyed by fire. Marriages and Wills date from 1834; Inventory of Estates from 1897; Orphans Court Records from 1843.

Rev. George E. Brewer

REV. GEORGE EVANS BREWER

Rev. George Evans Brewer was born near Covington, Newton County, Ga., October 31, 1832, and died in 1922 in his ninetieth year and is buried in Notasulga with other members of his family. He was the son of Rev. Aaron G. and Martha (Taylor) Brewer, the former born near Squancum, Monmouth County, N. J.; grandson of George and Rebecca (Schenck) Brewer, both of whom were members of the earliest Dutch families settling in the New Netherlands, a minister in the Protestant Methodist Church, being a member of the Baltimore convention which organized that body; and of George Taylor, a native of Ireland; great-grandson of Lazarus Brewer, of Monmouth County, N. J.; and great-great-grandson of Anneke Jans Bogardus, of New York.

Rev. Mr. Brewer was educated in the country schools and at Robinson Springs Academy, Elmore County. He taught school from 1851 to 1856. In 1856 he was elected superintendent of education of Coosa County, being the first under the new school law and was a member of the House of Representatives from the same county, 1857-59, and a member of the State Senate, 1859-63. In the fall of 1860 he was ordained to the ministry in the Missionary Baptist Church, and served his first pastorate at Wetumpka. In February, 1862, he was elected captain of an infantry company raised in Coosa County, and was first on detached duty at Pensacola, but in June, 1862, was assigned to Co. A., 36th Alabama infantry regiment, C. S. A. With this organization he served until the close of the War Between the States, much of the time in command. He was adjutant-general of Alabama during 1866, but resigned before the close of the year. He then returned to the active ministry, in which he continued without interruption until 1901, when he was appointed to the position of chaplain of convicts, by Gov. Wm. J. Samford, being retained in office by Gov. Wm. D. Jelks. After the expiration of his term in 1907, he again took up his ministerial work. He served as moderator at various times of the Central, the Tuskegee, and the Harris Baptist Associations.

He was a potent influence in the establishment of the School for the Deaf and Blind at Talladega and the hospital for the insane, now Bryce Hospital, at Tuscaloosa.

Mr. Brewer's deep interest in history was manifested by numerous writings both published and unpublished. Among the former was his "History of the Central Baptist Association," (1895) and "History of the 46th Alabama Regiment, C. S. A.," which appeared in *The Montgomery Advertiser*, 1902. He was employed in the State Department of Archives and History for several years, including 1917-18, at which time he wrote the "History of Coosa County" published herewith. The military files of the Department were enriched by voluminous notes from his pen.

He was married December 20, 1854, at Rockford, Coosa County, to Laura Ann, daughter of Judge Isaac Willis and Louisa (McCary) Suttle, of that county. She died in 1914, after a happy marriage lasting sixty years. Children: 1. Sallie Teresa, m. Henry Bradford; 2. Edgar, m. Mary Morgan; 3. Ella Rosa, d. young; 4. Samuel Oscar, m. Ollie Wilkie; 5. George Francis, m. Frances Meredith; 6. Mattie Laura, m. Dr. B. W. Allen; 7. Mamie Louisa, m. Thomas M. Espy; 8. Infant son, deceased; 9. Charles Milford, a Baptist minister, m. Chattie Filliford.

HISTORY OF COOSA COUNTY

Part I

(This work was not undertaken because the writer felt himself competent for it, nor from any expectation of pecuniary reward. On the other hand, such he felt to be his unfitness that with reluctance it was undertaken, and now after much time, labor and personal sacrifice the work is ended he feels ashamed to offer it with its imperfections.

(This work was undertaken at the solicitation of Hon. Thomas McAdory Owen, Director of the "Archives of Alabama," who is indefatigable in his efforts to gather the material for a complete history of Alabama. Being in earnest sympathy with this desire of his, and failing to get the consent of such as were deemed competent to undertake it, the author reluctantly consented to undertake, and has spent more than two years of the leisure at his command in gathering and preparing the facts herein presented.

(Hoping that with all its imperfections it will aid in preserving some facts that ought not to be lost, and may interest some searcher for events of the past, and help to preserve from oblivion those who ought not to be forgotten, it is respectfully offered to my State.

(The author is much indebted for aid to Dr. Owen, to Mr. Brewer's History of Alabama, and Mr. Garrett's histories, "Memorial Record of Alabama." Help has been sought in vain where it could have been rendered. Among those who have given valuable aid are Horatio Robinson, N. A. Green, Hon. Thomas Williams, O. P. Looney, Henry Pond and wife, Jasper McAdory, Stephen D. Ray, Levi Johnson, Mr. and Mrs. John Leonard, W. T. Johnson, H. R. Robbins, Mrs. Moore, of Birmingham, Mrs. Alice Oden, Mrs. Kate Grayson, Mrs. Kirkpatrick, Hon. J. C. Maxwell, Mr. Cabot Lull, Albert Crumpler, and Miss Annie May Clisby, for which the author is grateful.—The Author.)

CHAPTER I

THE ABORIGINEES

The history of any part of America must begin with the Indians, for they were here when the white, cultured, and writing races first reached it. Such history is meagre prior to the discovery by Columbus, for, though they occupied the whole continent, they had no history but vague tradition, and even that did not pretend to answer the question as to when or from where the Indian came to America. Various conjectures have been offered as to their arrival, but some seem absurd, and most of them improbable. The writer has as good a right to present his conjecture as any one else no better informed, and none are acquainted with the real facts.

Some things are recorded in the Bible, the book of books, which are suggestive of thoughts in regard to it. It is told in Genesis, the eleventh chapter, from the first to the ninth verses, that the whole earth was of one language and one speech, and they confederated to build a city and tower which should reach unto heaven, and to make them a name that they might not be scattered abroad upon the face of the whole earth. While they were prosecuting this design, "The Lord said, the people is one, and they have all one language; and this they begin to do; and now nothing will be restrained from them, which they have imagined to do. Go to, let us go down, and there confound their language, that they may not understand one another's speech. So the Lord scattered them abroad upon the face of all the earth; and they left off to build the city." In this account certain facts are established. It was after the flood. The facts are:

1st. The people, all of them, were homogenious, and were one in language and design, and (a fair inference) one in complexion, and with one purpose, to combine for mutual preservation.

2nd. That it was God's purpose to put such difference among them as that instead of remaining combined, they should become repugnant to each other, and scatter, and be separated.

3rd.   That one recorded difference was wrought by God's miraculous power upon them, that of giving difference in language, the object of which was to drive them from each other.

4th.   It is a fact that difference of language is easily overcome, while difference in color, habits, and tastes are not.   While the account does not relate the confounding of feature and complexion at that time, it is a reasonable supposition that it was done then, since they were scattered abroad upon the whole earth.

The thought is supported by the fact that the languages, complexions, and modes of thought and life are similar among those of similar complexions, except as they have been modified by differing circumstances under long existing periods.

5.   That they were scattered over the earth when these differences had been established, and those bearing a likeness are near each other, whether upon the Continents or Islands.

After this, in Genesis 10:25, it is said "the earth was divided."   This evidently does not mean the same thing as the *scattering abroad of the people,* for by God's own appointment the *dry land* was called *earth,* Gen. 1:10.   In the account of the creation it is said, "the waters under the heaven were gathered into one place," and were "called seas," Gen. 1:9, 10.   The earth could not have been divided then as now, for the waters are not in one place now, but divided into oceans, seas, gulfs, and bays, while continents, peninsulas, and other bodies of land separate them.   At the time it is said "the Lord divided the earth," there must have been some great convulsive power exerted by him, the result of which was the division into the continents and islands as we now find the earth.   The thought seems to be supported by the configuration of these divisions.   The shape of the western continent on its eastern side, corresponds to the shape of the eastern continent on its western side, as though once fitted together.   Wherever great bays and seas are found in the continents, not far off are found islands that look as though they had been thrown out of these openings.   The similarity of the inhabitants on these islands to those of the people on the contiguous continents would indicate that those people had wandered off with those of like features and complexion, and had been separated from their kind by the great convulsion. The supposition then would be that the red-men or Indians had been planted upon that part of the earth known as the Western Continent, before it was thrown off from the Eastern in the days of Peleg.

But be the conjecture true or false, the Indians were here when America was first touched upon by the whites, and had occupied it for so many centuries that even tradition faded away into perfect ignorance of when the red-man first became possessor of the soil. For many centuries it had been theirs. Like the races of other colors they had had their times of peace and prosperity——their times of famine and pestilence——their quarrels and wars——small tribes had grown into strong and powerful ones——while some that had once been powerful had become weak, blended into others, or had entirely passed away. Their traditions while not pretending to recite their early origin or early history, yet reached back considerably into the past, and told of many changes that had taken place. But there are neither monuments nor written history upon which to rely until the whites came upon the soil.

The first written history begins with the conquest of Mexico by Cortez, and Peru by Pizarro. That of this country by the invasion of Ferdinand DeSoto, the celebrated Spanish adventurer and general. With a view doubtless of accomplishing something that should equal if not eclipse the splendors of Cortez in Mexico, or Pizarro in Peru, he sailed from the island of Cuba, of which he had been the Spanish governor general, with a well equipped army, and landed at Tampa Bay, Florida, in 1539. From there he moved toward the west until he reached where Tallahassee now stands. From there he moved back in a northeasterly course until he reached what is now Savannah, Ga.; then northward to where Rome, Ga., is; then turned southwestward until he reached the Indian town of Coosa, between the mouths of the Talladega and Tallasseehatchie creeks. Resting here twenty-five days, he moved southeastward until he reached Tallassee on the Tallapoosa River. This was a prominent town, and here he met many of the chiefs and warriors of the natives. He was kindly treated for the twenty days he remained among them. Upon invitation of the powerful Indian king, Tuskaloosa, he moved southwestward to visit him. A few days march brought DeSoto to the king's city, Maubilia, on the Alabama River. But he was not met with hospitality, but a strong force of warriors at once gave him battle. This of course was evidently provoked by the way the Spaniards had forced the Indians into their service as slaves and pack-horses. The battle lasted for hours, and would have resulted fatally to the Spaniards but for the superiority of their weapons. As it was, it was one of the fiercest engagements ever occurring between the whites and Indians, resulting in the death of 2500 brave warriors, and a heavy loss to the Spaniards. From the nature of the country, it is likely that a portion of northern and eastern Coosa was crossed by DeSoto's men in going to Tallassee, and a portion of southern Coosa in the visit to Tuskaloosa. If so, this was the first visit of whites to Coosa.

The next authentic account of whites reaching this county was in 1714, when Bienville, the French governor in this part of America, and the founder of Mobile and New Orleans, came up the river, and about four miles below where Wetumpka now stands, built Fort Toulouse, on the Coosa River. By the cession of this part of their territory to the English by the French, the Fort came into possession of the English, in 1763, and was occupied by them as such, for a time, so that for about 62 years it had been a fortified post for Europeans. The object for its occupancy was for facilitating trade with the Indians, and the protection of the traders. The trade was principally in skins and furs of animals, and in corn. Though the Fort was not in the bounds of Coosa County, it was so near that of course there was passing from there into Coosa. In fact, there was more or less of inter-marriage between the whites and Indians. From these inter-marriages came some families well known as among the most prominent among the Indians after relations became more inti-mate among them. The Weatherfords, Rosses, Ridge, McGilliv-ray, McIntoshes, and Colbert were of English and Scotch blood, and Boudinot, and Leclerc Milfort, and Marchand of French.

Georgia claimed all the territory from its eastern border to the Mississippi as belonging to her under the charter granted to Oglethorpe. As the colony filled with population, the tendency was to continually press westward. The Indians opposed it as trespassing upon them west of the Ocmulgee. The result was frequent clashings between the English settlers and the Indians. So when wars were waged between England and France, the Indians were usually allies of the French. In the war of the Revolution, and that of 1812 to 1814, the Indians were allies of the English as against the colonists, because of this grudge against the encroaching colonists. In 1802, Georgia ceded all her claim to what is now Alabama and Mississippi to the United States. This made it necessary for the United States to send armies of invasion into this territory during the war of 1812-14, to put down the depredations of the warlike Indians. Some of them were, however, friends of the United States, and many of their braves were its allies, fighting against their own people. These Indians were the Muskogees, said to have been the most numerous, brave, and warlike of all the tribes north of the Gulf of Mexico. The Cherokees, Choctaws, and Chickasaws were also in the territory, but the general name of Creeks is applied to all of them, it is thought from the large number of creeks flowing through their country.

General Coffee attacked the Indians, November 3rd, 1813, at Tallassehatchee, now in Calhoun County, and destroyed all the warriors there, 186 in number. November 9th, 1813, General Jackson surrounded the Indians again at Talladega Town. He routed them with the loss of 299 warriors, and a loss to the whites of 15 killed, and 80 wounded. The Indians were again defeated at Hillabee Town, November 18th, by General White, when 60 warriors were killed. General Floyd invaded the country from Georgia about the same time, and built Fort Mitchell in what is now Russell County. From there he marched to Autossee in Macon County, and defeated the Indians, inflicting a loss of 200 warriors. He then fell back to Fort Mitchell. Reinforcing, he advanced to Callebee Creek, where the Indians attacked him, inflicting a heavy loss upon him, though they also suffered a heavy loss. There had been some other victories gained over the

Indians, both north and west. General Jackson had been delayed for want of supplies, but in January he again invaded their country with 900 whites and 200 friendly Indians. On the 22nd of January, 1814, he was attacked near Emucfau Creek, in what is now Tallapoosa County, by 500 Indians. The fight lasted all day, both sides suffering severely, but the Indians were finally driven off. He was suddenly attacked again on January 24th, near Enitochopco, a Hillabee village, as he was retreating toward Fort Strother. His army was at one time in great peril, but the assailants were finally driven off, and Jackson continued his retreat to Ft. Strother.

Having received reinforcements of the 39th U. S. Infantry, and two brigades of Tennessee militia, he moved again into their country and, on March 21st, established Fort Williams, where Fayetteville, Talladega County, now is. On the 27th of March, following the Chapman Road which he had opened, he attacked the Indians in their strong fortifications at Tohepoka, or Horseshoe Bend, on the Tallapoosa River. This was a very severe and bloody battle, the Indians fighting with desperate bravery, though surrounded on all sides by their foes. Five hundred and fifty-seven of their warriors lay dead on the field, and others were shot in trying to escape by swimming the river. Of Jackson's army, 54 were killed and 156 were wounded. The blow was so heavy that it about ended the war, as most of their warriors were dead. April 21st, Jackson returned to Ft. Williams. From there he opened the Jackson Trace that he might move his army to Hickory Ground, an Indian town where Wetumpka now stands. He built a fort on the site of the old French Fort Toulouse, which he called Ft. Jackson, which name it yet bears. This was just one hundred years from the time Bienville built his fort on the same spot. From this fort detachments were sent out to burn and destroy the towns and crops, and kill what remaining warriors could be found. The villages were generally deserted, and what Indians were left were generally suing for peace, for they were without food, and most of their leaders and warriors were dead.

In July, General Jackson having returned to Fort Jackson with authority to treat with the Indians for peace, the treaty was signed by the leading warriors and chiefs August 9th, 1814. The Federal government demanded as remuneration for expenses incurred in the war, a cession of territory embracing all the country claimed by Muscogees west of the Coosa River to the Tombigbee, and south of a line running southeast from the Coosa Falls, where Wetumpka now is, to a certain point on the Chattahoochee just below where the town of Eufaula now is. This opened the way for the whites to about half of the present limits of the State of Alabama. This treaty did not cover that part occupied by Coosa and several other counties of a later period. It was a very important concession from the Indians, and was made with much reluctance, and would not have been granted had they been in condition to resist. The whites rapidly came into this new territory so that there was soon a considerable population gathered upon the soil.

This left still an important part of Alabama in the possession of the Indians, which remained theirs until by a treaty with them, made in 1832, at Cusseta, now in Chambers County, the preliminary negotiations were entered into with the Creeks to cede to the United States all their land east of the Mississippi River. This was accomplished by formally signing the agreement on the part of their leaders at Washington, March 24th, 1832, in the presence of Wm. R. King, Saml. W. Mardis, C. C. Clay, John A. Broadnax, John Tipton, Wm. Wilkins, Saml. Bell, J. Speight, and John Crowell. This treaty gave to the whites all that part of the State now embraced in the counties of Coosa, Talladega, Benton (now Calhoun), Etowah, Cleburne, Tallapoosa, Randolph, Chambers, Lee, Russell, Barbour, Bullock, Macon, and Clay, called for a long time New Alabama.

By the terms of the treaty the Indians were not to be removed except voluntarily. The whites were not to come in as settlers until after the United States should survey the lands, and the personal possession of lands by the Indians be settled. The whites then within this portion were to move out after their crops were gathered, until after such survey and settlement. But the whites, in violation of this agreement, came in, and those already in refused to leave. When the government agents attempted to force their expulsion according to the treaty, there was resistance on the part of the settlers which induced a clash between the Federal and State authorities. Governor Gayle, then governor of Alabama, came to the defense of the settlers about to be removed. He claimed the attempt to be an invasion of the prerogatives of the State on the part of the Federal government, jurisdiction in the matter belonging to the State. Considerable discussion sprang up between him and Lewis Cass, then Secretary of State at Washington. Feeling ran high. The matter was finally settled at Tuscaloosa, during the session of the legislature in the winter of 1833, through conference with that body and a representative of the general government. The settlement agreed upon was that only those settlers were to be removed who were on lands reserved to the Indians, the others to remain undisturbed.

Out of what the Indians regarded as an intrusion on them, and a violation of treaty agreement, as well as through cheating and other bad treatment on the part of some of the whites, some hostility of feeling was engendered, and especially on the part of the young warriors. By 1836 it had spread so far, as to have brought serious apprehension to the minds of the whites as to their security against an Indian massacre. Certain rendezvous had been agreed upon in case of danger. The shooting of Jessee Suttle at his spring in Coosa, and one or two others in different parts of the new territory about the same time, brought about the crisis that resulted in the removal of the bulk of the Indians in August and September of 1836 to the Indian Territory. Some not carried off then were mostly removed in 1843, but as late as 1845, a few were still here to be moved, and Robert M. Cherry was a general agent of the government to contract for their removal from this section. The Franklins, near Rockford, and one or two others were all that were permitted to remain. Thus ended the occupancy of this fair land by a people who for untold centuries had made it their home, their hunting ground, and the place where their bodies were to sleep when green-corn dances,

hunting, and life were over. Here were all their memories——all
their traditions——all that made up life for them——all the graves
of their ancestors——everything that made life dear to them was
here. They had bathed in the beautiful streams——they had wandered over its hills, valleys, and mountains——they had followed
the turkey, deer, buffalo in the hunt——they had played as children——courted as young warriors and maiden——reared their
families——smoked the pipe with friends around their wigwams
——had played ball and other games on their festive days——had
recounted their deeds in the hunt, and on the war-path beneath
its wide-spreading shades and about its cold springs. Ah! how
many precious memories were gathered here for them. But all
was to be left behind, and they were to go far away to a land
unknown to them, beyond the "father of waters," where there was
not a tie to bind, or memory over which to linger, that a place
might be made for strangers who wanted a new home. Is it any
wonder they were loath to leave? Is it any wonder they sat at
times by the hour and brooded over the hardness of their fate,
and the injustice with which they had been treated by the white
man? Is it any wonder that their trust in the fidelity of the
white man to his promises and professed friendship was at a
heavy discount?

The writer has talked with some whites who lived among
the Indians, and shared their friendship and hospitality, and
knew their habits in their homes. All these have borne testi-
mony to their general kindness, except when moved to act dif-
ferently by wrongs inflicted upon them.

Stephen D. Ray, who lived among them from 1814, until
their removal from the country, has written some things of them
that may be of interest here.[1] He thus describes their dress:
"The garb of the men was a hunting shirt that reached to the
knees, with raw-hide leggings that reached to the hips from his
feet. The hair was cut close to the skin of his head, with a roach

---

[1] In Letters in Thomas M. Owen. Feb. 19, 1902.

from his forehead to the back of his neck. He wore no hat. The female dress was a jacket with sleeves, which reached to her hips, and a skirt from her hips to her feet. They went bare-headed, and bare-footed, and their hair floated loose around their shoulders. Their diet, in part, was soup made of corn, parched and then pounded into meal, boiled in an earthen pot. They sat on the ground around the pot, and ate from it with a spoon, one spoon serving for all, as each one would dip by turns and drink. The spoon would hold about as much as a tea cup. There was no salt or other seasoning in the soup.

"These Indians make beasts of burden of their wives. When they go to market among the whites, she carries the produce such as corn, potatoes, berries, fruits or other things in a basket fastened to her shoulders. If he owns a horse he rides and carries nothing. The wife, however, seems to think it an honor to thus wait on her man. The Indian man is the most indolent of human beings. He seems naturally averse to labor. His wife and daughters do all the work on the farm, digging it up, planting, and cultivating it with the hoe, a very poor one at that, while he lies up and sleeps, or is off on the hunt or war-path.

"Their way of approaching the house of a white person is peculiar. When they get in sight of the house and near, they sit down in the road or path, and wait, even for hours, for some one from the house to invite them in. If no one comes, they get up and march on.

"THE GREEN CORN DANCE"

"The Indians hold what we call a Green Corn Dance, once each year, about the time corn gets into the roasting-ear stage. It lasts about three days and nights, and they fast all that time. The chief sits on a raised embankment, with a drum, often made of an earthen pot covered with a raw-hide head, and one stick with which he taps on the drum, while the warriors, some hundreds in number, in single or double file move around him,

dancing and keeping time to his drum. This is an act of religious
worship to the Great Spirit, and a degree of profound solemnity
is observed through all of it. The last day they take the "black
drink," which is a dark tea made from some herb[1], which is very
bitter, and bring on nausea, producing violent vomiting. They
claim this purges from the sins of the past year, and prepares
them to enter the new year clean. This is followed by a feast.
The women come from all directions with baskets loaded with
corn, boiled in the shuck, with pumpkins unpeeled, boiled whole,
other vegetables, with meats, all without salt or other seasoning.
All participate in the feast, and thus ends their most solemn
religious season."

Mr. William Spigener of Wetumpka has a fragment of what
was once a valuable diary of Joel Spigener, one of the pioneer
settlers of Coosa. From this diary there follows a short extract
which properly stands related to this chapter, though it is not a
quotation, but compilation. Spigener tells of an Indian ball play
he attended in company with Charles Bulger, in July, 1833. This
play was about two miles above Hatchesofka Creek, on the Jackson Trace road as afterwards established. These two were the
only whites present. There were more than four hundred Indians. He says he never saw anything to equal the expertness
with which they played. The balls would fly higher than the
tallest pines. The play lasted about six hours. He and Bulger
bet fifty cents on one party, but did not know they had won until
the stake holder handed them the money.

He attended the green-corn dance at Jabouver Town House,
five miles above Wetumpka, in 1834. The name of the presiding
chief was Magilberree. At this dance a young man named Brown
was killed by another young man named Houghton. Brown's
parents lived in Georgia, and Houghton's in Wetumpka.

At the green-corn dance of July, 1835, at Alabama Town,
Joel Spigener and his whole family attended. He says it was a
very solemn religious rite. The Indians insisted on his daughter

_____
[1]Yaupon, to be found in Coosa County.

Eliza and Miss Caroline Paulden, a niece, to participate in the dance. They accepted, and went through the dance just like the Indian squaws. The chief of Alabama Town at the time of this dance was Sukabitchee, or Broadback.

There were a number of Indian towns in and around Coosa County, but some are unknown to the writer. The following are the ones about which something is known. Tuskegee was on the east bank of the Coosa, in the fork of the Coosa and Tallapoosa rivers. This town derived distinction by being visited so early as 1714 by Bienville, and as being the point where he built Fort Toulouse, the first permanent establishment of the whites in the interior of Alabama, from which point trade was so long established between the whites and Indians. Several events took place here which increases the interest investing this historic spot. It was here, in 1722, that the garrison under Captain Marchand, the French commander of the fort, murdered him in a mutiny. Here he was buried. He married Sehoy, princess of the distinguished tribe of the Wind. Their daughter, Sehoy, married Lochland McGillivray, a wealthy and intelligent Scotch trader, from which marriage was born Alexander McGillivray, the noted Indian chief of the Creeks.

This place was visited by Bossu in 1759, who traveled much among the Indians, Spanish, and French, and is the author of "Bossu's Travels." He was sent from Mobile with recruits for Fort Toulouse. Chevalier D'Aubant was to have accompanied him, and to take command of the fort; but being sick could not come with him. Bossu came up the river by boats with his recruits, taking fifty days for the trip. When he reached the fort, D'Aubant had also arrived, reaching it by a horseback route. Bossu remained here some time visiting the surrounding country. He records a speech of a chief made at the fort to other chiefs as follows: "Young men and Warriors! Do not disregard the Master of Life. The sky is blue——the sun is without spots——the weather is fair——the ground is white——everything is quiet on the face of the earth, and the blood of man ought not to be spilt upon it. We must beg the Master of Life to preserve it pure and spotless among the nations around us."

Bossu further says, according to Pickett: "The Creeks and Alabamas were a happy people. They lived with ease, had an abundance around them, and were at peace with the surrounding savages." In this connection Pickett also says of them: "They greeted him (Bossu) with friendly salutations, and offered him provisions, such as bread, roasted turkeys, broiled venison, pancakes baked with nut oil, deer's tongue, together with baskets full of eggs of fowls and turtles. The Great Spirit had blessed them with a magnificent river abounding in fish, with delicious and cool fountains gushing out of the foot of the hills, with rich lands that produced without cultivation, and with vast forests abounding with game of every description."

While Bossu was still at Fort Toulouse, D'Aubant's wife, becoming tired of the long separation from her husband, made her way from Mobile to the Fort. It lacked such comforts as were desired by her, so there was built a separate house for her, with a brick chimney. The remains of this chimney were to be seen until 1850. D'Aubant's wife was said to be a Russian princess, once the wife of a son of Peter the Great. The story is that the prince treated her so cruelly, that she feigned to be dead, was buried, but soon taken up by friends who were in the plot, and was spirited away. She traveled in different parts of Europe. under assumed names. She came to America incognito, and finally reached Mobile. D'Aubant had known the princess in Europe, and recognizing her, was married to her. They both lived at this fort for some years.

While Chievalier D'Arnville was in command of this Fort, a French soldier was killed by an Indian warrior. By agreement between the French and Indians, the killing of one was to be atoned for by the speedy execution of the one doing the killing. D'Arnville demanded this warrior of the chiefs. They claimed to be unable to find him. D'Arnville then arrested the mother of the murderer, as the next of kin, and said her life was to expiate the deed of the son. The chiefs claimed as she had not done the deed, she ought not to suffer the penalty. The commander reminded them of the agreement, and their own custom of taking the next of kin where there was a failure to get the principal. The woman was brought from the fort for execution. The relatives followed sadly, but praising the courage of the mother who marched forth so heroically to her fate. But just as the execution was about to take place, the young warrior burst through the cane, gave himself up and saved his mother. During Bossu's visit there was a reception of the emperor from Cowetta with much pomp by the French and the assembled chiefs of the Creeks at Fort Toulouse. This array of visitors crossed the Tallapoosa at Red Bluff, which was then and has been until recent years a popular crossing place of this river, known to the whites for so long as "Grey's" or "the lower Wetumpka ferry."

Additional interest gathers about this town, for after the battle of the Horse Shoe Bend, General Jackson marched from Ft. Williams, and rebuilt the old fort, giving it the name of Fort Jackson, and here made the treaty by which that part of Alabama west of the Coosa was ceded to the United States, as has been related. Here it was that William Weatherford, one of the noblest and bravest of the Creek warriors, surrendered himself so heroically, as related by Pickett, after having been the leading spirit among the Indians in the war of 1813 and 1814. I will give the story as Pickett relates it, tho some have questioned the correctness of the narrative as given by him. Pickett was on the ground, a resident near by, not many years after the event. He knew personally those who were parties in the event, and used much pains in trying to gather the facts. Here is his account of it: "Finding most of his warriors dead, their towns destroyed, their supplies wasted, and the women and children starving, and wandering homeless, he resolved to appear personally at the American camp. Mounting the splendid gray stud that had carried him so nobly, and for so long in the chase, and along the war-path, he started for the encampment. When within a few miles he saw a fine deer which he killed, and tied behind his saddle. He reloaded his rifle with the intention of killing Big Warrior, if occasion required. When he came to the outpost he inquired for Jackson's whereabouts. The soldier replied to him rudely, but an old man pointed out the General's marque. Weatherford rode up to the entrance where the Big Warrior was sitting, who exclaimed: 'Ah! Bill Weatherford, have we got you at least?' Weatherford fixed his keen eyes upon him, and said in determined tones: 'You traitor, if you give me any insolence, I will blow a ball through your coward heart.' General Jackson came running out of his marque, with Hawkins, and in a furious way exclaimed:

" 'How dare you, sir, ride up to my tent after having murdered the women and children at Fort Mims?'

"Weatherford said: 'General Jackson, I am not afraid of you. I fear no man for I am a Creek warrior. I have nothing to request in behalf of myself; you may kill me if you desire. But I come to beg you for the women and children of the war party, who are now starving in the woods. Their fields and cribs have been destroyed by your people, who have driven them to the woods without an ear of corn. I hope you will send out parties who will safely conduct them here, in order that they may be fed. I exerted myself in vain to prevent the massacre of the women and children at Fort Mims. I am now done fighting. The Red Sticks are nearly all killed. If I could fight you any longer I would most heartily do so. Send for the women and children. They never did you any harm. But kill me if the white people want it done.'

"When he had finished a crowd had gathered around and cried out: 'Kill him! Kill him! Kill him!'

"General Jackson commanded silence, and said: 'Any man who would kill as brave a man as this would rob the dead.'

"He then invited Weatherford to alight, and drank a glass of brandy with him, and entered into a cheerful conversation with the brave warrior in his own marque, and extended his hospitality. Weatherford gave Jackson the deer, and the two soldier became good friends. Weatherford took no further part in the war except to aid in restoring peace." (Pickett, pages 513-14-15.)

When the fort was built by Bienville he had eight cannon mounted on it. When the fort was abandoned, these pieces were spiked, mutilated, and left on the ruins. Some of these old pieces were carried to Montgomery, one to Wetumpka, and one to Rockford, and were used for firing salutes on the 4th of July and other occasions. Once in Montgomery, at the celebration of the election of John Quincy Adams as president, Ebenezer Pond was firing the salute when the piece burst, and came near killing Pond. The remains of one is now at the capitol. The ones at Wetumpka and Rockford were both burst in firing salutes[2].

It will be seen that this fort on the border of the Coosa has been rich in historic incidents surpassed by no other in the interior of the State.

Another Indian town in the limits of Coosa, located in the flat in the southern part of Wetumpka, was Hickory Ground. It was here, in 1745, that the Scotch trader, Lochland McGillivray, married the Indian princess Sehoy, daughter of Captain Marchant. After his marriage to her, he did business both here and at Little Tallassee, and accumulated quite a fortune.

Colonel Tait, a handsome, courteous, and popular English officer of the British army, was stationed here for a time in 1778, to keep favor with the Creeks, and hold them in alliance with the British during the Revolutionary War.

---

[2]Now in Military Room, World War Memorial Building.

In 1781, a party of Americans from about Natchez, Miss., numbering about one hundred men, women, and children, led by Colonel Hutchins, came to Hickory Ground. They sympathized with the British, and were in danger about Natchez because the opposers of British rule had obtained the ascendency there. They were trying to make their way to Savannah, Ga. They had wandered at times much out of the way. When they had reached the vicinity of where Birmingham now stands, they became afraid to venture among the Cherokee Indians, and turning from the mountains southeasterly, made their way toward Hickory Ground. One of the party was a Mrs. Dwight, who on at least two occasions during their trip, had proved herself quite a heroine. They came to the Coosa River about twenty miles above Hickory Ground and hesitated about what to do. Mrs. Dwight urged upon them to cross the river and pursue their way, and leading herself, they crossed partly by fording and partly by swimming. When they came to the town McGillivray was away. The Indians took them for a party of Georgians, who were hated by them, and so threatened to destroy them. The party begged earnestly for mercy, and disclaimed being Georgians, telling their story of escape from Natchez, and their efforts to reach the English at Savannah. The Indians, intent on their destruction, would have accomplished it but for a ruse practiced by a smart Negro body servant of McGillivray, named Paro, who was present. The Indians told the party they would not believe their story unless they "could make the paper talk," that is, by a written statement. The Negro, Paro, learned their story. He could speak English while the Indians could not. Getting some paper from one of the Hutchins party, he pretended to read from it the story of their flight, how they had suffered, and were then badly bruised up and worn out, and were only trying to get among their own people. When they heard the paper talk corroborating what had been said, the Indians gladly received them, fed them, and cared for them until, rested and refreshed, they were permitted to go on their way.

In April, 1790, Colonel Willett, representing the United States, visited Hickory Ground. He was sent by General Washington, then president, from New York, on a secret errand to McGillivray for the purpose of securing a visit from him to New York, in the hope of inducing him to treat more readily there with the United States, in behalf of his people. Willett moved cautiously and with tact arranged for a meeting with McGillivray. He came from New York to Charleston, and then worked his way on through the settlements and wilderness, until he met McGillivray at Graison's, a white man, ten miles from Fish Pond town. They stayed all night at Graison's, and came the next day to Fish Pond, where the Indians honored him with a national dance. From there they came to Hickory Ground, one of McGillivray's residences. From here Willett visited several Indian towns, and the ruins of old Fort Toulouse. His mission was successful in getting McGillivray to New York, where a favorable treaty was made between the government and Creeks through him.

There was another town, Little Tallassee, four miles above Wetumpka, on the farm afterwards owned by Howell Rose, and not far from where he afterward built his house near the Turnpike. This town also had incidents of interest occurring about it. The wealthy Lochland McGillivray had one of his principal stores here, and after making it the center of an extensive trade, he took up his principal residence here, and reared his family. Here his son was born, who afterward became the celebrated Alexander McGillivray, king and leader of the Creek nation. Being the birth place of such a man would have immortalized it had nothing else taken place in it. He was born here in 1746. At an early age his father received the consent of Sehoy, his wife, to send A'exander to Charleston to be educated. Among Indians the wife has control of their children during minority. The youth learned rapidly, and returned a well educated man. His father proposed to make a merchant of him, and sent him to Savannah to learn about conducting mercantile affairs. His tastes were not in that line, but his stay there in Charleston was of great advantage to him in his subsequently chosen career. Returning to Little Tallassee while yet quite a young man, the condition of things was such that it suited the Creek nation to make him king by right of his mother's position among the tribes. He was born with a very superior mind, and it had been very carefully cultivated. He was dignified, graceful, courteous, of broad views, but fully Indian in feeling. He was possessed of that quality, owned by few, the instinctive power to command. He was brave, but his ruling characteristic was diplomacy of which he was a master. He will compare favorably with the most brilliant minds in that glittering galaxy.

During the Revolutionary War he was an ally of the British with the rank and pay of a colonel. When the Spaniards possessed Mobile and Pensacola they gave him the rank and pay of a colonel. The difficulties between the Georgians and Indians induced Washington to send for McGillivray, in 1790, to come to New York, where he was given the rank of a Brigadier, and a stipend of $1200 a year to consent to the sale of an extensive tract of land to the Georgians for a small sum to be paid to the Indians. This aroused the fears of the Spaniards who wished the trade of the Indians, and their alliance in case of war. They gave him the same rank, and increased the pay from $1500 to $3500, to render ineffective his agreement made with Washington. Several of the fine letters of diplomacy written by him about this period, which showed his consummate skill as a diplomatist, were sent from Little Tallassee. Perplexed by the complications into which his duplicity had involved him, he died in Pensacola, February 17th, 1793, and is buried there.

Little Tallassee was also the home of Leclerc Milfort for a period of twenty years, from 1776 to 1796. He was a Frenchman of courage, ability, culture, and military skill. He came to Little Tallassee and married a sister of McGillivray, a beautiful Indian princess. Such was Milfort's skill and influence over the warriors that he led them in most of the battles fought, especially with the Georgians, while his brother-in-law looked after the general affairs of the nation. In 1796, Milfort returned to France, and was made a General of Brigade by Napoleon. He afterward wrote an account of his stay among the Indians, called "LaNation Creek."

Colonel Willett, while on the visit to McGillivray in 1790, also came to Little Tallassee, and stayed for some time in his nice home at this place. Here he was feasted sumptuously on fish, venison, strawberries, and mulberries. From here, on May 12th, 1790, McGillivray and Milfort set out to meet the great council which had been called to convene at Ositchy on the 17th of May, 1790.

Wewoka Town was on Wewoka Creek, fifteen miles above Wetumpka. No incidents of interest are known in connection with it.

Alabama Town was in the Knight and Whetstone neighborhood, west of Buyckville. At this town Joel Spigener and his family attended a Green Corn Dance.

Kialigee Town was near Kialigee Creek, not far from where the road between Wetumpka and Alexander City runs. This town was burned by the war party during the war of 1813 and 1814, because those living there were friendly toward the whites.

Thottolulgau, or Fish Pond Town, was a few miles north of Nixburg, not far from where Mr. Tuck lived. It has been stated elsewhere that Colonel Willett and McGillivray were honored on their visit here with a national Indian dance in 1790. This town gave name to Fish Pond Church, one of the first organized in Coosa County, and that has maintained its organization to the present. It sided with the anti-missionaries in the split.

Opillowan, or Swamp Town, was on Swamp Creek, twenty miles from the Coosa River. No incidents of interest connected with this town are known.

Pochusowan Town was on Hatchett Creek.

There was a town near Rockford, less than a mile west, where a noted chief, Redmouth, lived at the time and after the organization of the county. His name is preserved in that of Redmouth branch. T. J. Pennington now owns and lives on the site of the town. Redmouth was an intelligent, wealthy, and friendly Indian, whose Indian name was Choak-Chart-Hadjo. His will is the first on record in the book of wills for Coosa County, made March 6th, 1834.

Pumpkin Town was near where Weogufka Creek enters Hatchett. This was the town of which the white man, Clark, was nicknamed chief.

Salonoby Town was in the neighborhood east of Nixburg, and gave name to the Salonoby Creek.

Weogufka Town was on the creek of the same name, in what was the Lindsey plantation, near where Weogufka Church has so long stood.

There was a town 12 miles north of west from Rockford, near the Fixico Mining Company's location. Some signs are still to be seen. The mining company now doing business there takes its name from Konip Fixico, a chief.

There are signs of a town 6 miles west of Rockford, near where Jacob Bently lived, from which some bullets, burnt corn well preserved, and other relics have lately been taken.

On the place owned by John Ward, on Jacks Creek, there are indications of a town, from which relics have been taken in 1886 and since, exposed by the washings of the creek in the great flood of 1886. Some of these belonging evidently to English soldiers, indicating a date corresponding to the war with the Yamessees, when they were driven from South Carolina as far west as Alabama.

These are all the towns of the Indians known to the writer, or of which he has been able to learn.

There were a few whites scattered in different parts of the county, living among the Indians before the organization of the county, but the names and locations of but few are known. Greenberry Clark lived at Pumpkin Town, living and dressing like the Indians. He was nicknamed by the whites after they came in, as *the Chief of Pumpkin Town*. He afterwards became a constable among the whites. Alexander and John Logan, brothers, lived among them, probably in the neighborhood of Hatchett Creek, above Rockford. Eli, Jessee, and Adam Harrell were in the Oakchoy neighborhood, above Nixburg. Eli had been a Barbe business man. Kirk Gray and a Mr. Hobdy were out southeast of Nixburg. Solomon Robbins, Wm. H. Weaver, and Larkin Cleveland with his sons, Joseph, Benjamin, Robert, David, and Harvey, were at Nixburg or near it before or about the time of the organization of the county. James Lindsey was in the Hanover neighborhood. Archibald Dowling and Wm. A. Wilson were in Marble Valley. Washington Campbell and William Lovelady were near where Eclectic now stands. Albert and Robert Armstrong, Joel Spigener, and Thomas and James Wall were near where Buyckville now is at the time of the county's organization. W. H. Ray and Nancy Kennedy were just below Rockford at an early day. The Chapmans, Goodgames, and Lauderdales were about Sockapatoy quite early. John Underwood was a blacksmith among the Indians, and had his shop near where the Turnpike crosses Hatchett Creek. Jack McNeily was also one among the Indians in the neighborhood of Shelton Creek, on the road from Rockford to Syllacogga. Mr. Kibbler had a store near the Coosa and Talladega line, not far from A. B. Nicholson's place above Goodwater.

CHAPTER II

EARLY SETTLEMENT, ORGANIZATION, ACTS OF EARLY
COURTS, OPENING ROADS, ETC.

In 1819, Alabama had been admitted as one of the States
of the Federal Union. That part of its territory ceded by the
Indians in 1814, was becoming fairly well settled by the whites
in the middle part by 1830. Autauga was bordering Coosa at
this time, and was separated from it by the Coosa River. Many
had settled on the elevated lands near the river, the Halls, Elmores, Robinsons, Jackson, House, Fitzpatrick, Grahams, Steele,
Rose, Debardelabans, Tatums, McNeil, Spigeners, Zeiglers, Stou-
denmires, Whetstones, and many more, from among whom a
number became prominent in public life. But east of the river
there were few, because the land belonged to the Indians until
the Cusseta treaty, March 24th, 1832, when they ceded all that
had not been ceded in 1814. These newly acquired lands, tho
within the limits of the State, had not been organized into counties. This was done by an Act approved December 18th, 1832,
making it into the counties of Coosa, Talladega, Benton (Calhoun), Randolph, Tallapoosa, Chambers, Russell, Macon, and
Barbour. The Act as it relates to Coosa says: "Be it further en-
acted, That all that tract of country bounded as follows, to-wit:
Beginning at the Montgomery line at or near Wetumpka Falls
on the Coosa River, thence running up said river to the line dividing Coffee's from Freeman's surveys; thence east along said
line until it intersects with the township line dividing ranges 20
and 21; thence south along said line until it reaches the three mile
stake of township 18; thence west to the Montgomery corner;
thence west along said line to the beginning; which shall form
and constitute one separate and distinct county to be called and
known by the name of Coosa."

By an Act approved January 12th, 1833, Washington Campbell and Archibald Downing were appointed commissioners for
the county. On the same day was another Act fixing the time for
holding Coosa County courts on the first Mondays in June and
November. Another Act of the same day established the election

precincts at the houses of Archibald Downing and Washington Campbell.

The growth of Wetumpka demanded greater limits by 1837, so that the boundary line between the counties was changed by Act of the legislature in 1837, so as to give Coosa the depth of a section southward taken from the northern part of Montgomery, beginning where the line between sections 23 and 24, T. 18, R. 18 crosses the river, and running six miles east. Then a similar strip of one mile deep and six miles long was taken from the southern part of Coosa, and given to Montgomery.

The county lies near the center of the State and was bounded originally by Tallapoosa on the east, Montgomery on the south, Autauga on the west, and Talladega on the north. February 15th, 1866, Elmore County was formed, and the boundary was again changed. Elmore was taken from Coosa, Tallapoosa, Autauga, and Montgomery. All that part of Coosa lying south of the township line running between Townships 20 and 21 from the Coosa River eastward to the Range line running between Ranges 20 and 21, or the Tallapoosa line, was given to Elmore. From that time the southern boundary of Coosa has been the Township line between Townships 20 and 21. The county since the new organizations is bounded east by Tallapoosa; south by Elmore; west by Chilton; and north by Talladega and Clay. This change removed much of the wealth, population, and historical part of Coosa, and added it to Elmore. Under its first limits it contained about 1,000 square miles, under the new about 660.

There were no roads but Indian trails in the county. What has since been known as the Jackson Trace follows mainly the road opened by General Jackson in 1814 to facilitate his march from Ft. Williams near Fayetteville, Talladega, to Ft. Jackson below Wetumpka; and the Chapman Road opened by him earlier, when he went from Ft. Williams to invade the Indians in Tallapoosa. It is called the Chapman Road because the father of John A. Chapman was in charge of the pioneer corps under Jackson who opened it. Though there was travel along them as trails, they were not kept up as roads. The old Georgia Road must have been opened by the movers who came in so rapidly from Georgia and the Carolinas, for it was a public highway before the Commissioners began to open roads.

By an Act approved January 9th, 1833, James Lindsey, Joseph B. Cleveland, and Robert W. Cleveland were authorized to open a road from the lower end of the Wetumpka Falls to the store of Joseph B. Cleveland at Sylacauga. They were allowed two years to open and complete it. When completed and kept in order, they were allowed to collect toll; for four wheel carriages 75 cts., two wheels 50 cts., man and horse 12½ cts., loose or pack-horse 6¼ cts., for hogs, sheep, or goats 3 cts. per head. A forfeit of three times the toll could be collected of anyone trying to evade the toll. They were to forfeit the right to collect toll if the road was not kept in order. Their franchise was to last fifteen years. This road is the "Turnpike."

The physical features of Coosa differ very much in different parts. A description of these varying parts will be attempted. A high range of hills, almost mountains, rises out of the narrow level bordering the river in which the business buildings of Wetumpka are mostly located. They are rugged but covered with trees, which makes them a pretty background for the picture of the town. On their steep sides, from the first, a number of people have had their homes, looking quite picturesque nestling among the rich foliage which grows profusely on their steep sides. This range of hills extends from here to the Tallapoosa River though not everywhere so steep, and nowhere else so rocky. They have furnished a fine quantity of trees for lumber. To the north of this range, and from a line nearly east and north of Wetumpka there sets in a gently rolling section of country, and sometimes for miles almost level. The soil here is light and sandy, with streaks of pebble. Some places it has a good subsoil. All this was once covered with a fine pine forest. There is still a good deal of timber, but nowhere in large bodies now. Until since the introduction of commercial fertilizers these lands were not generally esteemed and sold at low prices. They are now very valuable, and production exceeds that of land once deemed so much better. There are many branches and small creeks of pretty clear water rippling over pebbly beds. Springs abound along the streams, and their borders are rather marshy, heavily fringed with bays, magnolias, laurel, ivy, gums, poplars, beeches, water and other oaks, and with rich evergreen vines, bamboo, jasmine, muscadine, and other vines. In the spring many of these trees and shrubs are laden with blooms that fill the air with fragrance, and are beautiful to look upon. In the dry seasons the sand drinks up the water so as to make the streams dry, or almost so.

The principal ones in this section are Corn Creek, Four Mile or Taylors, Yellow-water, Steep, Town, Hatchesofka, Hatchechubbee, Tunkehatchie, Little Wewoka, and Chaneyhatchie. Corn, Taylors, and Yellow-water are short, rising in what was the lower part of the county, flow westerly into the Coosa. Hatchesofka and Wewoka rise not far from Brooksville, and flow southwestward to the Coosa. Hatchesofka had Roger's, Smith's and another mill in the neighborhood of Gun's, upon it. The hills bordering it are large. Town Creek was west of Buyckville, and had Knight's mill upon it. It ran southwest into the Coosa. Hatchechubbee and Tunkehatchie rise about Central and Eclectic, and flow southeasterly into the Tallapoosa. Chaneyhatchie rises about Central, and flows nearly east to the Tallapoosa.

From this belt the surface becomes more broken; gradually the hills become steeper, until in the northern part of the county, and especially between Hatchett and Weogufka creeks they rise almost to the dignity of mountains. The soil is more varied in this portion, being generally more free from sand, and of a darker gray color with a clay subsoil. There are streaks of red and mulatto soil, with occasional pieces of sandy pine land. This whole region has more or less rock, flint, granite, slate, and dark gray stones. The eastern part of the county is not so broken, and is more productive. Along the streams are some very rich bottoms, and among the mountains are some very rich coves. The north sides of the steep hills are usually much richer than the south sides. Streams are numerous, and constant, fed by springs of water so cool that ice is not needed in summer to make them refreshing. The wells also of this section are likewise abundant in delightfully cold water.

Some of the rock is utilized in making fences, building chimneys and sometimes houses, and is easily put into shape for use. These rocks render cultivation more difficult, and make the roads rougher, and more unpleasant in traveling. Yet this rocky portion was more rapidly settled up, and farms paid a better profit in the early period of the country. Larger farms were opened, and the heaviest slave population was to be found in the eastern part, also better homes, schools, and churches. In this upper part of the country there was much very fine pine timber, but there was short leaf pine in parts, and more oak of different varieties with hickory, poplar, beech, chestnut, walnut and other varieties of hardwoods.

Some of its streams were bordered by fine rich bottoms, but others had the hills jutting in close to the stream. This is especially true of Hatchett. The principal creeks of the upper part of Coosa were the Salonoby, Oakchoy, Kowalija, Elkahatchie, Sockapatoy, Swamp, Wewoka, Jacks, Hatchemadega, Hatchett, Weogufka, Peckerwood, Finnicotchkee, and Point. Hatchett is quite a large stream even where it enters Coosa from Clay, near Goodwater. It is a hundred or more miles long, and carries a large volume of water that makes it difficult to bridge successfully. It could furnish water power for propelling a vast amount of machinery. It is so hedged in by high hills as to furnish but little bottom land. Weogufka is also a large stream rising in Talladega County. It is also bordered by high hills except in its first entrance into Coosa County where there is some bottom and moderately level land along its border. After entering the hills it has more bottom land than Hatchett. These two creeks run almost parallel from northeast to southwest across the county, and between them is the highest range of hills in the county, called the Weogufka Mountains.

Swamp Creek is also a large stream, rising about and above Nixburg, but is rapidly fed by a number of larger branches and small creeks so that it soon assumes good proportions, running into Hatchett north of what is known as the Devil's Half Acre. The Weogufka runs into Hatchett a few miles below where Swamp enters, so that by the time Hatchett reaches the Coosa

River it has the proportions itself of a river. Wewoka rises in the neighborhoods of Nixburg and Brooksville, draining a scope of country so abounding in springs that it soon takes on good size and where it crosses the Trace is a large stream. On Hatchett Creek are a number of mills. A long while ago there was a mill not far from Brownville, but the first one positively known to the writer was Samuel Pruett's, below Goodwater. Below this, J. C. Jones built at different times several mills before the creek crossed the Turnpike. At the Turnpike, John Sears and George McEwen had a good mill from about 1856. There had been a mill at the same site much earlier, but it washed away and the site was unused for years. Below, William Chancellor had one, and below that was the Shaffer mill, now owned by Lawson. There are others below, but only Hardy's is positively known. How many were on Weogufka is not known, except one near Mt. Moriah. Swamp was noted for mills, Robinson's, Parker's, Crumpler's, Holly's, Horton's, and Conoway's all being along it in the order named. Wewoka also had mills along it from near Brooksville, the first being O'Harra's, afterward Austin's, another, Curligh's, before reaching the Turnpike, Cox's and Lykes' from there to the Trace, and perhaps one or more below.

Kowaliga, of which the Salonoby and Oakchoy are branches, has its rise in the country east and north of Nixburg, and gathers volume so fast that by the time it crosses the county line it is a large stream and on its branches were Johnson's, Hardy's, and Hagerty's mills. It is a large stream with fine bottom lands. The Indian town of Kowaliga was near where Big and Little Kowalija unite. Elkahatchie has its rise east and south of Sockapatoy, and drains a broad scope of country by numerous small streams, which soon make it a large creek which has a southeasterly flow to the Tallapoosa as also Kowaliga has. The country drained by it was the richest part of Coosa, occupied by a number of well-to-do farmers. Sockapatoy Creek rises around Sockapatoy and Goodwater, and runs southwest through a rich though hilly and rocky country, emptying into Hatchett opposite to Hanover. Bradford's mill and factory were upon it. Peckerwood Creek is formed by streams from the northern part of Coosa, and the southern part of Talladega, and flows westerly near the northern boundary of Coosa, emptying into the Coosa River just below Talladega Springs. It has some good land along it. Tooney had a good mill on it. Paint Creek drains the northwestern part of the county, running southwesterly into the Coosa. There are other creeks in different parts of the county, some of pretty good size, but the ones named are the principal streams, except the broad and beautiful Coosa River which runs the whole western length of the county.

The following description of the country by an eye witness while the matter was fresh upon his mind, taken from a letter of Joel Spigener, written to Wm. K. Oliver, a brother-in-law in South Carolina, June 3rd, 1833, will be interesting here. He says: "Should I determine to settle in the Creek Nation, I think it advisable for you all to move out next spring. However, upon this subject I will write you in the future more particularly. About ten days ago I returned from exploring the Creek Nation. I saw there a beautiful, healthy, and fertile country. The country affords many beautiful millseats, and the best springs my eyes ever beheld. The range is good, and in many places inexhaustible. It is generally a well watered and healthy country, but like all other nations and climes there are objections, viz: It is generally a rocky, gravelly, and mountainous country——parts of it too far from market. The fertile lands are generally in too small bodies ——though upon the whole I think it is a very fine poor man's country. I like the country so well that I expect to go back in about a month. The greatest objection I have to settling there now is, you are compelled to play squat, that is to set down upon government lands. It is not known yet when they will be offered for sale."

Again, August 26th, 1833, he writes telling Oliver he had selected in the Nation places for himself, Oliver, and all the others, and says, "the land will produce from 600 to 1000 lbs. of cotton per acre, and from 15 to 30 bushels of corn." At that time and for years afterward, up in the fifties, there was but little undergrowth, for the Indians burned off the woods in the spring, which killed the bushes, leaving only the larger timber. The whole country was covered with grass, wild pea-vines, and cane, making rich pasturage for game, cattle, and horses. The cane which at first grew so profusely along the stream, and in many places on the uplands also, eventually died out, said by the old settlers to have just gone to seed. Up till the fifties the whites used to keep up the practice of burning off the woods in the spring, notice being given to interested neighbors when fire would be put out, so they might guard their fences. Keeping down the underbrush made it easy to ride through the woods and to see game, or cattle at a distance.

Game was very abundant, both large and small, and the early settlers were able to keep their tables well supplied with the meat of bear, deer, and turkey. As late as in the fifties deer were still right common, and even now, in the northwestern part, occasionally a hunter gets a deer. Wild turkeys, though scarce, now are yet to be had. Perhaps no part of the State had a better supply of fine timber both of the yellow pine and also hardwoods.

Campbell, Lovelady, and Downing, who were appointed commissioners for Coosa County by Act of the Legislature, and were by the Act authorized to purchase 160 acres of land for locating a court house, and to levy a tax for buildings, did nothing toward organization. This delay was caused by the clash between Governor Gayle of Alabama and the Federal government about the white settlers coming into the new territory contrary to the terms of the treaty with the Indians. This trouble was not settled until December of 1833, so the real organization of the county was not effected until 1834. There is no record showing how the first judge of the County Court was appointed, but Robert W. Martin was the first judge appearing on any records. By an Act of the Legislature approved November 28th, 1833, Alfred Mahan, Larkin Cleveland, Simeon Chapman, and George Taylor were appointed Commissioners for Coosa County to locate, in connection with the county judge, the seat of justice and acquire by purchase or otherwise 160 acres of land to be laid off in suitable lots, to be sold at public sale after thirty days notice in two public newspapers, reserving such lots as would be needed for public buildings. It was required that the place was to be called

Lexington, and was to be in eight miles of the center of the county. They were also required to have an election held at the precincts, on the second Monday in February, 1834, for a sheriff, clerk of circuit court, clerk of county court, an assessor and tax colletor, and four commissioners of roads and revenues for the county. On the same day, Asbury Coker was appointed by an Act to take the census of the county.

On the 16th day of January, 1834, an Act was approved authorizing the commissioners to select 160 acres for a county site under the grant of Congress, made in May, 1824.

Election precincts were established at the houses of Solomon Robbins, Hugh McMillan, George Taylor, and Thomas Walstin, by an Act approved January 18th, 1834.

In the absence of records it is presumable that the Judge of the county court had been appointed by the Governor, and that the election provided for in the Act of November 28th, 1833, was held, and the commissioners elected were: John A. Chapman, Larkin Cleveland, Thomas Lowery, and Jared B. Townsend; and Albert C. Mahan, clerk of the county court. The first record book of the county shows these names: A. R. Coker was sheriff, J. P. Daniel, circuit clerk.

The first records of the county show that a session of the commissioners court, in its first term, was held at Lexington in May, 1834, and that Robert W. Martin was County judge; A. C. Mahan, county clerk; and John A. Chapman, Larkin Cleveland, and Thomas Lowery, the commissioners that were present. At this term they appointed Gideon B. Benton as coroner; R. W. Cleveland, county surveyor; Thomas W. Walden, auctioneer; and Francis M. Hamilton, county treasurer. This is the only business recorded as being done at this session. This is from the records of the Commissioners Court of Coosa County, as filed in the Probate-office of the county. And what follows in regard to public roads and other matters are taken directly from the records of that office.

The next term of this court was held August 19th, 1834, when a public road was ordered to be opened from Bait's Ferry on the Coosa River, the nearest and best route to the county line of Coosa and Talladega to Talladega Town. Wm. A. Wilson, Thompson Coker, Abram Chancellor, Henry Logan, Archibald Downing, John Thomas, and John Cameron were appointed reviewers to mark out the road, and make return to the next term of court. This road still exists and is called the Bait's Ferry Road.

This same term of the court ordered the opening of a public road beginning at the county line in the town of Wetumpka, and run then in a straight direction to the county line of Talladega County, at or near Thompson Coker's. James Williams, George Lowery, John S. Baits, Enoch Autrey, Jessee M. Wilson, Albert Armstrong, and Joshua Monk were appointed the reviewers. This road is what is known as the Jackson Trace.

The same term ordered opening a public road beginning at the county line in Wetumpka, and thence in a straight direction to strike the county line of Talladega County at or near Kibbler's old store. The reviewers were Charles Williams, George Lewis, David Lauderdale, James Spraggins, Solomon Robbins, Adam Harrell, and George Taylor. This is the road known as the Sockapatoy Road. A. R. Coker, sheriff, was required to serve notice on those appointed.

At the December term of the court, Joseph B. Cleveland was appointed treasurer in lieu of F. M. Hamilton, who had resigned. At the same term of the court there is a notice that at the May term Thomas Walden, Alexander Black, and John McKenzie were appointed commissioners of the sixteenth section of Township 23, R. 20, but the court being informed of the removal of Walden and McKenzie from the county, Josephus Lauderdale was appointed vice McKenzie, and Charles Nix vice Walden.

At the February term, 1835, John Goodgame was appointed overseer of the poor for beat 4. The following sums were ordered paid the parties named for services from February, 1834, to February, 1835; A. R. Coker, sheriff, $50.00; J. P. Daniel, Circuit clerk, $50.00; A. C. Mahan, clerk, county court, $25.00; Geo. W. Jones, county bailiff, $6.00; J. A. Chapman, court bailiff, $4.50. This court also appointed William H. Ray a commissioner in lieu of Jared B. Townsend. George Lewis, A. C. Mahan, and Daniel Robbins were appointed overseers on different parts of the Sockapatoy Road; and Michael Reynolds on the River Road.

At the May term, 1835, the county tax was ordered to be raised from fifty per cent of the State tax to one hundred per cent. This term also ordered the opening of a public road from Rockford to the county line in a straight direction to the Tallapoosa court house; and Fanch Cleveland, John Gilliard, James Goggans, George A. McDaniel, Wm. Patterson, George Melton, and T. T. Wall were appointed reviewers. A new road was also ordered from Rockford to the county line at Samuel Lovejoy's, with Joseph Ray, James B. Morris, Adam Harrell, Jessee Bradshaw, Archibald Kimball, Samuel Lovejoy, and William Weaver as reviewers. Also another from Rockford to House's Ferry on Coosa River, with J. P. Daniel, R. W. Martin, W. H. Ray, A. R. Coker, G. A. McDaniel, T. T. Wall, and A. B. Hamilton reviewers. Also one from Rockford to Sockapatoy, and from thence to the nearest and best route to the county line, in a straight direction to the Randolph court house, with John Smith, E. F. Heard, James Spraggans, Davis Campbell, John Gilliard, Fanch Cleveland, and John A. Chapman to Sockapatoy; and from Sockapatoy to the county line, William Winslett, Charles Williams, Charles Nix, Isaac Lamb, Josephus Lauderdale, A. S. Elly, and Stephen Shelton the reviewers. This court appropriated $125.00 for the purchase of books of record for the county. This court also appointed as managers of elections, at Rockford: T. T. Wall, Fanch Cleveland, and G. A. McDaniel; in beat 3, Wm. A. Wilson, Abram Chancellor, and John D. Wilson; at Moore's Store, Wm. Richards, George Allen, and Russell Joes; and at Williams' Ferry, James A. Wall, Isaac P. Pond, and Joel Spigener.

It will be noticed that several of the new roads ordered were to start from Rockford. This was because Rockford had become the county site, and Lexington had been abandoned as such since 1834. Lexington was on the south side of Hatchemadega Creek in what afterward became a part of Albert Crumpler's plantation.

The writer is not informed as to whether the county ever had any buildings there or not, or where the courts held their sessions. The sessions of the Commissioners Court for 1834 were held there, and the spring and fall terms of the Circuit Court for 1834. The commissioners records do not show how the change was made, but from an Act of the Legislature, approved January 9th, 1835, it would appear that the commissioners had made the change, and had chosen Rockford for its county site. The Act referred to, approves the act of the Commissioners Court of Coosa County, by which Rockford was made the seat of justice for the county. From then on it has held its place, and these roads were to make it accessible.

No record has been seen of the sale of the lots at public outcry if such ever took place. The first record of a deed to a lot in Rockford was made on the 9th of February, 1837, to Dr. John S. McDonald, by the commissioners court.

At the August term of the commissioners court for 1835, George W. Melton was allowed one dollar a day for two days, for carrying the chain in the survey of the town lots of Rockford. Joel Spigener was appointed county surveyor in lieu of J. B. Cleveland who had left the county. Another new road was ordered from Rockford to the James Williams Ferry on the Coosa, and James Williams, George Lowery, Wm. A. Wilson, Abram Chancellor, Daniel B. Dennis, Archibald Downing, and Joshua Monk were appointed reviewers.

At the adjourned term of the court held on August 16th, 1836, it was ordered that one-fourth the present assessment of tax be appropriated for support of the poor. Wm. Robertson was allowed ten dollars per month for keeping one pauper. This court ordered a new road from Thompson Coker's running south to House's Ferry on the Coosa. The reviewers were Wm. Maherg, Nathan Coker, Allen Wood, John Looney, Enoch Autrey, Archibald Downing, and A. J. Cameron. Also one from Funderberg's Ferry to the county line in the direction of West Point. The reviewers were Joel Spigener, Lucian Pinkston, Jas. A. Wall, John Hurley, Alexander Smith, Westley Marshall, and Jessee Bradshaw.

In December, 1836, Solomon Robbins was made a commissioner in lieu of Larkin Cleveland, resigned. This term of the court paid Robertson $150.00 for keeping Patsey Hamilton, a pauper, for one year, and he was paid $200.00 a year for each of the three following years, for caring for her.

At the August term of the court, 1837, the commissioners were Jessee Hickman, James Goggans, and Wm. M. Moore, and the court appointed Wm. C. Bulger as a commissioner in lieu of Jessee Hickman. This court ordered a new road from Sockapatoy to the Weogufka Town House, to run by the house of James Lindsey, where Hanover now is. The reviewers were Wm. R. Moore, David Crowson, John Council, James Lindsey, Albert G. Wall, David Mitchell, and John Smith. A road was also ordered from Rockford to Weogufka Town, and the reviewers were John Kelly, J. B. Cleveland, Hillman Franklin, George Smith, Elijah Smith, Wm. Patterson, and Robert W. Cleveland.

Richard Stewart and A. H. Ripetoe were the proprietors of the turnpike in April, 1838, and the road was reported by James Lindsey and A. Chancellor to the court to be in the condition required to authorize collecting tolls. At the July term of this year, the court appointed the following election precincts, and managers of elections, viz:

Wetumpka: Mungo D. Simpson, George Taylor, and Creed M. Jennings.

Kimbrell's or *Bradshaw's*: Daniel Rowe, Cadwell Sanford, and Moses Grier.

Terry's: James A. Wall, Sr., Malcom Smith, and David Hargis.

Robbins': Wm. Richards, Solomon Robbins, and Wm. C. Lee.

Rockford: Richard Stewart, Richard Plunket, and Fanch Cleveland.

Goggins': Isaac W. Suttle, A. C. Mahan, and Reuben Jordan.

Sockapatoy: E. F. Heard, Wm. S. Caldwell, and John A. Auld.

Jas. Lindsey's: Thompson Corbin, Jas. Lindsey, and Benj. Foscue.

A. Chancellor's: Washington Jones, John Looney, and John D. Wilson.

L. Clark's: Littleberry Clark, J. Stickney, and Thomas Hannon.

At the August term of 1838, John McMillan, James Prather, Reuben Jordan, Nathan Bozeman, Edward Ogletree, Joseph Tuck, and Albert Crumpler were appointed reviewers to open a road from the southwest corner of Section 18, of Township 23, Range 21, to the nearest and best point so as to intersect the Sockapatoy Road at Nixburg. And also Jessee Harrell, Robert Dobbins, James Swain, Daniel Hogan, Howell Johnson, Russell Spears, and Glenn Barnett to open a road commencing at or near Jessee Harrell's, and running the nearest and best route so as to intersect the road from the Georgia Store, at the county line on Sec. 13, T. 22, R. 20. James Goggans was paid by the court two dollars for drafting plats of the town of Rockford. Also ordered payment to Richard Plunket $525.75 for building the court house. The county paid for the material. This building was a two story wooden building, the court room above, reached by two pairs of steps ascending from opposite sides in front, landing on a piaza in front. The offices were on the ground floor. It stood near where the present court house stands.

The next year Ebenezer Pond was the County Judge, and James Goggans resigned as commissioner, and W. W. Morris was appointed in his place. The Point Creek Road was ordered opened at the August term in 1839, with Israel Pickens and Wm. A. Wilson overseers. This term authorized the reception of bids for building a stone jail. The one at that time was a heavy log jail. The following January the contract was let to A. Lyle. He forfeited his contract, and on March 22nd, 1841, a contract was made with Miller and Heard to build it for $2,745.00. It was received in August, 1842. It was built of large blocks of the native granite, so abundant about Rockford. Several times prisoners have worked their way out. About twelve years later iron cages were connected with it, and it has since been safe.

At a term of the court held February 1st, 1841, James R. Powell and Harrison Ripetoe, proprietors of the Turnpike, surrendered their right to that part of it from Rockford to Wetumpka, in accordance with an Act passed at the preceding session of the legislature, and it was made a public road. At the same term Felix G. McConnell made complaint against the condition of that part between Rockford and Sylacauga. Elijah Smith, Benj. Foscue, and Nathaniel Cook were appointed to review it and report. At the April term R. C. Goodgame and Wm. H. Ray reported that part in bad condition, and no apparent disposition on the part of the proprietors to improve it. Elijah Smith and James Pylant were appointed to look after it, and in May, Pylant reported it repaired, and the proprietors were authorized to collect toll. In December, 1846, Benj. F. Cleveland, who was then proprietor, surrendered his right of property in it to the county, and that part of the road was then made public, and the whole road has so remained ever since.

The Chaneyhatchie Road was established August 16th, 1841, to run by D. Calhoun's, J. D. Letcher's, and D. Williams'.

The Roger's Mill Road to Wetumpka was established December 6th, 1847, with Alex. Smith, Donald Ferguson, George Graham, and John H. Townsend as reviewers. The Chancellor Road to Weogufka was ordered open at the May term, 1849; and the Gray's Ferry Road to Nixburg was ordered at the same time; also the road to Tallassee leaving the Turnpike near Alexander Graham's, and running by Roger's and Holtzclaw's, and Lyle's Mills, and near Central. The reviewers were Henry McCain, Saml. P. Dennis, Elisha Trice, Luke Haynie, Henry Mann, Jordan Thornton, and William Lyle.

In 1843, William Weaver, J. W. Suttle, and Aaron Yates were members of the court. On January 17th, 1844, they granted the establishment of a ferry at Wetumpka, owing to the bridge having been swept away by a flood of water. A month later they allowed a toll bridge erected across Weogufka Creek on the Trace.

A. G. Hallmark, John S. McDonald, and James Goggans, who had been appointed for the purpose, reported, September 11th, 1848, that they had bought 160 acres of land from Asa Edwards for building a poor house for the county. This was on the south side of Swamp Creek, on the Turnpike Road. In February, 1849, Rev. Albert Crumpler made a contract with the county for keeping the paupers. This contract was continued until Crumpler left the county after the war. After that time the paupers were removed to Rockford at Dr. McDonald's place, where they were kept for a number of years. The writer is not informed how they are now provided for.

March 4th, 1850, the court granted the Plank Road Company the right to use the public roads or such parts as were needed conditioned that the company would make a good road by the side of the plank road where they were so used, for the benefit of the public who might not wish to use the plank road. This road began at Montgomery, keeping mainly along the upper Wetumpka or Judkin's Ferry Road, crossing the Tallapoosa River at that ferry. After crossing the river and reaching the hills, it kept near the flat river lands at the foot of the hills, coming into the public road again near Harrowgate Springs, and thence to Wetumpka. After passing through the business part, instead of going as the old road over the spurs of the hills, it kept round the edges of them, making the road now used as a public road, and ran in front of the Penitentiary, and left the Turnpike Road so as to strike the Corn Creek flats, crossing the Sockapatoy Road at the Thrasher place, and intersecting it again at the Pogue place. It is now the public road. It soon left the Sockapatoy Road and made out through the more level lands to Central, intersecting the old road again near the Mark E. Moore place, continuing on through Brooksville and above Bozeman's. From here it passed to the right, leaving Nixburg west, because in some way the citizens of Nixburg had incurred the displeasure of its president. It came into the Sockapatoy Road again at Boling Hall or Graham place about three miles above Nixburg. From there it followed mainly the Sockapatoy Road, passing Bradford's Factory, and from thence to Mt. Olive, and from there to Sylacauga, sometimes using parts of the Chapman Road, and thence to Talladega, a distance of nearly ninety miles. Since the plank road was abandoned as such, most of its bed has been used as the public road, because the grading made it preferable to the old routes.

This road had for its president and principal manager, John G. Winter, a capitalist and banker of Columbus, Ga. The road was in construction from about 1850 to 1854. A large number of hands were employed, and sawmills erected along the route, and moved from time to time as necessity required for cutting lumber for the road. The road was graded to a comparative level, about twenty-five feet broad. Heavy scantling stringers were laid lengthwise in a few feet of each other, for sills, and upon them was laid a floor of heavy plank. The limit of a load was about what a wagon would hold up. The speed was the capacity of the team. When the road had been completed to Sylacauga, a distance of seventy miles, a large barbecue was given at Sylacauga, and everybody invited. It was desired to show what could be done on the improved road. On the day of the barbecue William L. Yancey was to make the address of the occasion. Relays of horses and buggies had been provided, the horses every six or seven miles, kept harnessed and ready for immediate change. Colonel Yancey started with the driver from Montgomery just at sun up, reached Sylacauga, stayed two hours for speaking and dinner, and returned to Montgomery at sunset, making the one hundred and forty miles, with a stop of two hours between suns.

There was also built about the same time a plank road from Wetumpka to Tallassee, a distance of twenty-one miles. These roads were very popular, and were well patronized, but the expense of construction and keeping in repair made it unprofitable, and in a few years they were abandoned.

During the successful running of the plank road, Wetumpka did something that offended Mr. Winter, and to punish the offense he opened just in front of the Penitentiary a very large department store, stocked it heavily, and put prices down, to divert the trade from Wetumpka. He was more than a mile out from the city on the route whence nearly all the trade came. For a while large quantities of goods were sold there. But eventually

Winter's *Bank of St. Mary's* failed, and with it came the failure of the store and road, and the end of his revenge. The failure of the bank was severely felt in all this part of the State, and especially Coosa, as the St. Mary's money was the leading medium of circulation for some years, and a quantity was afloat at the time of failure.

Other roads were opened later, and changes were made in existing roads, but these were the main thoroughfares for the convenience of the people, and development of the country. Roads are important factors in the well-being of a country, and there is but little development and progress where these arteries of travel do not exist. The better the roads of a country, better schools, churches, and homes are found. The facts in regard to the roads have been thus extensively noticed, and the names of the parties in charge of the work given, that both may be remembered by those who have enjoyed the advantages in later years of the labors of these pioneer toilers who made the wilderness to become the habitation of happy families, and prosperous communities.

The first Probate Court which took the place of the County Court was held June 28th, 1850, with I. W. Suttle as the first Probate Judge. The session of the legislature of 1849-50 had provided for putting away the County Court, by substituting this new court with its larger sphere of duties. The commissioners were still continued, and the Probate Judge was its presiding officer.

A new brick Court House was built in 1858, by Patrick Coniff of Wetumpka at a cost of $10,434.35. The brick were all overcast with a coat of fine cement, that has stood the storms and seasons of more than forty-five years. This house still serves the county for its courts and offices; but there were large and costly improvements added in 1906, making quite a favorable change in its front and rear, also giving much more room in the interior. This improvement cost more than $10,000.00.

It will doubtless be a matter of interest to those now living in Coosa, and those who may come on later, to have a real transcript from the early courts held in the county, and that they may, the following is copied from the records, and though lengthy, it will not be devoid of interest.

The first circuit court held in the county was at Lexington, south of Hatchemadega Creek, three miles below Rockford, the present court house. There were two terms held here. The first was opened March 24th, 1834, with Judge John W. Paul presiding; A. R. Coker, sheriff; and William D. Pickett, prosecuting attorney general for the eighth judicial circuit.

"The following named persons had been summoned as jurors, viz: William Wall, Joshua Monk, Thomas Edwards, John Carleton, Robert Armstrong, William Pressnal, Victory Thompson, James Williams, Henry Logan, Archibald Kimbrel, James Morris, James Shelton, James Spraggins, John C. Demasters, Stephen Shelton, William Brown, Elim Malone, William Wilson, Robert Lauderdale, Lamkin Williams, Charles Williams, Alexander Honeycut, George Melton, Charles Nix, Davis Campbell, Jas. B. Morris, Geo. W. Cameron, Gaynor Gray, Westley Marshall, H. W. Harris, John S. Bates, James Taylor, Hillary Williams, John Curtis, George Taylor, Joel Harvill, Isaac Lamb, Patrick Quartermus, Absolom Nix, John Cameron, John Campbell, Ambrose Nix, Anderson Bates, Larkin Carden, Washington Benton, James Dourning, William Cooper, and Moses Kelly."

"The following were selected as the grand jury: William A Wilson, *foreman*, Moses Kelly, Wm. Wall, Alexander Honeycut, Thomas Edwards, Ambrose Nix, Robert Cooper, John Cameron, Charles Nix, Jas. B. Morris, James Williams, James Campbell, Larkin Williams, James Shelton, and Robert Lauderdale."

The entries on the docket are as follows:

"Tuesday, March 25th, 1834.

"This day appeared Elisha Lipscomb into open court, and took the oath required as an insolvent debtor, after rendering in a schedule of his property and effects, and it appearing also to the satisfaction of the court that the requisite notice had been given by the said defendant to his creditors."

The first case was:

"The State of Alabama
    vs.   Larceny
Samuel Kennedy   "This day came the State by Wm. D. Pickett, her prosecuting attorney general for the eighth judicial circuit, as well as defendant in his own proper person, who, having been charged on the bill of indictment, for plea says he is not guilty.

"And thereupon came a jury of good and lawful men, (to-wit) Joshua Monk, Robert Armstrong, John C. Demasters, John W. Marshall, Gaynor Gray, Isaac Lamb, Hugh W. Harris, Absolom Nix, James P. Chapell, Joel Spigener, Wm. Weaver, Thomas Wall, who having been duly sworn well and truly to try the issue joined, upon their oaths say, the defendant is not guilty. It is therefore considered by the court that he be discharged from custody, and go home without day."

The second case is:

"State of Alabama
    vs.
Chofolup Harjo   "This day came said defendant with Jimmy Larma, and Osa Harjo, his securities, who acknowledged themselves indebted unto John Gayle, Governor of the State of Alabama, and his successors in office, each in the sum of five hundred dollars to be levied of their goods and chattels, lands and tenements——to be void on condition that the above bound Chofolup Harjo shall make his personal appearance before the honorable the Judge of our Circuit Court, at a court to be holden for Coosa County, in the town of Lexington on the fourth Monday in September next, then and there to answer a charge of the State of Alabama exhibited against him by the grand jury, and give his attendance from day to day, and from term to term, and not depart the court without leave."

Eleven jurors whose names are given as having been summoned, and failed to appear, as jurors, "were ordered held bound to John Gayle, governor, in the sum of twenty dollars each, to be recovered from them unless good cause should afterward be shown why they did not appear."

"Solomon Robbins, James Spraggins, Hugh McMillan, and Thomas Williams were bound over in open court in the sum of two hundred dollars each to John Gayle, governor of the State, to appear at the next term of the court in Talladega County, to give evidence in behalf of the State against Steinmassagee, charged with murder."

The second term of the court was held at Lexington commencing on the 22nd day of September, 1834. Judge Anderson Crenshaw presided over the court. A. R. Coker was sheriff. William A. Elmore was appointed to act as prosecuting attorney in the absence of the regular prosecutor. Of those summoned as jurors, "there were present Solomon Robbins, James Kiggrah, William Nix, George Lewis, Wm. F. Floyd, Washington Bates, Elijah Cansey, Jessee Harrell, John Honeycut, James Buchannon, Greenburg Armstrong, Daniel Robbins, B. B. Bonner, Gideon D. Benton, Jno. D. Wilson, Squire C. J. Carden, George Lowery, Thomas Warren, Alexander Logan, John M. Rennie, Jessee Bradshaw, Absolom Whitehead, Abram Chancellor, Jessee Wilson, John Logan, Samuel Lovejoy, and Emory McGraw."

Those selected and sworn in as the grand jury, were "Solomon Robbins, *foreman*, Alexander Logan, Wm. Nix, George Lewis, Wm. F. Floyd, Geo. E. Causey, Jessee Harrell, John Honeycut, James Buchannan, E. G. Armstrong, Daniel Robbins, B. B. Bonner, G. B. Denton, and John D. Wilson."

"William H. Weaver appeared in open court and procured a license signed by two of the circuit judges of the State of Alabama, authorizing him to practice law in the State. He took the oath prescribed by law.

"The court then adjourned to the next day."

This was the last court held at Lexington, for by appointment of the Commissioners Court, approved by the legislature, Rockford had been chosen as the permanent seat of justice. The extracts from the minutes of the first court held at Rockford will be of interest, showing the beginning of the long series of court sessions which have followed in the course of the succeeding 71 years, where so much has been done of interest to the lives and property of so many thousands.

"The State of Alabama,

"March A. D. 1835, Monday the 23rd

"Be it remembered at a circuit court began and held for the county of Coosa, at the Court House, to-wit, Rockford, it being the 23rd day of March, in the year of our Lord one thousand eight hundred and thirty-five, and of American independence the fifty-ninth year, and the fourth Monday of said month, before the honorable John S. Hunter, one of the circuit judges of said State:

"This day appeared A. R. Coker, sheriff of Coosa County. who returned the venira facias served on the following persons. to-wit, B. Turner, Davis Campbell, Wm. Logan, Simon Posey, Squire Casey, Daniel P. Dennis, Joel Spigener, Manning Ray, Joel Gullege, William Blake, Hooper Caffy, John B. Lewis, James C. Campbell, George Gray, Jeremiah Gray, Isaac Lamb, Charles Nix, John Goodgame, Absolom Nix, James Chandler, Isham Edwards, Robert Lauderdale, John Smith, Wm. Stamps, Wm. F. Robertson, John Pate, Jarnett Townsend, Almon Crumpler, B. B. Bonner, M. J. Bulger, Levin Tarlington, Simeon Turner, Victory Thompson, Robert Cooper, Westley Marshall, William Suttle. John C. Bulger, Thomas Edwards, William Nix, George Taylor, James C. Gulley, John Ellison, George A. McDaniel, James B. Morris, Joseph B. Cleveland, William Richards; among whom the following persons were drawn as grand jurors, to-wit: Joseph B. Cleveland, foreman, John Smith, William T. Stamps, Jared Townsend, Joel Spigener, Wm. Richards, John Goodgame, John C. Bulger, John C. Pate, Levin Tarleton, Robert Cooper, Wm. Suttle. Isom Edwards, James B. Morris, and Simeon Posey.

"For sufficient reasons appearing to the satisfaction of the court, it is ordered by the court that William T. Robertson, Davis Campbell, and Almon Crumpler be excused from further attendance as jurors this term."

This was the commencement of the public life of Rockford, which though always small as to population, never numbering over a few hundred, has exerted a wide influence in the county, and has been the home of men of much more than local influence and reputation. Its bar for years was noted for the talent to be found in it. For many years Lewis E. Parsons, Sr., John T. Morgan, George Walden, Judge Abram Martin, William L. Yancey, Seth P. Storrs, Robert M. Cherry, Thomas Williams, William Kyle, Sampson W. Harris, Neil S. Graham, W. W. Morris, J. Q. Loomis, W. W. Mason, W. L. Penick, E. R. Vernon and others were regular members and attendants, with the frequent attendance of W. P. Chilton, S. F. Rice, John A. Elmore, J. J. Hooper, J. J. Falkner, and others widely known. Of later years Lewis E. Parson, Jr., Felix Smith, Osee Kyle, John Parker, Edwards Archibald Bentley, Evander Jones, W. D. and Thos. Bulger have been its leading men.

Rockford, for a place of its size, has always kept up good schools. Society has been good, and the style of its people was much beyond that of most places of no more wealth, and so remote from great centers. The Methodists were the pioneers in building a church. On the 18th of April, 1843, the ladies without denominational distinction held a fair to raise funds for building a church house. The Wetumpka band furnished the music free of charge. The editor of *The Argus* was complimented with a beautiful cake. The editor in his description of the fair says: "It would have done credit in its decorations, articles for sale, and splendid management for a place of much more pretentions than Rockford. It realized to them about $300.00 for their church building." This was not exceptional, for its social functions, barbecues, public dinners, May Day celebrations, Fourth of July celebrations, Temperance rallies, etc., were generally a surprise to visitors because of the taste, bounty, and hospitality that attended them. The Baptists had no church until 1850, but, when organized, it soon became and has ever since maintained the leading place in the community. No other church organizations were effected there, but for years Rev. Johnathan Mitchell, a Cumberland Presbyterian, kept up a regular appointment. More will be said of Rockford in other connections, though it might be well to say here that she was not permitted to hold her place as the Court House without a struggle. By an Act of the legislature in 1839-40, an election was held on May 1st, 1840, as to removal of the Court House. Three places were in nomination in the race—Rockford, Nixburg, and Wetumpka. Rockford received 337 votes, Nixburg 223, and Wetumpka 154. Neither place having received a majority, the Act provided that the one receiving the lowest vote should be dropped, and another election held as between the remaining contestants. This made the election between Rockford and Nixburg. The next election was held on the 2nd Monday in June, 1840, when Rockford received 439 votes, and Nixburg 395, which settled the question in favor of Rockford.

EXTRACTS FROM RECORDS, SHOWING SOME OF THE

FIRST ENTRIES

It will evidently be a matter of interest to others, as it was to the writer, to see some of the early entries of record in the county.

The first will recorded in the first Book of Wills of the county, is that of an Indian named Coak Chart-Hadjo—called by the whites Redmouth. This will was made March 6th, 1834. He willed to his wife and children certain lands near Rockford, and all other lands owned by him; eleven negroes valued at $3,100.00; his hogs, horses, cattle, sheep, etc. John A. Chapman was appointed in the will as the guardian for any minor children he might leave.

This same Indian sold to Joseph Cleveland at one time 9 negroes for $3,000.00.

The next record in the book of wills is the appointment of Ellender Lawby a guardian for her children.

March 24th, 1835, M. L. Bulger was appointed administrator for the estate of an Indian named Foshatcheyoholo.

The first recorded deed in the first Book of Deeds of the county is a deed of gift from Nancy Chapman to her children of a half section of land, being the east half of Section 17, T. 23, R. 20 in the Tallapoosa Land District. This deed was made July 4th, 1834, and was witnessed by James W. Smith and H. B. Hamilton. The names of Robert W. Martin, Judge of the County Court, and A. C. Mahan, clerk, appear in approval. She makes her mark, an evidence she could not write. It is remarkable how many of the early conveyances are signed in a similar way, showing a heavy percentage of illiteracy even among those in easy circumstances.

FIRST DEED ON RECORD IN BOOK OF DEEDS OF COOSA COUNTY

1st. This Indenture made and entered into this fourth day of July, 1834, between Nancy Chapman of the County of Coosa and State of Alabama of the first part, and Simeon Chapman, Allen Chapman, Anderson Chapman, Lutice Goodgame, William Chapman, John Chapman, Griffith Chapman, Martha Chapman, Joseph Chapman, Mary Ann Chapman, and Rachael Chapman of the second part witnesseth that for the love and affection I bear to the said parties of the second part, and for and in consideration of the sum of one dollar to me in hand paid by the said parties of the second part, the receipt whereof is hereby acknowledged hath given and granted, and by these presents doth give grant unto the said parties of the second part, their heirs and assigns forever all that certain tract or parcel of land lying and being in the county of Coosa, known and designated as the E. ½ of Sec. 17, T. 23, R. 20, in the Tallapoosa Land District with this provision, That I the said party of the first part, and my son John A. Chapman, is to have the right and exclusive privilege of living on said land, and enjoying the rents and profits of every description arising out of said lands so long as the said party of the first part, and said John A. Chapman and Rachel his wife may live. In witness whereof I, the said party of the first part hath set my hand and seal, the day and year above written.

Signed, sealed, and delivered and acknowledged in presence of us.

James W. Smith   her
H. B. Hamilton   Nancy   X   Chapman   (Seal)
                    mark

This was proved before Judge Robert W. Martin.

The second record in this Book is a copy of a receipt from Nimrod E. Benson, Land Receiver, for $100.37½ from Enoch Autrey for E. ½ of N. W. ¼ of Sec. 28, T. 20, R. 18. This is followed by a deed from Autrey to Joel Spigener for the same piece of land for $200.00. A. R. Coker and A. J. Hamilton are the witnesses. James P. Daniel is Clerk of Circuit Court before whom Autrey and wife acknowledge the transfer. His wife, Susan Autrey, signs away her right of dower or other claim. Both Autrey and wife sign by making mark. The receipt from the Receiver is dated October 16th, 1834; the deed to Spigener is in October, 1834; Mrs. Autrey's conveyance May 25th, 1835; and Mahan's certificate of recording is November 19th, 1835.

The third is likewise a receipt from N. E. Benson, Receiver, for $100.37½ from John Curtis for the West ½ of N. W. ¼ of Sec. 28, T. 20, R. 18, which was also sold to Spigener for $200.00 October 16th, 1834, and transferred on the 18th. He signs by mark.

The fourth record is the deed of Samuel Kennedy and wife to Wm. H. Ray, of the N. W. ¼ of Sec. 1, T. 21, R. 18, for $300.00. On the 25th of October, 1834, W. H. Ray deeded to Nancy Kennedy the S. W. ¼ of the S. E. ¼ of Sec. 21, T. 21, R. 18, for $100, and the deed received for record the same day.

The next recorded, is a conveyance from Albert and Mahaley Armstrong to Joel Spigener of the E. ½ of the N. E. ¼ of Sec. 29, T. 20, R. 18, for $100, May 26th, 1835. Both sign by mark.

The next recorded, was made November 14th, 1834, by Robert and Elizabeth Armstrong to Joel Spigener of the W. ½ of the N. E. ¼ of Sec. 34, T. 20, R. 18, for $97.67½. Armstrong signed by mark but his wife wrote her name.

These are followed by deeds from T. T. Wall and several others to Joel Spigener, and some from Spigener to other parties in 1834 and 1835.

The first Indian deed recorded was made February 24th, 1834, to Larkin Cleveland from Ochusyoholo, a Creek Indian of Oselonoby Town, who was numbered 9 on the census-roll. The second was to Cleveland of same date, from Nogochee, numbered 22 on census-roll. Each was for a half section, at $300. The witnesses were J. Bright, W. R. Curty, and L. R. Lawler.

The third was from Luwartarch and Chocholelee to James Buckhannon, for a half section 14, T. 19, R. 18, sold for $150, April 25th, 1835.

This is followed by the record of a lease from Absolom Nix to M. L. Bulger, on the 18th of January, 1835, for four years, to the S. W. 1/4 of Sec. 6, T. 21, R. 20. Bulger was to build a double log house for dwelling, clear 20 acres of land, besides a garden, and to plant fifty fruit trees.

In April, 1835, Wm. H. Weaver bought a half section of land from each of two Indians of Wewokon Town, one named Narboche Emarthlar, numbered 55, and the other Ufalla, numbered 1. Solomon Robbins and Wm. H. Bright, witnesses.

J. M. N. B. Nix, Mark E. Moore, and B. D. Chapman were each purchasers of a good deal of Indian lands. Richard L. Powell bought a half section of land near Nixburg from Woliga Fixico, widow of Coono Fixico, a Creek chief. B. S. Griffin and B. D. Chapman were witnesses.

One of the largest land deals of that time was the purchase by Joseph B. Cleveland in February, 1836, of $2,500.00 worth of land from Albert H. Ripetoe. E. E. Wilson and Wm. T. Stubblefield were witnesses.

The first recorded sale of negroes in the county was from Edward J. Felder to James W. Taylor, to satisfy a judgment against Felder in favor of Samuel Glover of S. C. There were eleven sold.

In 1837 and 1838 many records appear of indebtedness to State Bank and Branches. Among them one from Johnson W. Hooper, in which there is a lien upon certain slaves.

The first marriage license issued in Coosa was by A. C. Mahan, County Clerk, December 8th, 1834, authorizing the marriage of William Stringfellow to Louveancy Ellington.

The second was issued by Mahan, January 7th, 1835, in favor of Isom Edwards to Mary Fletcher.

The third was by Mahan, September 4th, 1835, to John M. Byers and Theresa Fitzgerald.

The fourth has not the day of the month but was in 1835, and the parties were William C. Bulger and Nancy Berry Donald.

The fifth was March 2nd, 1836, and the parties were Robert Lumpkin Martin and Elizabeth Robbins.

CHAPTER III

WETUMPKA

A history of Coosa County would be very incomplete without a good deal being said of Wetumpka, for from the very first until 1866 it had much to do with making Coosa what it was, for it was for the period mentioned, the point where its greatest business centered, its largest wealth and intelligence was located, and its most progressive spirit emanated. It was situated at the lower end of the shoals of the Coosa River, which gave the beautiful Indian name to the town, Wetumpka, or "roaring waters." For more than sixty miles above, there is a succession of shoals that render the river unnavigable for steamboats. At Wetumpka these waters make their last leap over the barriers of rocks that for so far had impeded this way, and as they rush foamingly on their way, it is with the loud laugh of joy that from henceforward they are to flow smoothly on their way to the Gulf. This laugh never ceases day or night except when from heavy rains the river rises clear above her rocky barriers. The Coosa is formed by the junction of the Etowah and Oostenaula at Rome, Ga. The river is navigable from Rome to Greensport, just above Childersburg From there to Wetumpka only canoes and flat boats can run, and then not at the ordinary stage of the river. For a number of years, however, flat boats would be built along the length of the shoals, and when the water rose sufficiently, under skilled pilots, they would be floated to Wetumpka, and sometimes even lower down, freighted with the marketable products of the people along the way. On reaching the market, when the cargo was disposed of, the boats would be sold, and the crew make their way back across the country. For years a fine trade reached Wetumpka in this way, until railroads opened a better way of getting the up country products to distributing points.

About 1830 or 1831, Theoderick Johnson, a Virginia, opened up a store on the west side of the river. He was a brother-in-law of Rev. John D. Williams, so long a prominent citizen. He was soon joined by some others on the same side of the river. From the first he realized the favorableness of the location for business.

and encouraged settlement. In 1831, William Suttle, a son of Jessee Suttle of Bibb County, with two brothers-in-law, George Johnson and William Howard, came from Bibb, and settled on the east side of the river. During the year George Johnson, being a carpenter, built the first store house in the place on the east side. A Mr. John Horton, in 1833, built a mill, both saw and grist, on the bank of the river. He also had the first boarding house, a two roomed log house, near the blacksmith shop, just above what has been known as "chicken-row." At first both sides of the river showed the same activity, and quite a number of stores were on the west side of the river. But as the new territory was populated, the larger part of the trade came from the country on the east, so that eventually all the business was on that side, but the west continued as a place of residence, and the churches and schools were also on that side.

Besides those already named as being there in 1831, there were also Wm. Bugg, James Loftin, and A. A. McWhorter, Joseph A. Green, A. G. Due, James Bradford, Monro and Joseph Parker, and George Taylor there as early as 1833. In 1834, the following persons, well known and long remembered, had established themselves, viz: Eli Gaither, Bennett S. Griffin, Thos. Burton, Mr. Gallagher, Mr. Holiness, W. W. Morris, R. M. Cherry, Seth P. Storrs, Samuel House, W. T. and Americus Hatchett, Rev. J. D. Williams, Dr. Burroughs, Dr. Boissau, Dr. Penick, Richard Smoot, Patrick Conniff, and early in 1835, Mr. Lacy and Dr. Fitzgerald. The Doctor was moving to Wetumpka during the "cold Friday and Saturday" in February, 1835, and had difficulty in keeping his family, white and black, from freezing. All the parties named in this list were conspicuous citizens of Wetumpka for years, some of them for a life time. Thos. Burton was a man of wealth, and once had quite a block of brick stores on the west side of the river, which was afterward removed to Montgomery. Mr. Gallagher built quite a large hotel, which was well appointed and patronized for some years. This hotel was about where the residence of the McWilliams afterward stood, but covered much more ground. During the year 1834, Miss Mary Meritt had a good school, employing an assistant. But in the spring of 1835 she died after a short illness, and is said to have been the first one buried in the cemetery, which has since become the final resting place of so many. Leander Bryant was also an early comer, but whether before 1835 is unknown.

It will not be out of place here to mention some of the firms that did business, and others in public life who were identified with the interests of this business place while it was a part of Coosa but without respect to the order in which they came. Among those of prominence were Theodoric Johnson, Eli Gaither, Cook and Jennings, House and Lundy, T. P. Dale, Heard and Due, Wm. Crocheron, Saml. Carnochan, Jennings and Stringfellow, Pearse and Taylor, O. E. Lacey, Norman Cabbott, A. J. Terrell, Silas B. Cater, Pitt Saunders, Thomas Stamps, Logan and Stone, W. T. and A. Hatchett, McConnegha, jeweler, Wm. H. McElroy, William and James Douglas, A. G. Due, A. G. McWilliams, Butter and Leak, Melton and Braswell, Ready and Houghton, Houghton and Allen, Catling, Due and Tulane, Jas. B. Taylor, Leeper and Flemming, Peter and Levi T. L. Hudgins, Blassingham Haggerty, Richard Smott, William and James Trimble, Milton Cooper, Boswell, Smoot and Dawson, McKinney Thomas, Felix Simmons, Edward Camp, Samuel and James Adams, J. B. Hubbard, Mr. Cassidy, Due and Cattott, Wm. H. Odiorne, A. A. McWhorter, Cabbott and Lull, Shulman and Goetter, Cabbott, Lacy & Co., Due and Taylor, A. J. Terrell and Co., Catlin and Cater, T. Johnson, I. Lingerman, W. B. Cooper, Jacob Adlers, John and M. McArns, W. B. Pardee, Ennis and Daughtry, James M. Bradford, Zeigler and Mason, A. J. Due, Woodruff, C. M. Jennings, W. H. Thomas, Harrison and Keith, John Weis, J. B. Hart and Sons, R. M. Cain, Clark and Cain, F. M. Finch, L. A. Saxon, C. F. Enslen, A. G. Campbell, Wm. Stringfellow, D. C. Neal, C. J. Woodruff, Seaman and Saxon, Brooks and Sedberry, and Francis Mann. Patrick Conniff and Mr. McQueen were contractors. Baxter and Peter Schwine were for a long time butchers. The latter, through jealousy, murdered his wife and a negro and then committed suicide while in jail.

Among the lawyers who lived at Wetumpka were Seth P. Storrs, W. W. Morris, A. B. Dawson, William S. Kyle, R. M. Cherry, Sampson W. Harris, William L. Yancey, Thomas Williams, Samuel S. Beeman, Neil S. and Malcom Graham, M. D. Simpson, J. Q. Loomis, A. J. Porter, George Mason, and W. S. Sarsnett.

Bennett S. Griffin and Wm. Mastin, though farmers and living just out of town, spent much of their time in the city, and were active in all of its public affairs. There was a Mr. Thompson, a portrait painter, who resided here many years. He was a fine painter who put a peculiar beautiful finish to his paintings that made them easily recognizable.

Among the physicians who for years ministered to the sick were Drs. Borroughs, Boissau, and Penick who were here in 1834, and later Drs. Fitzgerald, Harris, Thomas and Edumnd Mason, Lightfoot, Townsend, and Robert Williams.

Wetumpka was incorporated under an Act approved January 17th, 1834, embracing the east side of the river, and an election of five councilmen was ordered to be held on the 2nd Monday in February, 1834. George Johnson, Ebenezer Pond, and Thomas Hatchett were to hold it. The Act incorporating the west side was approved on the 18th. The corporate limits embraced all the land laid off in lots by the general government on both sides of the river. The managers of the election on the west side were John M. Byers, Lemuel Bradford, William Harris, Bennett Griffin, and N. H. Crocheron. This was perhaps because the east side was in Coosa, and the west side in Autauga. An Act was approved January 30th, 1839, by which both sides of the river were made one corporation, with three wards on each side of the river. This Act also established a city court which began operations February 3rd, 1839, and continued until 1884. A. A. McWhorter was appointed the first judge, but resigned September 9th, 1839; and D. C. Neal was appointed to the vacancy, and elected in 1840, and held until the court was abolished, 1844.

On the same day, January 17th, that the city incorporation was authorized, an Act was approved incorporating "The Wetumpka Bridge Company." The incorporators were James G. Lyle, Isaac Pond, Benjamin Fitzpatrick, A. B. Northrop, Francis

Gray, George Taylor, J. W. Loftin, Thomas E. Clark, G. W. Brown, Charles Cromelin, J. A. Green, and J. L. Bradford. The corporation still exists, so that it has had a continuous existence for about seventy years. Its first bridge was washed away in a freshet in January, 1844, and the river had to be crossed by a ferry boat and bateaux until rebuilt. This was done as soon as possible. The second structure was a covered bridge which stood till the unprecedented flood of 1886, when it was swept away. It has been replaced with an uncovered iron bridge.

The first paper started was by Mr. Henry Lyon in the early part of March, 1835, called *The Times*. Although the town as such was less than two years old, it had a population of 1,200, two churches, three hotels, and an Academy. About a year later two other papers, *The Courier* and *The Family Visitor*, were started. *The Family Visitor* was started by Rev. J. D. Williams.

One who had known Wetumpka only the past fifty years would hardly be able to believe that there had once been blocks of business houses on the west side of the river, extending up toward the cemetery, and westward from the bridge. The Gallagher hotel on that side was also the largest hostelry ever in the place, for then there were large crowds of travelers that visited the town. Many of the men, though, later moved to the eastern side, and others to Montgomery. Even residences were moved to Montgomery. W. L. Yancey moved his home, putting it on Perry Street, where it now stands.

The schools were separated in December, 1836, and both a Male and Female Academy were incorporated. The incorporators of the Male were Wm. H. Houghton, A. B. Northrop, L. Q. Bradford, Norman Coe, Edmund I. Fielder, John D. Williams, and Alvin A. McWhorter; of the Female, Robert B. Houghton, Leander Bryant, James Bradford, James Townsend, John Goulding, Irby Q. Kidd, and A. Crenshaw.

The churches and schools have been on the west side, and it has usually had more residences, because the land is level and the water much better. It would appear that the water on the east side ought to be the best, flowing out from the foot of the high hills, but the reverse is true. But so closely identified have both sides been from an early date, that a distinction will not be attempted, except when necessary.

The trade of the place reached a long ways, embracing for many years most of it from Coosa, Tallapoosa, Chambers, Randolph, Talladega, Shelby, Autauga, and even much from Cherokee, and Benton (now Calhoun). It was not a rare thing to see wagons from Macon, Jefferson, Bibb, Blount, and even Heard, Carrol and Troup of Georgia. The largest part of this trade was by wagons, and during the fall, winter, and spring, to get through with a vehicle from the warehouses in the lower part of town to above what was known as "Chicken Row" was a difficult undertaking. The roads leading in were usually crowded with conveyances both ways.

The flatboat trade, which at one time was very heavy, was so often delayed for want of sufficient water, that as early as January 9th, 1836, The Wetumpka and Coosa Railroad Company was incorporated with the view of furnishing transportation around the Coosa shoals. The capital stock was not to exceed $1,200,000. They were authorized to cross the Coosa River at any place between Wetumpka and the Ten Islands. Later they were authorized to extend the road through Talladega and Benton (Calhoun) counties to the State line between Georgia and Alabama, or to the Tennessee River at any point above Gunter's Landing. The grading was soon commenced and a very good road bed was graded for about twenty miles, the marks of which can yet be seen in places stretching up on the west side of the river. But the fearful financial crash which came on in 1837, and lasted through several years put an end to "The Flush Times in Alabama and Mississippi," and to this railroad enterprise, ending the aspirations of Wetumpka to being the great central emporium of Alabama. Had this road been pushed through, and had Daniel Pratt been encouraged and aided in locating his cotton factory there which he wished to do, which in 1836 was after built in Prattville, no doubt the place would have been the great trading center of the State; would have received the capital when removed from Tuscaloosa; and have continued the lead it had of Montgomery till 1842; for it was the head of navigation; all boats up the river came there; the freight rates were the same as to Montgomery; and a very muddy road, crossing a bad river, had to be passed over in getting to Montgomery. By the census of 1840 it had one-third more population than Montgomery, it having in round numbers 3,000, while the latter had 2,000, and its business activity was much greater. It had a bank as early as 1836. The first two churches were the Methodist and Baptist, but it was not long before the Presbyterians and Episcopalians had one.

A good class of steamboats were visitors to the place from the time business began, and the number and equipments improved as trade and travel improved. Some of these boats became almost floating palaces, for the passenger lists were large until at a date just preceding the Confederate War, steam-cars began to reduce it. The cabins were beautiful and finely furnished, and the table fare was superior to that of hotels. All boats from Mobile came to Wetumpka as regularly as to Montgomery. There were bar-rooms on board for the accommodation of passengers who drank, and in those days nearly everybody indulged in a dram. One of the most uniform ways of expressing welcome to a guest was to participate in a drink either from the little brown jug, or the beautiful cut glass decanters and glasses adorning pretty sideboards supplied with whiskies, brandies, and wines. About the first thing after greetings, when friends met near a bar-room, was to tip the social glass over the counter.

There was much card playing and gambling indulged in on the boats, and some persons spent much of their time going up and down the river to indulge the propensity for gambling. Regular black-leg gamblers almost lived on the boats for the purpose of fleecing the green ones they could draw into a game. Many a man who entered the cabin with a good supply of money, would land stripped of it. Such was the evil that in the late fifties the legislature prohibited card playing on boats, in hotels, and other public places. Often parties of pleasure were formed who would take a trip to Mobile and return. These were usually accompanied by a musical band, and much time was spent in the cabin cleared of tables, while the dancers glided in graceful motion over its floors to the sweet strains of music.

Among the boats on the river in those days were the Dispatch Queen of the South Dixie, John Duncan, Niagara, Factor, General Gaines, Bass, St. Nicholas, Jewess, St. Charles, Montgomery, Legrande, Magnolia, and others, the names of which are not remembered. There were usually three or more making the trip weekly. Sometimes opposition boats would start, and the competition for passengers became lively, bidding against each other, so that the fare would be made very low, getting down to one or two dollars for the round trip. But this would be too expensive to the owners to last long. About 1860 a splendid double decked boat was built for the river called the Southern Republic. It had two decks and cabins and made a striking impression on the beholder. It had a fine caliope attachment, and on approaching a landing or leaving it, some popular piece of music would be played for notice to interested parties. It was frequently played between landings for the entertainment of passengers.

In the Seminole war with the Indians in Florida, 1836, a military company was raised in Wetumpka called "The Borderers," led by Capt. W. J. Campbell. After the return its existence as a military company was continued for some years.

When the Indians were about leaving their old country under the compulsion of the United States, for their home assigned them in the Indian Territory, in August, 1836, Mr. Holiness, a citizen of Wetumpka, was married to an Indian maiden princess of the McIntosh family. He went with his bride and her tribe to their new home in the West. The marriage took place in the Baptist church, and Col. Thomas Williams, an eye witness, says no more handsome couple ever stood before the altar of that church to be made one in the holy bonds of matrimony. Unusual interest was felt as a popular white was going to leave his home in the city, and cast his fortune with the expatriated Indians.

Hotels and boarding houses were in good supply and demand because of the large amount of travel and traffic. Besides Horton and Gallagher, who have already been named, there was at different times and places catering to the public: Echols, Batchelor, Blake, Saxon, Pogue, Roach, Mrs. Phillips, and Mrs. Roberts. The leading hotel after Gallagher's was what was called the "Coosa Hall," until its destruction by fire, now "Riverside Inn."

In 1836, A. B. Dawson, Sampson W. Harris, and W. W. Mason came to Wetumpka, and became men of much more than local note. By this time Wetumpka had become prominent, and advanced in all directions. The financial crash that began in 1837, and continued for several years, led to the failure of several of her most wealthy citizens, and to the crippling and destruction of some of the projects for her enlargement.

This was a fine point for fishing, and several large shoal traps were placed in the river which often supplied more than the local demand. Not infrequently quantities would be furnished to Montgomery and other points. The writers remembers being in Wetumpka, once, and seeing bateau loads of them landed, and by the time they could be removed the traps would need to be emptied again. Schools of fish had come up the river to the shoals in the effort to find shallow water for spawning, and in swimming around, the current would wash them on the traps. This was the most noted catch on record. It was about 1850. Joe Skinner was owner of some of these traps, and for years was engaged in the fish business. He told the writer that on the day spoken of, he took from his traps 2,300, and Judge Neal still more from his.

In the spring of 1839, William L. and Benj. C. Yancey embarked in the newspaper business in Wetumpka, and threw so much vigor into it as to bring Wetumpka into more prominent notice than ever before. It will not be amiss to draw on its files for some culling that will add interest to this chapter. Access to these files was had through the courtesy of Dr. Thomas M. Owens, Director of Archives of Alabama, who has complete files of Yancey's paper.

In the salutatory, the purpose of the paper is declared to be, "in its political feature to represent the original Democratic Republican Party, opposed to national banking, protective tariff, and internal improvements by government. The advocacy of a strict construction of the Constitution, and the firm maintenance of State Rights. Its principal business will be to build up all the interests of Wetumpka, so as to make it a leading city of the State."

In its first issue it strongly advocated the election of Wm. R. King for the vice-presidency, who had for more than twenty years been a United States senator.

The legislature had decided upon the establishment of a Penitentiary, and had located it at Wetumpka. It had been a matter of much local interest as to the side of the river which it should be built. But about the time of the Yancey purchase it had been decided to build on the east side, where it now is, by a vote of two of the commissioners to one. *The Courier*, a paper published by Charles Yancey, condemned the selected site as sickly, and made general charges of unhealthfulness about the east side. *The Argus* denied the charges, approved the location, and administered a rebuke to *The Courier* for working to the detriment of Wetumpka by such declarations of unhealthfulness.

The paper reported the receipts of cotton at Mobile from May 4th to 8th at 2,000 bales. At that time most of the cotton south of the Tennessee Valley in Alabama was floated down its rivers to Mobile. Cotton at this time, at Wetumpka, was worth from 11 to 14 cts.; bagging, 22 to 24; hams, 15 to 18¾; sides, 14, shoulders, 11; nails, 9 to 10; butter, 37½; corn, 75 to 1.00; coffee, 16; molasses, 45 to 50; rice, 8; sugar, 9 to 10; whiskey, 60 to 65.

In about a month from the sale of the paper to Yancey there appears a notice of the death of M. D. Simpson who had been a former proprietor and editor. It speaks of him as having been of much prominence and influence, highly esteemed, and whose death was widely mourned. The present commandant of the

Soldiers Home, Capt. James M. Simpson, is a son of this gentleman.

There appeared an order in the paper that was not uncommon then, commanding, by order of Lt. Col. O. P. Hackett, the 68th regiment of militia to attend a brigade encampment to be held at Dudleyville, Tallapoosa County, on June 3rd, 1839. This encampment was held, and before breaking up, a visit was made by it to the battlefield of Horse Shoe Bend, and the remains of Montgomery, for whom the capital of the State was named, and who was killed in the battle and buried there, were taken up carried to Dudleyville, and there buried with military honors.

Another notice, though common then, sounds strangely now, was for the sale, at public outcry of five negroes, on the 10th of June, by John Driver, administrator.

Another notice common then, but unusual now, was of some horses "strayed" both by Wm. A. Wilson and Joseph Cleveland. Under the law of "Straying," when strange domestic animals came upon one's premises, the owner of the premises could take them up, and advertise the animals with a description for a certain time, and if not claimed by a lawful owner in the time they became the property of the one "Straying" them.

About the same time there was an editorial calling attention to the law, approved February 1st, 1839, making it a penal offense to carry a deadly weapon concealed about the person, and urging compliance with the statute.

The paper gave an earnest support of Arthur P. Bagby for governor, Dixon H. Lewis for Congress, and A. B. Dawson for the House of Representatives, who was opposed by W. W. Morris and Samuel Graham.

At this time a line of coaches was being run from Wetumpka to Eatonton and Greensboro, Ga., by way of Dadeville, Lafayette, and West Point; and another from Montgomery to Abbington, Va., by way of Wetumpka, Talladega, Rome, Ga., and Knoxville, Tenn., by the enterprising Col. J. R. Powell.

In the issue of *The Argus* of May 22nd, 1839, there is an editorial endorsement of the sentiment of a Georgia correspondent of the "Standard of the Union," in his opposition to Henry Clay for president on the ground of Clay's political sentiment being at variance with democratic sentiment, and also that of many southern whigs; "Clay is a consolidationist rather than States Rights; a liberal rather than strict constructionist of the Constitution; for protective tariff; for national bank; for hearing petitions of abolitionists; and for hostility to the interests of Georgia in her dealings with the Indians."

A public and enthusiastic dinner was given at Wetumpka, May 28th, in honor of Bagby, at which the attendance was large. After dinner a number of toasts were drunk, and among the most prominent ones offering them were Col. S. P. Storrs, Capt. Leander Bryant, Judge Ebenezer Pond, S. W. Harris, and R. M. Cherry.

A paper in June of that year speaks in very complimentary terms of the public examinations of the pupils of the Wetumpka Male and Female Academies, presided over respectively by Mr. Wallace and Mrs. Bradford, with their assistants.

Another characteristic of those days was the celebration of the 4th of July. It was then a universal holiday, and most uniformly celebrated in some public way, usually by a barbecue in each community, with the reading of the Declaration of Independence, an oration, music, and other festivities. Christmas was not looked forward to more eagerly than the celebrated Fourth. As a sample of how it was observed, the following is a substantial account of the observance in Wetumpka in 1839, preparations for which had been making from the latter part of May. When the day came it was ushered in at five o'clock in the morning by booming cannon, repeated at intervals through the day. The military company, "The Light Artillery Borderers," were on parade. At 10 o'clock the procession formed in front of the Court House of the city, and marched over the bridge to the Baptist church, where prayer was offered by Rev. Mr. Heard of Mobile. The Declaration of Independence was read by Mr. Franklin Fisk; followed by an eloquent oration from Wiley W. Mason. The procession was again formed, and marched back across the bridge to the barge of the Dispatch, on which it was carried to the grounds of the barbecue, where a bountiful and sumptuous repast was partaken of, prepared under the supervision of Messrs. Ryland and Hubbard. Music lent its charm to the feast. A beautiful original poem, from a gifted lady was read. The cloths were removed, and then came the drinking of about forty toasts, patriotic, humorous, to the "Borderers," to individuals, and in regard to the removal of the capital to Wetumpka. There is an account of a splendid celebration at the same time at Harmony Springs, where Johnson J. Hooper was the orator.

The first bale of cotton of 1839 was received at Fort Gains, Ga., July 29th. So it appears that before the use of commercial fertilizers cotton was marketed sometimes as early as July.

Some papers of the year 1902, in July, speaking of the long prevailing drouth of the season, that so fearfully cut off the crop of the year, say "it has not been equaled since the drouth of 1839. The drouth of 1839 had lasted for more than two months by the 9th of October, and supplies of all sorts had run out in Wetumpka, even paper upon which to issue the periodicals, except half sheet issues. The means of receiving freight was by the river, and it was too low for boats to run, and lower than it had ever been known. The drouth was not broken until the 11th of November, and it was December before the boats could resume their trips. In the latter part of November cotton was from 7 to 8 cents, but by the 25th of March, 1840, it had fallen to 3 to 6½.

The Penitentiary of the State stands closely related to the history of Wetumpka, for it was located there at its first establishment, and has ever since remained there. During the year 1839, the Commissioners to build the Penitentiary, A. A. McWhorter, William Hogan, and Malcom Smith, had let the contract to W. H. Thomas for $84,899.00. The cornerstone was laid with imposing ceremonies by the Masons, March 4th, 1840, escorted to the place by the Borderers. Prayer was offered by Rev. Mr. Holman, and an address was made by A. B. Dawson. The land upon which it was built was owned in times of Indian possession by an Indian named Slab. On the 27th of October, 1841, the keys of the Penitentiary were formally turned over to the Commissioners, and the occasion was publicly celebrated by a dinner. William Hogan was made the first Warden.

To January, 1842, but one convict had been incarcerated. His name was William Garrett from Autauga County, a harness maker from New York. He was charged with harboring a runaway negro, and was sentenced for twenty years. He had a wife in New York. He once escaped, but was recaptured. He was finally pardoned by act of the legislature, because grave doubts had arisen as to his guilt. Four additional convicts were received on the 22nd of March, 1842, and still others later. On the 24th of December, 1842, eight convicts made their escape by lashing together two pieces of timber, nailing cross pieces at intervals on these for steps, and' tieing a rope to the end going over the wall, by which they could lower themselves to the ground. This was done while the Warden and guards were at dinner. Seven got out then, but the eighth, hearing the guard approaching, hid himself in a pile of lumber until night, and then made his escape. One, in descending, fell and hurt himself so he failed to make good his escape. By January 10th, 1843, all but two had been recaptured.

In February, 1843, there were 28 convicts in the walls, 12 of whom were from Mobile. Of these, six were making wagons; three were blacksmiths; three shoemakers; four tailoring; three at cabinet work; three coopering; one a painter; one a cook; and two at miscellaneous work. Other industries were added, such as saddle and harness making, tinners trade, etc.

A. M. Bradley succeeded Hogan as warden in January, 1844. Sometime during the year 1844 the wooden workshops in the yard were burned, but replaced. The convicts in those days were not congregated together in large cells as now. There were long rows of narrow cells, each occupied by only one at night, and each cell had its separate door and lock, and then a strong chain ran in to a staple in each door through the length of the line of cells. There was quite a clanking night and morning as these chains were being rapidly run along the tiers of cells. The convicts were not allowed to converse with each other, or visitors to talk with them except by special permission.

The condition of the Penitentiary financially was not satisfactory to the legislature, the cost of maintenance being so far in excess of income. To January 1st, 1846, it had cost to maintain it $53,546.44, while the receipts from its products had been only $21,565.75, leaving a balance against it of $31,980.69. In January, 1846, Thomas Cargyle was made warden. In February of that year an Act was passed authorizing the lease of the institution; and it was leased by John G. Graham in the same month, and he was lessee and warden until 1852, when his six-year lease expired.

From 1852 to 1858 the lessees were Moore and Jordan, with Mr. Moore as warden. They engaged largely for a time in the manufacture of rope and bagging, but it was a financial failure, involving the lessees in heavy loss. It also proved unhealthy for the convicts.

In 1858, Dr. Ambrose Burrows and Mr. Holt were lessees, Dr. Burrows as warden. He was killed in 1862 by a convict named Karminsky. Dr. Burrows had whipped him for misconduct in accordance with the rules of the system. He vowed revenge. Watching his opportunity, at a time when Dr. Burrows was off his guard, Karminsky, with an axe in hand, at one blow nearly severed the Doctor's head from the body. He was tried for the murder in Rockford, and hanged in the yard of the Penitentiary, in the presence of the convicts.

The State resumed control upon the death of Dr. Burrows, and appointed Dr. M. G. Moore warden. The war came in 1861. The supply of men for soldiers was getting scarce, and a proposal was made to the convicts to pardon those who would enlist as soldiers in the Confederate service. Many enlisted. With those left Dr. Moore manufactured many articles useful for the Confederate needs so that he was able to turn into the treasury about $80,000 in Confederate money. Alabama, at the request of Mississippi, owing to greater security at Wetumpka, received all of Mississippi's convicts. These remained at Wetumpka until the spring of 1865, when the Federals threw open the doors of the Penitentiary and turned loose all the convicts of both States. When thus released, one named Marooney refused to leave, and stayed alone at the Peniteniary, faithfully guarded it, and protected the property as well as he could until relieved by proper authority. Dr. Moore continued to act as warden until in June, 1866, when Gov. Patton leased it to Smith and McMillan. This was an unfortunate lease, as the $15,000 advanced them by the State was never repaid, and the valuable machinery was wrecked and almost worthless. In 1866, by act of the legislature the lessees were allowed to sub-let the convicts, and thus was begun the system of letting the convicts out under contracts. The history of the Penitentiary as connected with Coosa ended with the formation of Elmore County in 1866. It is well enough to say that the Penitentiary proper has ceased to be the place of confinement to any large number of convicts, but is mainly the hospital for those of chronic sickness. There is a small farm and large garden attached, where those who are able work.

In the latter part of 1839 there is a reference in *The Argus* to the continued financial depression which had continued from 1837, and that was leading to many business failures, and the financial ruin of many individuals. Another article in the paper shows the wonderful contrast between the revenues of the United States then and sixty-four years later. They wede in the aggregate in 1839, $35,661,427.82. After deducting the expenditures there was left a balance in the treasury of $1,536,384.93. Even as late as 1860 the whole revenue was only a little over $60,000,000, and that met all demands of what was then called an extravagant administration, and left a surplus in the treasury. Now the Post-office Department alone expends more than twice the whole revenues then. More than a billion dollars are required now to meet the current expenses. This shows an unwarranted degree of extravagance.

William L. Yancey, who had been living in Lowndes County,
moved to Wetumpka in the early part of 1840, and became more
intimately connected with the editorial conduct of the paper, and
more closely identified with the interests of Wetumpka and
Coosa. It was perhaps during this year that he lost so many
slaves by someone poisoning the spring on the plantation from
which water was largely used.

A petition from the citizens of Coosa, Talladega, and Benton counties to the legislature to do away with the charter of
the Turnpike Road, and make it a public one is referred to in
the paper. On the 25th of March, 1840, there appears in the
paper an interesting account of the marriage of Victoria, the
young Queen of England, to Prince Albert, with a lengthy description of the scenes and ceremonies. It hardly seems credible
that one crowned and married so long ago, should have held
the sceptre for such a while. But God seems to have lengthened
out her life for she was no less a wife and mother in her own
family, than a queen in her empire. She deserves to be remembered not for brilliancy but for excellency.

Great floods of rain fell in the spring of 1840, and the
paper complained of the great interruption to travel from high
waters. It said some gardens about Wetumpka were ten feet
under water, and the roof was all that could be seen of one
of the warehouses. The next spring, that of 1841, had even a
greater flood, coming down in tradition and history as "the
Harrison freshet," because it extended over much of the country
about the time of his inauguration as president. But neither
of these reached the heighth of the one in 1833, which was the
highest known until the great freshet of 1886 which entered so
many of the stores, and carried away the second bridge which
had stood since 1844.

On the 6th of June, 1840, the editor of *The Argus* and some
other Wetumpkians were a party of excursionists who were to
take a trip over the first completed twelve miles of the Montgomery and West Point Railroad. The party consisted of about
sixty. As they went and returned the people were gathered

along the line of the road to see the then marvelous sight of people flying along, drawn by steam. It was to them a new and strange revelation. Less than ten years before the first railroad in the United States had been operated. The trip was made to the terminus, and then returning about half way, the train stopped, and the excursionists partook of an enjoyable dinner spread by the managers of the road. Hon. Abram Martin presided at the table and over the toasts. Upon reaching Montgomery on the return, James E. Belser made a speech of thanks on behalf of the excursionists to the railroad officials. This road has been a great factor in giving importance to Montgomery. Though trains were running on the road as early as 1840, the connection by rail to Atlanta was not completed until about 1853, when the Atlanta and West Point was completed. The connection between the termini was made by a number of stage coaches, which gradually shortened their run as the roads approached each other. The writer has passed over the route when the staging was from West Point to Newnan, then to Grantsville, then to Hoganville, and last to LaGrange.

There was much sickness in Wetumpka in the fall of 1840, and it prevailed to an unusual extent in the country, reaching up into the hills which were regarded as immune against the type then prevailing. The record for the year was bad in the line of sickness.

The Fourth of July, 1841, came on Sunday, but on Monday, the 5th, there was quite a noted celebration in lieu of the 4th. The prayer was offered by Rev. Benjamin Foscue, a Primitive Baptist preacher of good property from the upper part of Coosa. The Declaration of Independence was read by James R. Powell; and the oration was delivered by James W. Graham. The dinner was spread near Valley Brook Spring. Upon the removal of the cloths W. W. Morris was made president, Judge E. Pond and A. Kendrick were made vice-presidents. After drinking the toasts, which ended the celebration, the people were addressed by Wm. L. Yancey, then a candidate for the legislature, and he thrilled them by his speech, and for the first time the people became apprised that a great orator was among them.

The population of Coosa the first of 1842 was 6,995.

In the early part of April, 1842, Wm. J. Campbell was buried at Wetumpka, his body having been brought from Rockford, where he died. He was sheriff of the county, and said to be one of the best in the State. He was buried with military honors by the "Borderers" of which he was captain in the Florida war, and after their return to Wetumpka, until elected sheriff.

The Argus tells of the high and complimentary terms in which *The New York Express* speaks of the prompt action of Alabama in paying a debt of $800,000 due from her in New York during this season of still continued money depression. What made it so notable was Alabama's heavy losses by bank failures, and the disposition so rife in places of repudiation.

The 4th of July celebration was 1842 was held in the Presbyterian church, and the ladies furnished the dinner, selling tickets at $1.00, the proceeds being for the benefit of the church. They also had a fair for its benefit, and realized $815.62. But somebody put off on them a worthless $5.00 and two $2.00 bills.

During the year a "Total Abstinence Society" was formed, that steadily grew in numbers and influence for a time. Its president was A. A. McWhorter, and the secretary was James W. Graham.

The Argus of the 6th of July tells of a very cold spell of weather for the time of year, and that a flock of 500 sheep that had not been long sheared were frozen to death in New York. The paper of October 5th of this year tells of peach, cherry, and other fruit trees being in full bloom. On the 11th of October is the notice of the marriage of William M. Lindsey of Weogufka, a prominent young man of that community, to Miss Martha E. Calfee. They were both afterward evidently known over the country. The November number of the 15th tells of the death of the wife of Alexander Smith, from the bloody flux that was so fatal among the Scotch settlers of what was known as the Carolina neighborhood. Cotton was then worth only from 4½ to 5½ cts.

The Argus, in January, 1843, tells with sadness of the rumored death of the young and popular Queen Victoria of England. Those were not the days of telegraphic news, so it was sometime before it was learned that she was not dead, but a dastardly attempt had been made by a young man of about twenty years of age to shoot her, while riding out with Prince Albert.

Snow fell to the depth of several inches on the 23rd of March, 1843, and it was cold for some time. This snow was extensive. The writer remembers on that day in South Carolina, the fall was about six inches, and well remembers the snow battle of that and successive days by the boys on the playgrounds of Bethany Academy. It was made possible by rolling up a number of large balls on the grounds. During the time of these snows, and before and after appeared the wonderful comet that has come down in history, noted for its brightness, the great length and curvature of its tail. Some humorous fellow said "warm weather need not be expected until the departure of the comet, as the cold was produced by the incessant fanning of its enormous tail."

The gold fever ran high during 1843, and there was much search for it both in Coosa and Tallapoosa. There was considerable mining done about Goldville in Tallapoosa. There was for a long time signs about Rockford and elsewhere where search was made for the precious metal.

The Argus complained during part of this year about the scarcity of chickens, and the high price, $2.50 per dozen. But it said turkeys, both wild and tame, were plentiful and cheap, ranging from 37½ to 75 cts. Fish were abundant and cheap, the traps doing well.

R. M. Cherry, a lawyer who lived partly at Wetumpka, and at Rockford, lost his wife by death, September 18th. She was a Miss Crenshaw. Cherry was a long while a prominent lawyer, and was the commissioner of the general government, through whom the last of the scattered Indians were removed in 1845.

The church building of the Baptists in Wetumpka was burned on the 7th of December, 1843. The Episcopalians kindly offered them the use of their building, until they could rebuild. The building erected was the pretty structure in which they have ever since worshipped.

W. J. Couch of Wetumpka was this year, 1843, elected Secretary of the Senate. Joseph D. Phelan was Clerk of the House. Wm. L. Yancey was in the House, and made the speech upon the State Bank and its Branches, the most important question before the body, that produced the most profound impression of any made during the session. His argument seemed to throw new light upon the minds of even the old legislators upon the banking question. From this time his reputation as a speaker was established. Phelan afterward became a citizen of Coosa, so that Coosa certainly had a prominent place in the legislature of 1843.

Wetumpka lost her first bridge on the 15th of January, 1844, which greatly inconvenienced the people, as well as inflicting a heavy loss on the stockholders.

On the 29th of February the death of the wife of W. W. Mason took place, and her loss was deplored not alone as a bereavement to her highly esteemed husband and the family, but such was the loveliness of her character, and so useful in the community had her life been, that it was felt to be a public calamity.

On the 20th of March of this year Colonel Yancey sold *The Argus* to Mr. B. B. Moore. The paper was about nine years old at the time of the transfer. The law partnership that had existed between Sampson W. Harris and Wm. L. Yancey was also dissolved during this year, and a partnership in law was established between Mr. Yancey and his distinguished half brother, Samuel S. Beeman. They were both good lawyers, and gifted in oratory.

January 5th, 1845, a fire took place in Wetumpka that proved quite destructive. It swept away all from the bridge, and in front of the Coosa Hall to the foot of the hill, and up to what was long known as "Chicken Row." Insurance was not then so common as now, and the result was but a light amount of insurance. The loss was very heavy, for heavy stocks were carried in those days. But with energy and pluck, the work of rebuilding was begun, and soon, Phoenix-like, she had arisen from her ashes to her busy life again, with many better buildings than the ones consumed.

In 1845 and 1846, Wetumpka made earnest effort to get the capitol. There was a disposition to move it from Tuscaloosa on the part of many. Wetumpka and Montgomery were eager to become the location for it. Wetumpka and Coosa sent Col. Howell Ross and Col. J. R. Powell as strong influential men to work in their interest. They worked earnestly, but Montgomery was successful, and from then on, with her railroads and the capitol, she has left her long time rival far behind in the race for power and distinction. From then Wetumpka barely held what she had for some years, say till about 1857. Then a good deal of wagon trade commenced going through to Montgomery, and her trade declined rather than grew. During this time the lower ferry over the Tallapoosa was a very profitable possession, having about as much as could be done till a late hour in the night to put across the travel.

Another terrible conflagration occurred on the 11th of June, 1852, when almost the same area was burned over. The Hagerty Block, and the Coosa Hall were not burned this time, but all from the bridge to where the court house now stands, and on up to where Mr. Hubbard lived, went out in smoke and ashes. There was some suspicion that one of the merchants, Felix Simmons, had started the fire. McKinney Thomas had given utterance to his suspicions. Simmons watched his opportunity. Having provided himself with pistol in one hand and whip in the other, he met Thomas in the street, and inflicted a castigation upon him.

As early as 1836, Wetumpka had a bank of issue, and during the years of prosperity its circulation was large. But during the long period of depression following the crash of 1837, the bank succumbed, went out of business, and for a long time struggled with its depreciated notes.

For a number of years, running through the fifties, merchants paid taxes on their gross sales. During much of this time there were four houses, those of Due and Cabbot; Pearce, Taylor & Co., Houghton Allen & Co., and McKinney Thomas, whose sales exceeded $100,000 each per year. There were others whose sales were over $50,000. A. G. Due, started, a poor boy in the early days of Wetumpka, and worked his way by energy and tact to the front, which was held by him to his death, though he died without much estate, having liberally used his gains to build up the place, and to hold its trade during the days of decline. At one time he was associated in partnership with a Mr. Heard. They were large cotton buyers as well as merchants. Heard was found guilty of changing the weights on cotton receipts. He made his escape between suns to void punishment. Due was not a party to the fraud, and therefore did not suffer in reputation, and continued business alone for sometime after Heard's departure. He and Charles Cabbot then formed a partnership that lasted till Cabbot's death.

Allen was a clerk for Wm. and James Douglass when they were leading merchants of the place, and became afterward one of the leading merchants himself, of the strong firm of Houghton and Allen. Rice was also a clerk who arose in business capacity so as to become one of the firm of Houghton, Allen and Rice. Rice afterward went to Memphis, Tenn., doing business there after the war. He has a son who is a prominent minister of the Presbyterian church, now in Atlanta. Houghton went to Boston after the war, and became a member of the strong publishing house of Houghton and Miflin.

The social life of Wetumpka was highly enjoyable, owing to the culture and refinement of its people, among whom it was a pleasure indeed to mingle. While there was taste, ease, and comfort, there was an absence of that stiffness and exclusiveness that so often eliminate pleasant intercourse. What was undertaken in a social way, or for public improvement of schools, churches, and the like was well done. They took an honorable pride in their churches, and were liberal in the payment of their pastors. Among the most noted of the Presbyterian pastors was Rev. Robert Holman who was with them in the palmy days of the city. He was very popular among all the people. He died in his fortieth year, July 5, 1842, and is buried in the cemetery at Wetumpka, and over his remains there is a pretty monument erected to his memory by the young men of Wetumpka. Dr. Mitchell was for a time the pastor of the Presbyterians. He was afterward for many years the principal of their high school at Florence, Ala. Dr. George Foster was pastor among them for several years before, and during the war as well as after it, but finally resigned to become the head of the Orphans' Home at Tuskegee.

Dr. McDougal was pastor of the Episcopal church, as well as being for many years at the head of a flourishing school. The Baptists had a number of ministers, but among those longest identified and best known were J. D. Williams, Dr. W. A. Chambliss, Dr. D. W. McIver, P. H. Lundy, Platt Stout, Geo. E. Brewer, and Rufus H. Figh. The Methodist Episcopal Church South was from an early date a strong body, and from time to time some of their strongest men ministered to them.

Candor requires it to be said that with many good things to the praise of the place, that liquors were freely sold both wholesale and retail, and the indulgence in intoxicants led to the ruin of many of the young men reared here, and who came to the place to enter business.

There was always enough military spirit in the community to keep most of the time a well drilled volunteer company. For a few days before the war, and during the early part of it, Prof. Davie had a good school with the military feature attached. The school furnished some officers to several of the companies that went from this section, and Davie at last gave up the school to become captain of a company. "The Wetumpka Light Guards" was a well drilled volunteer company which had been organized for some years. Upon the secession of the State it was sent with other companies by Gov. A. B. Moore to Pensacola to seize the forts and Navy Yard there. After Confederate troops were sent to hold these, it returned to Wetumpka. But hostilities beginning between the States, in the spring of 1861 it volunteered into

the Confederate service, and became part of the 3rd Ala. Regt.
When they started for Virginia they went as far as Montgomery
on the pretty double-decked Southern Republic. A large crowd
of friends and citizens gathered at the warehouse on the wharf
to see them off. A beautiful silk banner was presented to them
on behalf of the ladies of Wetumpka by Rev. Geo. E. Brewer,
which was received and responded to by Lt. Henry Storrs. This
was followed by tender farewells as parents, brothers, sisters, and
friends parted, not knowing they would ever meet again. Tears
flowed from almost every eye while blessings were called down
upon the dear young men leaving home for the carnage of war.
When the company was aboard the boat and the men standing
upon the decks and about the guards waving their farewells and
throwing kisses to those who were soon to be seen no more, or
if at all, in the distant future, the irrepressible Nick Carnochan
called to a friend standing on the bank, and said, "Tell mother
the next time she hears of me I'll be in Abraham's bosom," thus
punning on the name of Abraham Lincoln.

In 1866, Wetumpka was cut off with that part of Coosa
which was taken to form the new county of Elmore and became
the county seat. Its history from thence forward belongs elsewhere than in Coosa. It has continued to be of much business,
though not of the importance of former years. But of recent
years there has been a material reviving in increased business,
population, and building, stimulated by the flourishing Agricultural School of the District. Many good residences and business
houses have gone up, and there is a general air of improvement
in all directions. The United States has expended a good deal
of money in recent years in clearing out the shoals and building
a lock with a view to opening up the navigation of the Coosa
over her more than fifty miles of shoal water, so that navigation
may extend to Rome, Ga.

CHAPTER IV

SETTLEMENT AND SETTLERS OF COOSA

As stated elsewhere, there were a few scattered white families living among the Indians at the time of the cession of their lands to the whites. There followed immediately a rapid influx especially in the eastern, middle, and northern parts. In Indian times and afterwards there was a settlement about two miles east of Wetumpka called New Georgia, the home of some prominent families. North a few miles were Hon. Howel Rose and George Taylor, more fully noticed elsewhere, and a Mr. Thrasher. These were men of good property and farms. Just north of Thrasher was John Pogue, long identified with Wetumpka. There were also Washington Barton, Wm. Mastin, Richard Smoot, and Bennett S. Griffin whose lives are interwoven with that of the county. There also lived in the vicinity Jared Townsend, one of the first elected commissioners, as also Thos. L. McGowan, John Thompson, Dr. Thomas, Westley Marshall, Solomon Wood, and William Lovelady, one of the first officials of the county. For six miles east it was almost an unbroken wilderness, and so remained till after the war, covered with fine timber. The range of hills running east of Wetumpka has had few settlements to the present. A jug factory was on one of these hills for a long while, owned by a Mr. Mulder. One of his sons still runs it. Then came in a right good settlement, some there early and others later. Among these were Charles Gregory, Samuel Welch, Henry Gilmer, Rev. Rovert Stewart, and William Townsend (noticed elsewhere) and their families, in the vicinity of Hatchechubbee Creek. There were others not now remembered. Eastward toward and around Good Hope church, and in the country lying north of the Tallassee Plank Road, there were the Shepherds, Pink Floyd and sons, William Lyle and sons, Pink Lett and sons, Owen Swindall and sons, Rev. Mr. Nichol, Seaborn Wingate and H. A. Jackson, Luke McNeil, Robert Lett, Luke and Hugh Haynie, Frederick and Benjamin Timmerman, Rev. Joseph Norton and his father, Mr. Clayton, Y. D. Harrington, James Ramsey, Mr. Osborne, the Lancasters, Mr. Fiefder, William White, and Mr. Ellis. None of these figured in public life, but were good sub-

stantial citizens, whose hospitality was such as to make a stop
at their house a real pleasure. About where Eclectic now is,
there were the pleasant homes of Seaborn Kidd, Wm. Haynie,
Dr. Whetstone, Eli and Fletcher Williams, and where a good
resting place awaiting the one who had come through the almost
unbroken forest of splendid pines to the east. On the old Georgia road, T. U. McCain, Jordan Thornton, and the Shepherds,
each of whom were long, well, and favorably known. Their
families had seen the country change from a new to one established. Around and near Central Institute were William Reeves,
Abram Callaway, William Barnes, Major Peevy, John D. Letcher,
Rev. James Peter, David Bozeman, Daniel Carmichael, Uriah
Williams, Rev. Barney Elliott, Rev. Benjamin Lloyd, Mr. James
Mann and sons, Mr. Watkins, and Dr. Watkins. Many of these
lived around there until death; and many of those now in the
country are their descendants. This community became very
prominent after the location of the Central Institute. This drew
others of means, influence, and culture until the superiority of
the community as a place of residence was attested by the numbers who sought homes here. Some of these were President A.
T. Holmes, Profs. B. T. Smith and B. Savage, Revs. Joseph Bankston, Bright Skipper, T. J. West, Platt Stout, with John A. Pylant,
Wm. M. Lindsey, William Thomas and sons, Mr. Green Holifield,
Stephen Hickman, Mr. Wideman, Swep Wall, and others. Mr.
Davis had a machine and gun shop on the Sockapatoy road about
two miles away, that did a good business, and through the war
was very useful. He afterwards bought the Central school building, and established his machinery in it. Above the village Mr.
Walkley owned a good home, where he raised nice fruit. He was
a scholarly man, and was highly esteemed as a teacher. He was
made principal in the female department of Central. One son is
now prominent in business circles. Above him, Dr. Edwards had
a good home, and a tan yard. From here, for years, the forest
was almost unbroken to the fine old home of Mark E. Moore.
When built, his was one of the best homes in the county. It became the property of Jas. R. Powell after the transfer of the stage
line to the Plank Road, and was kept as the stage stand and
boarding house. Above this, Braddock Harris early established
a blacksmith shop where he did a good business owing to the

heavy travel on the road. He had a well of fine water near the road, which furnished many travelers and their thirsty teams refreshing draughts. To this point from Wetumpka the Plank Road passed over a comparatively level country. It was more broken along the original route of the Sockapatoy road.

In the early fifties, John T. Brooks began a mercantile and milling business, both saw and grist, had wood and iron shops, and soon a thrifty village, Brooksville, took the place of the woods. For a good while he did a fine business, but ultimately failed. The business has been carried on by others, so that it has continued a good center for local trade all these years. Some of the men of this region were here either among the Indians or just after. Among these were W. H. Ray, John Corbett, William and John Suttle, Archibald Kimbrell, Grigsby Hughes, Mark E. Moore, William Blake and son, Isaac Blake. Wm. Blake and his wife, who was Miss Rhoda Suttle, were the parents of nineteen children. Lumpkin Martin, a son-in-law of Solomon Robbins, and father of Darius Martin, was here quite early. These were all substantial and reliable citizens, and most of them still have representatives around. There came in a few years later Benjamin Hodnett and his father, Joseph Smart, a son-in-law of William Suttle, J. H. Willbanks and his brother, Capt. J. R. Cross and William Cross, the Archers, D. M. and Thomas Harris, Mr. Bross, James Walston, R. J. Simmons, John Conner, and the Casons, one of whom became sheriff. Rev. Bright Skipper and Colonel Austin also lived about here for a time.

Charles K. Cotton, and the Parkers (Joseph and Monroe) were east of Brooksville, and always maintained a good school west of the place, from an early date, were the Rogers (Washington and his father and brothers), and the Ellises, familiarly known as "Uncle Ben and Nathan," and also W. G. Ellis. North of Brooksville was the home of Nathan Bozeman, one of the early and prominent citizens of the county. He first settled near Fish Pond in 1833. In a few years he settled the home near Brooksville. It was a noted place on the road for years both for the appearance and comfort of the place, and the fine orchard. Here was reared his sons, Col. Nathaniel Bozeman of Arkansas, Col.

David of Central, Dr. Nathan of national fame as a surgeon, and his daughters, Mrs. M. L. Bulger, Mrs. J. D. Letcher, Mrs. Jasper McKinney, and Mrs. James Jordan. James Jordan and Mr. Sarsenett, father of William Sarsenett, once prominent as a lawyer and politician, and son-in-law of Hon. George Taylor, lived between Brooksville and Nixburg. The people settled around Nixburg more rapidly perhaps than in any other portion of the county. As early as 1832, Solomon Robbins settled, the first white man among the Indians, and lived at the same place till his death in 1880 at the advanced age of 82 years. A further notice of him appears later. Soon after him came in Larkin Cleveland and his grown sons, Joseph, Benjamin, Robert, and Harvey. They were here and took an active part in the organization and early history of the county, as did some of their posterity after them. Also among those early settlers were Henry Lee, the hotel keeper and merchant of Nixburg, and his son-in-law, Dr. Elias Parker, also Charles, William, Absolom, and Ambrose Nix, for whom the place was named. Robbins had four sons, Solomon, Jr., Peyton, Thomas, and George. About 1843, Alexander Smith bought the Larkin Cleveland place just to the east of Robbins, and raised his large and useful family there. The place is still held by his son. William Crawford lives at the Robbins place. Richard and Zachariah Powell came in some later, as also Henry and Epps Temple, John Logan, Rigdon Edwards, the Littles (Asa, James, and Robert), Thornhills, Hollidays, Richards, Days, Walden, Gus Morgan, Jerry Garey, Kendricks, Grahams, Halls, Robinsons, Crumplers, Leonards, Townsends, and many others not now recalled. It was a fine substantial set of citizens, above the average in intelligence, property, and public spirit. Good schools and churches were kept up, and for years there was a regular camp meeting held. In 1835, Monroe Parker came into the country east of Brooksville and Nixburg. In the same year George Johnson and William Howard with their father-in-law, Jessee Suttle, came into the Oakchoy neighborhood, northeast of Nixburg. Here Johnson built his mill that still stands, the first in this part of Coosa. It was not a great while after till Hagerty also put up one on Salonoby, and some later Mr. Hardy had one, as also Dr. Parker and Dr. Robinson. About the same time Russell and William Spears came in, as also Mr. Hobdy, and Adam, Jessee, and Eli Harrell, if they did not precede. A son of Eli Harrell, William V., now owns a farm in Talladega, but spends much of his time with a daughter, Mrs. Barnes, in Woodlawn. He is well preserved though he has passed his three score and ten. He was nicknamed "Buck" when a boy, because of his fleetness, and his ability to dodge a ball in playing. His father was once the captain of a barge run in Florida waters. Adam was a steam doctor. He later went to the Knight and Whetstone neighborhood west of Buyckville. William, on growing up, went to Louisiana and engaged in steamboating from New Orleans to Shreveport. He was a major in the Lewis Battalion during the Confederate war. Eli was the first owner of the mill on Salonoby, known later as the Hardy Mill.

As early as 1836 there were quite a number of settlers in the surrounding country, noted among them was Joseph Tuck who lived to be old, and who accumulated a good property. Allen Thomas married his only daughter and child. Those long and well known in this section, among others whose names are forgotten, were Adams Hill, Daniel Hogan, L. Salter, William Richards, Mr. Wilkinson, the Ogletrees, James Goggans and his sons (Peter and William), John J. Myers, John Driskell, Thomas Peterson and son, Mr. Wilton, Jackson and William Justice. William Justice married Margarett Johnson, daughter of Hon. George Johnson. They had a good family of children, and the present senator from Elmore County, Dr. Justice, is a son. In the same section were Stephen D. Ray, a son-in-law of Jessee Suttle, who lived in the same section till his death at over ninety. He contributed by his memory much help to the author in preparing this work. Mr. Radford, B. B. Bonner, J. Hickman, Manning Ray, James Benson, Dr. Thomas Espy, G. G. Gresham, John Goldthwait, Joseph Billups, and Daniel Robbins, were here not only early, but many of them spent their lives here, and have descendants to the third and fourth generations still in old Coosa. An incident memorable in the history of Nixburg occurred in May, 1836, the killing of Jessee Suttle at his spring in the presence of his wife. He was the father of Judge Isaac W. Suttle of Coosa, of Judge John W. Suttle of Bibb, William Suttle, and of Mrs. George Johnson, Mrs. William Howard, and Mrs. Stephen D. Ray.

He bought a piece of land of an Indian, Pothleoholo, in 1835, and settled upon it. When he paid the purchase money M. L. Bulger desired him to pay a debt he held against the Indian from whom the purchase was made. But this could not be done, for the government required the money paid to the Indians in the presence of the government agent. So the money was paid to the Indian. As was common, he was soon drunk. On sobering, his money was gone. Being without money or land he demanded one or the other again, but of course Suttle refused as he had paid. It is said that it was not unusual for Indians to be made drunk when in possession of money, and to be relieved of it by unscrupulous white men. They were wronged in other ways by many of the whites. There was also a good deal of talk of removing them to the Indian Territory in violation of the terms of the treaty. All these things had stirred the Indians up, until there was strong apprehension of them rising up to massacre the whites. Some understanding was had among the whites as to what was to be done, and certain rendezvous had been agreed upon in case of hostilities. This Indian, incensed at his loss, felt like inflicting vengeance somewhere, and so Suttle was on the land that had been his, and he did not know who had gotten his money, decided he would revenge himself on Suttle. Suttle had not yet built a house, but lived in the two Indian cabins on the place. On the 16th of May Suttle was cleaning out a good spring near the cabins, and his wife was with him. While so engaged the Indian slipped near, and shot Suttle to death at the feet of his wife. She took her granddaughter, Matilda Howard, who lived with her, and ran to her son-in-law, George Johnson's home. He and a neighbor, Howard Johnson, took their families and the widow, with all haste, to Nixburg, to Solomon Robbins' house, the place agreed upon as a rendezvous for this section. They scattered the news as they went. The news spread rapidly, and consternation seized upon the settlers, and the families of the whites were rapidly concentrated at Robbins'. His house was the shelter for the women and children, while fortifications were hurried by the men. M. L. Bulger's wife, while on the way to refuge, was so injured by the horse running away, that she died from the injuries. For two days there was constant dread of attack. Once alarm became intense as a cloud of dust was seen arising from the route out westward. On coming in sight it was discovered to be a party of mounted Indians. But on opening a parley with them they were found to have been on a fishing excursion, and knew nothing of the excitement prevailing. Larkin Cleveland had instructed the women, that if the men failed in the defense, and it became necessary for the women to escape from the house, to make a hole in the floor, near the chimney, and go out there, as the Indians would be less likely to see them there than if they attempted to go out by the doors. During a prolonged period of excitement occurring while a meal was being prepared the meal was of course neglected by the excited crowd. A half-witted woman among them gave her attention to the neglected cooking, and saved the bread. After the excitement passed she said, "The biscuits would have all been burned up if I had not attended to them."

For two days Suttle's body lay where it had fallen, but by then matters had quieted somewhat, and a party went and brought the body to Nixburg, and it was buried in what is now the cemetery, the first grave opened in it.

The killing of Suttle in Coosa, with one or two others in the newly settled country, together with exciting, alarming, and exaggerated reports from different places, led to the removal by governmental authority of the bulk of the Indians to the Territory, in the summer of 1836. Very many of these people named were members of the two strong churches of Shiloh and Fish Pond. Much of the land was hilly, but very proudctive. Oak and hickory was more abundant here than south.

To the north and east, and further off from Nixburg, the lands continued to be good and induced a number of substantial men to settle upon them. Among the very early ones were Rev. James F. Edens (a preacher of strong convictions, and bitter against the mission movements), Mr. Reuben Jordan and his sons (Dr. John A. and James), and Dr. Reuben, the Spiveys, Moses Favors, Meshac Ward, the celebrated maker of bells for stock, Elijah McLemore, Moses and Ransom Meadows, and Mr. Towns. Later was Dr. James Kelley, long the leading physician in all the upper part of the county, and who was the teacher and helper of so many young physicians, Lennard Marberry, a wealthy planter, and his son, Thomas, Harris McKinney, Reuben, Allen and Frank Maxwell (also men of wealth and prominence), Isaac Smith, another Jesse Stanley, William Rogers, Ezariah Pinson, Mr. Ogletree, Rev. Bright Skipper, Mr. Wilkerson, Milton Russell, John and Anderson Colley, Albert Holloway, the noted singer for more than half a century, besides others who helped to make this Elkahatchie community the equal of any portion of the county in whatever makes a country desirable. Descendants of most of these are still to be found about here, who have succeeded in maintaining the name and reputation of their ancestors. Towns had a mill and cotton factory on Elkahatchie. The mill is still kept up, but the factory went down before the war. It has been quite a place for July celebrations and picnics. Mr. Taylor and Wm. T. Hatchett, sons-in-law of Marberry, lived here for awhile, as did W. W. Mason and Rev. J. D. Williams.

Near where Kellyton is, Mr. Webb from quite an early day in Indian times had a store and for long years after. A grandson is now a professor at Auburn. Brice M. Burgess had a tan-yard. But Kellyton, named for Dr. Kelly, has been built up since the Central Railroad penetrated the country. It has never become a place of much business, being too near both Alexander City and Goodwater, but it is in the midst of a good and thrifty country. There lived early hereabout Archibald Kelly, Iver D. Patterson, Thomas Childress, William S. Caldwell, Hamilton Ware, John C. Burgess, who was killed while tax collector, it is supposed, for the money of which he had a considerable sum on hand the evening before disappearing. No clue could be had. His horse and buggy were reported found in the neighborhood of Kingston. Mystery surrounded the affair, and some prominent men were suspected. William Winslett, John M. Benson, Peter Robinson, Alexander Black, and Charles Hagan and his son, Edward, were also here early. Coming later, but not much later, were Stephen D. Hughes, John William and Joseph Shaw. William White and son, Capt. John H. Clisby, Doss Martin, Martin Bull, William Selman, Mr. Gaddis, John Auld, Dred Thomas,

John McNeil, and still later, Buck Martin, Mr. Brown, Mr. Corley, Monk, and the Thompsons.

Goodwater is now the leading place for business in the county, having several blocks of stores, ginneries, mills, and other public works, with a good graded school, and several churches. It became a place of importance after the Central Railway of Georgia reached it, about 1880. For some years it was the terminus, remaining so long enough to give it a good start in business, which it has more than held. While the terminus, it had a large country untouched by trains which found this its most convenient market. While the country was in possession of the Indians a Mr. Kibbler had a store near here, and from then on some business has been done. William Adkins, known as "Little Billy," a dwarf in size, but full of pluck, settled here early as a shoemaker. He stuck to his trade, practiced economy until he was able to begin a small mercantile business, gradually enlarging and prospering, until in the fifties he had accumulated a fair property. He talked up his place, worked for its interest, and no doubt his tact and energy laid the foundation for the town it has become. The place takes its name from a bold spring of cool water which flows out at the base of its high hills.

An industrious population was scattered around from an early period. A. B. Nicholson, a thrifty farmer, was in the valley above the town. Timothy and Noah Ford lived near. Noah went in the forties to Louisiana, but Timothy remained till his death, and sons and grandsons are still among the people. George Gray, Geo. B. Nash, Joseph Adair, and M. Bailey were here quite early, and not much later John Grimes or Graham, the McClouds, McNairs, John T. McElwrath, and Dr. Baker, all North Carolina Scotch, settled and remained here, as have also some of their descendants. John M. Pascal, Prior Nabors, Samuel and Robert Pruett were long citizens. Dr. Baker was a fine physician, a good citizen, and man of much public spirit. His wife was Mary Jane McAdory. Dr. John N. Slaughter married Celia McAdory and also lives at Goodwater.

A newspaper has been published at Goodwater, but the writer has failed to get needed information about it. There was also a volunteer military company, but the history of it has not been obtained. There is a bank here. New life has been taken on in recent years.

An elevated ridge runs west dividing the waters of the Hatchett and Sockapatoy creeks. A road ran along its crest through an almost unbroken wood until the business of the place enticed settlers. Now most of it is cultivated, and good homes are scattered upon it. The writer was traveling this elevated ridge one night, and witnessed a grand display of the Borealis Lights, which for beauty and splendor surpassed anything of the kind he has ever seen.

Westward from Goodwater there were but few people living until the Mt. Olive and Hanover country was reached, but now people are settling more in there, and opening up farms. South and southwest is what is known as the Sockapatoy country, in which were some of the earliest settlers, and which rapidly filled up with others. Solomon Chapman, who opened for General Jackson in 1814 the road bearing his name, was a Tennessean who came into the country, if not before, immediately after the cession of it. He and his sons, John A., William, and David, especially John A., were important factors in shaping up the county, and had good helpers in Joseph, Josephus, and Robert Lauderdale, Rev. John McKenzie, Robert Goodgame, William and Gabriel White, Burrell Ware, and John Thomas. By 1836, Joseph H. Bradford and Daniel Hogan came from Tennessee and settled below, but it was not long until Bradford had built his mill and cotton factory near, adding these enterprises to his large farming interest. Samuel S. Graham, John Martin, William Selman, Patrick McKinney, John Bell, John, Jonathan, David, Reuben, and Isaac Mitchell, and John D. Letcher were all here early, and did duty here as useful citizens most of their lives. Jonathan Mitchell and Letcher moved lower down pretty soon, Mitchell living at Nixburg, and Letcher at Central. Another early settler was a Mr. Moss who was killed by Burrell

Ware in 1839, which created much excitement, as murders were not so common then. A little later Mr. Garnett and his sons, Dr. William and John, Col. Thomas Smith, a dentist, John Gaddis, William B. House and sons, and Abram Hester and sons, good farmers, were added forces. In the fifties Col. William Garrett, a distinguished Alabamian, and Simpson and Moore, lessees of the Bradford factory, came into the community. The factory was abandoned a few years after the war, but the old stone building and dam are there yet. Jefferson McKenzie and John Bell merchandised a long time at Sockapatoy, and John N. Slaughter taught a fine school. McKenzie and Slaughter are now at Goodwater.

South and west from here there was much forest land, and the hills were usually steep and rocky, but the lands were good, and a number of farms, some of them large, were scattered about. Thompson Corbett, his son-in-law, Stephen Gray, Mr. Wiggins, John and Albert Thomas, Robert and John Goodgame, and Mr. Measels all had good farms, and later the Crews, and still later Spigener were in here and added merchandise to their business. Not far away were Joe and Spratlin Porter, Hiram, James, and Reuben Phillips, Charles Murray and John Griffin. Lower down was H. Massingale, Jeremiah Busbee, Robert Willingham and his father, Mr. Dorsey and his sons. Rev. Joseph Hill came very early, and was one of the pioneer preachers. He had at one time a good property, mostly in slaves. Their freedom and extreme old age left him poor, so he had to be helped in his last years. He was near one hundred years old at his death. He would doubtless have been neglected, but for the remembrance of him by Stephen D. Ray, who brought his case to the attention of the Central Association, and carried the help given by the brethren to him yearly. Ray himself died in 1902, between 90 and 100 years old.

A little west of these last named was the home and mill of Daniel Crawford. This mill has long converted the corn and wheat of this country into breadstuffs. John Ward, the Lecroys, Benjamin Manning's family, and others have come into this section which so long lay a virgin forest. On Hatchett which borders westward the country just spoken of, Elijah Smith had a mill quite early. Not far off lived Stephen Thomas, who was killed during the war by a party looking up deserters. There were several in here, and he was suspected of harboring some of them, though it was not known that he did. Killing him was not perhaps premeditated, but it stirred up feeling, not assuaged till some of the leading parties left the country. His sons, Calvin and Carney, also lived here, but afterward moved near Rockford.

At the heavy freshet of 1886, on Jack's Creek, in the farm of John Ward there were heavy washes. In one of these there was unearthed a quantity of relics, showing among them parts of guns, soldier caps, and kegs of powder from which the wood had rotted off, but the powder was caked in the shape of the kegs, and English coins bearing date with the war of the Yamasee Indians in South Carolina. This tribe was largely destroyed, and their remnants, according to Wilson's History of the United States, "were pursued by the whites as far west as what afterward became Alabama." All the dates on relics and coins pointed to this period, and the only reasonable conjecture of their presence here, was that they must have been brought and left by this pursuing party of English and colonists. These relics were in the hands of Judge John S. Bentley when seen by the writer.

Calvin Jones, father of Dr. Julius Evander, and Watt Jones lived at different places along Hatchett Creek, and built several mills on that stream between Goodwater, Mt. Olive, and Hanover. He was an enterprising man, and valuable citizen.

On the west side of Hatchett Creek and north of Rockford is the region known as Hanover beat. The settlers here who lived among the Indians were Alexander Logan and James Lindsey, father of W. M. Lindsey. Lindsey was a man in good circumstances, and early built a good home on the Turnpike, afterwards owned by John A. Pylant, and then by Jasper McAdory, who still lives there. In 1838, Lindsey built a still better home a mile or more on the roads from the place sold to Pylant toward Sylacauga. This was a well finished two story house, the best in all the upper part of the county. It had good guttering with the date of the structure upon it. This afterward became the home of Isaac Willingham, a much loved citizen, who was murdered by one of his slaves during the war. The murderer was taken to Rockford and burned. The place was afterward occupied by Benjamin Kimbrough who married a daughter of Isaac Willingham who bought it from Lindsey. Kimbrough's widow still lives there. Alexander Logan lived till a few years back in the lower part of the neighborhood, reaching a ripe age. Two sons, John and James, lived to be men of ripe years in the community, and other children and descendants are still in the section. John A. Pylant, Mr. Norwood, Mr. Mathews, William Samuels, Guy Smith, and Rev. Matt Butler, lived here from an early period. Samuels is still there. J. R. Steely, John and Patrick Smith, and John Chancellor were also early settlers, and somewhat later came in Russell and William Hand, Joel, William, and Mark Murphy, Williamson Spears, Uriah Darden, the Conoways, Abraham Atchley, Daniel and George Thompson, Dr. Wm. Garnett, and John Garnett. Descendants of these are still in the country. One son of Darden has been an honored commissioner of the county, and he has a son who is a promising young Baptist minister.

A portion of this country lies well, and the people used to raise an abundant supply of home subsistence and fruits. They have usually had good schools, and the Methodists and Baptists have had good strong churches. Andrew Chapel, the Methodist, has always been strong. Poplar Springs, the Baptist church, was for some years the strongest numerically in the Central Association. The people here were very social and hospitable. On the west of the Turnpike there is a high range of hills, or succession of ranges, called the Weogufka hills or mountains. Higher up they cross the Turnpike, and run up into the region long known as the Mt. Olive country. Along the Turnpike, after passing the Lindsay place, there were few settlements for some miles as it was mountainous. From an early period, there was a hatter named Robinson, who lived on the side of one of these mountains, and the remains of his old home may still be seen. Since the war several good settlements have been made.

East of this range of hills and west of Hatchett there is a country less broken, and the soil is good. Quite a number of people who are prosperous have lived in here from a period early in the history of the country. Among them are remembered Larkin Newman, Peter Vardeman, Mr. Works, Mountain Hill, John, Wyatt, and Mr. Bailey, Mr. Adkins, W. A. Richards, Mr. Woody, Michael, Frank, John, and Clem Corley, Carey Cotton, Wm. C. Brown, Rev. J. C. Fulmer and sons, Asa Waldrop, Rev. Robert Carlisle, long a leading Primitive Baptist preacher, and sons, Thomas King, Mr. Finch, Rev. Benj. Foscue, another Primitive preacher, and Hon. Fred Foscue. The last two went west in the early fifties. Most of the others have long lived here, and their descendants are clinging to the old homes. Robert Pruett came into this country after the war, and farmed and merchandised, accumulating a handsome property. A large set of saw mills for more than twenty years has been established a few miles above Mt. Olive, at Hollis, and has cut an immense amount of lumber, and furnished a market for much of the spare products of the farms. The lands are good, and farmers self-sustaining. The country has taken a noble pride in keeping up good schools and churches. Much of the soil is red and fine for apples and other fruits, and grapes. Mountain Hill lived for many years just north. Also Mr. Works, one of whose daughters married Dr. Peter Goggans, and was the mother of the well known Dr. J. A. Goggans of Alexander City.

After leaving Mt. Olive the Plank Road passes through a gap in the mountains, and reaches the old Chapman Road, and there strikes another comparatively level belt of country lying on both sides of Weogufka Creek, which is known as the Macedonia and Stewartville country. There is now a pretty good population living in here, and they are generally thrifty, though the settlers were for a long time scattered. Fox Shelton was here at an early day, near Shelton Creek, where it crosses the Turnpike, and he kept for a long time the Shelton Inn. Mr. Richards was also early on Weogufka, near where the Turnpike crosses it. He was a well to do farmer, and paid some attention to fruit. The writer has seen very fine apples and peaches grown on this farm. Jack McNeily was a blacksmith who ran a shop in this region among the Indians. Later Mr. Geo. Ross, Obed Thomas, and Thomas Kennedy were farmers in good circumstances, who did well, but left for more advantageous parts after a few years. Stewart came in before the fifties, and gave name to the voting precinct when established. For some years Thomas Lambert, who represented the county, was a Republican in days of reconstruction, and was made State geologist during the same period, resided here. He was poorly equipped for the place as geologist. Rev. Mr. Vanzandt, a Methodist Protestant minister, also in the legislature during that period, was a resident of this neighborhood. A. J. Porter, who was a gallant Confederate captain, and a man superior to the other two mentally, also represented the county several times, and was a member of the last Constitutional Convention, as a Republican. He has had his home here from about the time of the war. Mr. Wood was a citizen here for years, and was killed by a mob during the war because of his Union sentiments, though he was known as a good citizen otherwise. This unjustifiable killing had much to do in making some adopt the Republican party who perhaps would not have done so otherwise. Guy Smith, an old citizen of Indian times, came here about the close of the war, and remained until the news of the thrift of Cullman enticed him there. Jack Smith and a brother, with Tap Bullard, are old settlers. William and Moses Stone are thrifty farmers who have lived here since soon after the war, as has Joseph Dunlap. Lee Blocker, one of the thrifty commissioners of the county, resides in the lower part of this neighborhood.

Passing down Weogufka from Stewartville there was for several miles a scope of finely timbered country that to the war had but very few people in it. About 1855 or 1856, Doss Martin and Capt. John Clisby moved into it and opened up good farms. Mr. W. A. McBrayer was an old settler. About the same time William Hughes, and William, Robert, and James Thompson came in. These were brothers of Hon. Daniel J. Thompson. On the east side of Weogufka there were some early settlers. Among them Henry Blankenship, a Revolutionary soldier, who with Mr. Casey were the only ones who lived in the county, so far as known by the writer. There were three sons of Mr. Blankenship, Mark, Reuben, and James. There were six Bazemores, Thomas,

Ephraim, Jackson, Meredith, Frank, and Joseph. Robert and Alfred Massey were here also tolerably early. Mint Spear, Epperson, and Curleigh were also citizens for a long while and from an early period. A Mr. Lesley was among them and noted for his large family of about twenty children, and that at a reunion of the family some years back there were 340 of them. Weogufka was noted for large families, besides Lesley's. There was Evan Calfee with sixteen children, Benj. Callaway with 21, Robert Taylor with 25, and W. A. Wilson with 12. There was a Mr. Webb, well known, who also lived in here.

Further toward Rockford was George Davis. In the valley on the west side of the creek was Mr. Wood, stepfather of William M. Lindsey, long well known and loved in the county. He was the son of James Lindsey of Hanover. Wood died and for years Lindsey, his mother, and his family lived on their fine old farm; but afterward he lived at Central Institute; and from there he moved on the Jackson Trace where he lived till his removal to Texas in 1868. Lindsey married a daughter of Evan Calfee who lived on an adjoining farm on the opposite side of the creek. He was the father of sixteen children. Among his sons-in-law were some of Coosa's most prominent men. Among them Hon. George Taylor, a nephew of his, George Taylor, Jr., Mr. Bazemore, W. M. Lindsey, and Patrick McKinney of Sockapatoy. McKinney was a wealthy farmer, and was robbed by "Rosseau's Raid" of a considerable quantity of gold, all his horses and mules, a quantity of provisions besides other things. Calfee was a member of the House in 1857. George Taylor was a member of the Secession Convention in 1861. Just west of Lindsey lived Benj. Callaway and wife, noted for their large family of useful sons and daughters. They lived here till death at an advanced age. Many of their posterity are still in the county. William Hood also spent most of his life here. Lower down the creek was John Bowden, a native of Ireland, and a fine citizen. Close by him was Robert Taylor and his brother John, both brothers of the older George Taylor. Robert Taylor was the father of twenty-five children, but by three wives. Near them for years Wm. A. Wilson lived on a fine farm on Weogufka. He was in the county at its organization, living in Marble Valley, but owned large plantations at different times in different parts of the county. He was much in public life, and served once as sheriff. He also had a family of twelve children. Mr. Jennings also lived in this beat, owning a good farm on Finniclochkee Creek. There are many more peo ple in later years living in this portion of the country. David Griffin, another prominent citizen, lived for years in this beat. He tied T. T. Wall for sheriff in 1857, Wilson, the sheriff, giving the casting vote to Wall. Many of these were members of Weo-gufka Baptist Church, which for a good while was a leading church in the Association. There was a small Methodist church in the neighborhood.

To the northwest from here was Lewis beat, which was gen-erally hilly, the land poor, and it was thinly inhabited. Thomp-son Coker, John S. Baites and his son Mitchell were here as early as 1833. John N. Lee lived on the Trace a long time. Farther west was George Lewis. The Dupriests were well to do farmers on Point Creek, as was also Messrs. Tait and Waldrop. B. D. Harrison, S. Baxley, and P. Martin had their homes in this beat, and there were others, but there were never enough people in here to maintain good schools and churches.

Marble Valley, which was north of this, was different. From the first it had some population. Much of the land was level, or gently rolling, and productive. There is a fine bed of marble underlying part of it. William A. and Jessee Wilson, brothers, lived here when the county was organized, and with Archibald Downing were connected for an ordinary lifetime with the affairs of the county. From almost the first Mr. Barrett, Jack Brasier, Mr. Pate, William Finley, William and Jessee Morris (both of whom were living a short while since, quite old men) lived near the post office, and were men of good position among their fel-lows. At one time a Mr. Manning did business at the Valley. His son, J. C. Manning, has figured largely in Populistic and Re-publican affairs in Alabama for the past ten years or more. John Upshaw has for a number of years been prominent, living nearer toward the river. Among those who long resided here, and who are represented still by descendants were Thomas Jordan, Charles Pate, Mr. Posey, Mr. Baxley, and James Harrison. John Looney was among the first settlers on Peckerwood Creek, where he owned a good farm and fine mill property. He was a substantial citizen, who was a commissioner of the county longer perhaps than any other man in it. He raised a fine family, and his sons have proved worthy of their sire, and their sons are taking a good stand also, promising to perpetuate the name in honor. The daughters and their children are also among the honored ones. Rev. L. H. Hastie, a son-in-law, has lived more than forty years in the neighborhood. He was recently burned to death in his home. Near Mr. Looney lived Allen Wood, also an early settler, who spent his years from manhood to a ripe old age among these people, rearing a family of sons and daughters who have maintained themselves in the esteem of those who know them. Mr. Wood was peculiar. He was a man of fine mind, full of quaint humor, and was a power in elections, able to find out how men stood, and controlling friends to his side directly, and opponents indirectly. He owned a good farm. John Cooper was also an early settler here, in easy circumstances. He owned a good farm, on which there is a fine bed of marble, but not much of it has been taken out. He lived to a good age, and also reared a family of sons and daughters, whose lives bear the fruits of good family training. Some of his sons and grandsons still are among the leading men of Marble Valley. Here is Union Springs Baptist Church, one among the oldest in the county.

The country below Weogufka and Lewis beats for some miles is very rough and broken, and was but sparsely settled. It has, of later years since the war, had more settlers, and there are some good farms opened. But this country will be more valuable for minerals than anything else. At an early day there was a small settlement in the neighborhood of Flint Hill, between Weogufka and Hatchett creeks, where there was a weak church and school. W. T. Stubblefield, who was for a long time clerk of the circuit court, was here among the Indians. The Franklins, half breeds, were also living near. Henry Jones, a man of some property, was further southwest, and his son Hardy, who afterwards became a preacher. He had a neighbor, Robert Parker, a considerable hunter. Near Hatchett Creek Robert King settled, and prospered well for awhile. Below him was a very fine old citizen, Mr. Castleberry, who was an old resident here. Isaac Jones, a man in easy circumstances, and father of Mrs. John Willis and Mrs. John A. Logan. Jacob Bentley, an uncle of Judge John Bentley, lived below him, and still lower down, Simon P. Shaffer, father of Dr. John P., lived for some years, putting up a good mill on Hatchett Creek. This mill was afterwards owned by Calvin Jones, then Charles Cox, and now by Matt Lawson. All this country was very hilly, and up to the last knowledge of it by the writer, but few people lived in it, though it is said the population has increased. The Fixico Mining Company has its plants in here. A Mr. Posey had a lovely home in here from an early day. Farther southwest Rev. E. T. Aiken owned a farm on the Trace, given to him by the Central Association in compensation for missionary work. The farm was good soil, but much of it was very steep hillsides. Below him for many years lived William Conway who owned a mill on Swamp Creek, not far from where it empties into Hatchett.

Passing southward we come to Traveler's Rest, more popularly known as the "Devil's Half Acre," and from here south and westward there were more people. Some of these were here early in the county's life. John Kelly owned a farm, store, blacksmith and wood shop, a distillery and bar-room. Here was the place for gatherings on public days, and often on Saturdays, and there was much drinking, rioting and fighting, consequently the name. Elias Kelly, for long years a justice of the peace, lived near. J. M. Paschall came here from the Sockapatoy country and was killed by some negroes in 1866. Stephen Pearce bought John Kelly out at the expiration of his term as sheriff, stopped the whiskey trade, and the place after that was civil. John Cooper, Mr. Rutlege, and Greenbury Clark lived in this section. Moses Hamilton once owned a large farm between Hatchett and the Coosa, which was afterwards owned by William Hardy and his descendants. William A. Wilson once owned a fine farm in here on Weogufka. Dred Allen was also a man of prominence for many years. Henry Logan was here among the Indians, and Ellis, his son, grew up here, and was once sheriff of the county and went as captain to the Confederate War in the 13th Ala. Regt. On Pinchula Creek, John Varner had a good farm from the first settlement of the country, and died here, having raised a family who succeeded to his estate.   Jessee Ellis, one of the early tax collectors, lived in this beat.   Jack and Joel Gullege were early settlers in this beat, and both remained citizens of Coosa for most of their long lives, each being above ninety years old.   A family of Hulls have lived here for several generations, and another named Estes and the Batsons.   Some of all these families live about here yet.   Henry Norrel came about 1850, and lived here and in Rockford until his recent death.   He had several sons to succeed him.   Among the prominent men of good property who lived here was James Lykes and Vine Smith.   Lykes owned a fine mill on the Trace on Wewoka Creek.   By mistake the post office named for this mill is called Sykes Mill.   Smith owned the ferry so long known by his name on the Coosa.   It is now owned by Mr. Higgins, a son-in-law.   Rev. A. G. Rains has been a citizen for thirty years.   Wm. Ward long lived in the beat, and so did Robert Massey and his son, Alfred Massey.   John Collins came into the lower part of the beat after the war.   Several of the Hannons, John, William, Beall, and their father, were here from quite early.   On the east side of the Trace there were a good many families, prominent among them were Andrew McCord, Williams Chancellor, who came from near Rockford just after the war, and Mr. Willett, who had sons, J. L., Wm., and J. E., still in this section.   All this portion of the country, though hilly, is not so broken but that most of it can be cultivated satisfactorily.   There has been a large supply of fine timber, much of which has been destroyed, much made into lumber.   For a number of years, Mr. Wadsworth of Chilton has been cutting extensively, and floating across the Coosa to his large saw mills.   He has a tram road that hauls the logs for miles around.

This brings us in our southward movement to Buyckville beat, the one lying north and northwest from Wetumpka, and which was a prominent part of Coosa until the formation of Elmore, when it became a part of the new county.   Most of the land here was more level, and susceptible of better improvement than the beats north of it.   Parts of it, however, are broken, and in places the hills are steep.   In original fine timber it was unsurpassed.   Here a number of whites settled with the first opening of the country. Among the pioneers were Jas. A. Wall, long a highly respected citizen on the Turnpike, where his house was for years a stage stand. His son, T. T. Wall, was of age and living here before the organization of the county, and was from the first one of its public men, filling among other offices the sherifalty twice. Conrad and Eddy, both physicians, were also sons, and he had grandsons, James Swept, and Dink, besides others who have also been well known citizens. Joel Spigener came in 1833, buying lands both for himself, William K. Oliver, and other relatives. It was not long until his brothers, Captain Samuel and William Spigener, and Mr. William Knight, Mr. Whetstone, Arthur De Bardelaben, Edward Buyck, and others from about Orangeburg, S. C., were here also, and for years were among the most thrifty men of the country. Lucien Pinkston, William Dunlap, William Moore, Alexander Graham, Lewis Gholson, Joseph Holloman, Solomon Chapman, and Green Holifield, were here also in the thirties, and some of them with the first comers. Most of these men left sons and daughters, and these in turn families again, so that several generations of them have successively had homes here. Gholson had a mill a little below a spring which furnished the water needed for propelling it. The mill afterward became the property of Charles Buckner, an old settler in the county. It was afterward owned by Henry Gilmer, who died here. The spring was the boldest one the writer has ever seen outside of the blue limestone country. Among those who came in a little later, but who were influential, were Mourning Holly, Thomas Stanley and sons, Henry Hoffman, Dr. Davie, Captain McKenzie, Charles Cox, Sr. and Jr., the Ruffins, Rev. Moses Gunn, a prominent Primitive Baptist preacher, and his sons, Moses and Dr. George, Elijah Holtzclaw, father of William, General James, and John; John Sears, a millwright who put up the Lykes mill, and was its owner for years. He built several other mills and was the best millwright of the county. He was for years the one who superintended and changed the machinery at the large Tallassee cotton mills whenever changes were needed. He was highly esteemed by all who knew him for his integrity, piety and general worth. Mr. Moon and son, Tandy, with Fred Lykes came in later. For a number of years Wesley G. Deloney, a son-in-law of Charles Cox, Sr., was highly esteemed by all. But in later years from some cause his life was revolutionized much for the worse, much to the regret of all, for both he and the Coxes were highly esteemed and prominent. He became a leader of the Republicans of the section after the war, drank and was quarrelsome. He fell into a cellar in Wetumpka that led to his death. Above Buyckville among the good citizens were Mr. Collins and sons, John and Andrew, Mr. Barnett and Mr. Bonner, William Johnson, Flemming Goolsby, William Cardwell, George McEwen, M. Watts with his sons, Thomas, Joe, and Robert, the Cardens and Cardwells, with others not now remembered. The village from an early period had a good school. Among the early teachers were Conrad Wall, William Holtzclaw, Geo. E. Brewer, and Isaac Hall, who for more than half century taught about here. Fred Oliver later brought the school to its best point. For several years in the fifties there were more dancing parties than in any other part of the county, and there was also a good deal of drinking. On Saturdays it was not unusual for a number to be found playing crack-loo in the store fronts, and yet the place was not given to rowdyism. A few years later there were some religious revivals, and dancing, drinking and gambling gave way. Joel Spigener was prominent in the county from the first. He kept a regular diary, that if it could be found would be of great value in preparing a work like this, for in the diary he noted not only events personal to himself, but events in different parts of the county that attracted attention at the time. The writer has seen some fragments covering several years, and tried hard to find it all. Some things from it will be of interest. In a letter to Fred Lykes, dated April 26th, 1833, he tells of a cloudy rainy spell lasting ten days, in which the sun had been seen but once. The spell had been introduced by a hail storm that destroyed the crops. The Tallapoosa, Coosa, Alabama, and Tombigbee were higher than had ever been known by the whites. He tells of a terrific wind storm on Saturday, the 6th of April, that destroyed houses, fences, killed stock, and crippled some of the people, but none were killed.

In a letter to his son Joel, May 7th, 1855, he says, "There has not been enough rain in five weeks to bring up cotton. Corn worth $1.25 per bushel, flour $12 to $14 per barrel, salt $3 to $4 per sack, cotton 9 cents. Coosa River lower than I have ever seen it. Boats cannot get to Wetumpka. I sold 125 bushels of potatoes at 80 and 90 cts. per bushel."

In December, 1859, he tells of eating fine watermelons on several different days, the last one mentioned being the 25th of December. These were raised and kept by himself.

Some springs he noted marking fifty and more lambs. In 1861 he had 144 head of sheep. In the fall he would fatten sheep and beeves for market. In June he had twenty stands of young bees, and twenty-seven of old ones.

On the 27th of July, the ladies of Buyckville organized an Aid Society to make clothing for the soldiers, and Spigener gave them fifty pounds of wool.

He notes the hanging of Mack Holifield at Rockford, March 26th, 1862, for committing rape on Mrs. Barnes, near Buyckville.

He mentions a large meeting held in Rockford, April 2nd, 1862, to aid in raising volunteers for the Confederate army.

He makes a note of the death of George Taylor at his home near Wetumpka, June 15th, 1862. Also that at Brooks' Mill, near Brooksville, they made brandy during the war.

He refers to taking hides to the tan-yards of Albert Crumpler, near Rockford, of Mr. Dennis, near Rogers Mill, and deer and sheep skins for dressing by James Carroll, near Rockford.

He speaks of saving two watermelons from October, 1862, to February 15th, 1863, and that they were good at the latter date.

In February, 1863, he notes that cotton sold in New York for 92 cts. per pound, and bacon at $1.50 in Mobile.

In 1863, he notes paying Charles Cox $2,700 for securing a Mr. McCollers, as a substitute for his son Joel in the army.

He notes killing fat wild hogs several winters from the woods, sometimes as many as a dozen in a season. He notes that sweet potatoes sold in Montgomery, March, 1866, at $3.00 per bushel. On the 13th of March he notes the death of C. J. Woodruff, for years a prominent business man of Wetumpka.

He notes the shooting that took place at Buyckville, January 12th, 1866, between W. G. Deloney and Moses Clipper.

He tells of the marriage of Thos. S. McDonald of Rockford to Miss Julia Spigener of Buyckville, November 15th, 1866, and of the death of Mrs. John S. McDonald at Rockford, March 31st, 1867.

He caught in his turkey pen on February 17th, 1867, nine wild turkeys. These pens were made of rails and covered with a hole under the bottom rail of one side from the outside reaching to the inside. This trench leading in was covered on the inside by boards or something else for some distance in, and the pen was baited with grain, and so was the trench leading into it. The turkeys that entered, after eating what they wanted, in trying to get out would be prevented by the covering, and walking around looking through the rail cracks they would walk over the covered trench, never looking down for way of escape and thus were safely prisoned.

He notes the death of Major Elijah Holtzclaw near Buyckville, May 19th, 1867. He was the father of Gen. James Holtzclaw of Montgomery. Also, in the same month, the death of George Mason, a prominent lawyer and editor of Wetumpka. Also in January following, the death of Dr. Jno. S. McDonald of Rockford, one of its first settlers.

East of Buyckville and west of Central there was a section of country known as the Rogers' and Carolina neighborhoods. Antioch, a strong Baptist church, was in the Rogers section, and around it lived three brothers, Joseph, Robert, and David Rogers. All were well to do farmers. Joseph had a good home not far from the church, and was the dispenser of a liberal hospitality.

For many years he was a commissioner of the county. He removed to Mississippi before the war. Robert Rogers lived two or three miles from the church, and, besides his farm, owned a good mill on Hatchesofka where the Rogers' Mill road crossed it. The mill now is known as the William mill. He was also largely connected for some years with building the Plank Road. After his death about 1854 or 1855, his widow married Mr. Dennis, and on his death, married Mr. Black, both prominent men in the community. She lived till a few years since, and died near Dallas, Texas, over ninety years old. Below them, and also owning a mill was Malcom Smith of North Carolina, who came out with the Scotch of North Carolina, who gave name to Carolina church and community. He was a relative of the Grahams, and Alexander Smith. He was a man of means, and had a good home. After his removal to Prattville, his son, Neil Smith; owned the home and farm until his death a few years since. At an early date he employed a good teacher, and boarded a number of young men that they might get the benefit of this good teacher. Just east of Smith's place there were the Batchelors, Peeples and others, some of whom are still there, and among the best and most progressive farmers of Elmore County. Lower down was Henry Macon, an early comer from Georgia, whose wife was a near relative of Governor McDaniel of Georgia. His sons, Oslin and Pleasant, also lived near; and descendants are still living around. A Mr. Collier was a substantial farmer not far from the church, and an early comer. Some of his descendants have continued in this county until now. Mr. Rawles, the father of John and Dr. Jabez, was a citizen here. A few miles north along and near Little Wewoka, there were several families who came in pretty much together, all of Scotch descent, and most of them related. For a long time the neighborhood was called Scotland. They were Presbyterians and soon had a church called Carolina. They were all in easy circumstances, and some worth a good property. As a rule they were intelligent and cultured. George Graham was among them, and died on the old homestead after a residence of more than half a century, and the home is still occupied by a son or grandson. He was the father of Mrs. W. C. Brown, of Mt. Olive, long an honored citizen. There were two other Grahams, relatives, who died comparatively young, but each left a family, the widow of one, a sister of Judge Archibald McMillan, married John H. Townsend, a fine citizen, and early settler. The other widow afterward moved to Louisiana, and her son, Evander, did well, becoming a lawyer and judge. Alexander Smith, of whom more is said elsewhere, came with the others. A fatal epidemic of bloody flux prevailed in this neighborhood in 1842, resulting in the death of many, among them, the wife of Alexander Smith, John and Jas. Graham, Mr. McMillan, father of Judge Archer and Neil McMillan. Dr. McClure's father was one of this company of early settlers, but went out in the scourge. The Doctor succeeded to the estate. Lochland Smith, a brother of Alexander, was also one of the colony, and lived here until about 1852, when he and several others went to Louisiana. John H. Townsend lived here until sometime in the fifties when he moved near Talladega Springs, where he lived till his death. The writer boarded with him, and taught at Carolina in 1851, and remembers the year as a green spot in memory, owing to the pleasant home and neighborhood. Living was bountiful. The farms yielded well,——fruit trees flourished——fish were plentiful in the streams, and deer, wild hogs, and turkeys. with smaller game were bountiful——the woods kept burned in the spring made fine pasturage where plenty of cattle, sheep, goats, and hogs were raised, so that fresh meats, domestic and wild, were always to be had. The deer were so close that the teacher would have time for a drive before or after school. By a drive is meant that deer usually have certain directions in which they run. The driver, as he was called, took the hounds into the brakes of cane and shrubs along the streams, and rousted out the deer. The places of running out into the open were usually known, and called "stands." At these stands a hunter was placed before the drive was made, so that the deer, fleeing from the chase of the dogs, came by, the hunter was to shoot it down. It was not very unusual for several deer to come out by one stand, and at other times they might scatter and come out at different stands. As late as 1851, the writer knew of as many as seven coming out at one stand. Small game was abundant.

The strong attachment of the Scotch for their kin and friends is well known, and it has become a proverb to say "as clannish as the Scotch," when close adhering friendship is alluded to. An incident occurring about Carolina in these days is illustrative. Some lady relatives on one occasion were together when one alluded to a visit of a kinswoman whom she said she liked, but not as well as she could if she would not let her children go so dirty; but, for this, she was ashamed of her. Another of the party rebuked her, saying: "You ought not to talk that way, for they are our kin, and I love her, and hope God will bless her and the children, *dirt and all.*"

There also lived in this community Mr. Lattiker, blacksmith, Jack Salter, John Lane, James and William O'Hara, one of whom owned the mill afterwards owned by Colonel Austin. This neighborhood met that of Brooksville and Nixburg.

West of this, on both sides of the Turnpike, there were a number of settlers, among them Green Holifield built a good home on the road on moving from below Buyckville, and opened a good farm. It afterwards became the home of Andrew Collins, later of William Johnson, and is now owned by Lafayette Johnson of Montgomery, who spends his summers there. Mr. Barnett, the father-in-law of Matt Lawson, long lived on the west side of the road as also Mr. Barnes. On the east side Moses Clipper owned a good farm, on which he lived for a number of years. Two large families of Curleighs were a little farther east for a number of years. Several of the sons died in the Confederate service. The same is true of a Mr. Blankenship. There were a few others in this section whose names are not remembered. There was a small mill in there, owned possibly by the Curleighs. There were several sections of land in virgin forest at the last acquaintance of the writer.

Immediately on the road was the good home of David Lawson, a well to do farmer, and a noble, hospitable man who lived here for a number of years and died. He had a family much respected for their solid worth. William Lawson, a prominent planter and politician of Montgomery, is a son, as also Matt and

David. Mrs. Alfred Massey, Mrs. Jane Humphries, and Mrs. Lafayette Johnson are daughters. Near him lived another good citizen, Mr. Pool, who has been a resident on the same place more than fifty years. The home is still occupied by a son. Not far from them lived Mrs. Lysle, the mother-in-law of Lawson, and his brothers-in-law, John and David Lysle. In this neighborhood Judge McMillan had a good farm which he left for Rockford when elected to the Probate Judgeship. Quite near them lived Calvin Humphries, a fine farmer and man, who held the place of commissioner longer than anyone else except Mr. Looney. He also represented the county in the House in 1859-60. He reared a family of several sons and daughters, who stood well while living here, and in the countries in which they have moved. T: T. Wall and William Spigener were once in this region, and also a Mr. Christie who came from below Wetumpka. The lands owned by these three are now the property of J. C. Maxwell and Judge Austin.

Fol'owing the Turnpike toward Rockford from here on, the country becomes more broken and rocky, but the soil being good it has supported a population of thrifty families. Among them may be named the two Spears, who lived here since the early fifties until their deaths, and have been succeeded by their children. Sterling Spears, a son, became a prominent preacher after the war, who was growing in power and popularity when cut off by death before the meridian of life was reached. One, Alexander, still lives there, though nearly 100. Near them Daniel Hamilton, a son-in-law of James A. Wall, had a home when most of the country was a wilderness, and he had for a neighbor Frank Morgan, who lived on the Turnpike where what was known as Morgan's Creek crossed it. This immediate country, or a good deal of it, was and is owned by sons of Jones Stephens, a fine citizen who lived farther east for many years, and by Stanley Jackson, a son of Stephen Jackson, who was also a highly esteemed citizen of long standing. On the west side of the road, and pretty much opposite to these, a Mr. Murchison settled here among the Indians. He had two sons, William and Rora, who were about grown in Indian times, and lived to be men of mature age, and there are descendants of theirs still in the country, one,

Rora, Jr., who is especially a very prominent and influential man yet in Coosa. All this family were public spirited. There were some Avans and Thomases, also early settlers here. Among the descendants of Thomas is the present pastor of the Union Springs Baptist Church. Another man here who was for years a man of influence was Henry Semple. Neil Gillis and Henry Lybrand were long well known, and were among the early comers to the country. Lybrand gave name to the hill at whose base he lived, said by Samuel Graham, once assistant State Geologist, to be the highest point of land from Montgomery to the Talladega mountains. "Lybrands' Hill" will always be remembered by those who marketed over this road. To the west of the road, and in the neighborhood of Shady Grove Church, there were among those long resident several of the Deloaches, William Hand, Wade Bussey, G. W. Bearden, Wiley Coward, Elijah Devaughn, Greenbury, William, F. M., Allen, Sr. and Jr., several Holbys, Sion R. Bullard, T. A. Kelly, J. J. Grant, L. Chadwick, and C. J. Crew. On the east side of the road, and out in the Concord Church neighborhood, was Dr. George Gun, Mr. Thomas Mosely, Jack Gilliland, Abner, John, and Simeon Penton, with their descendants; Mr. John Payne, Peter, Henry, Wesley, and John Bird, James Corderey, Mr. Flemming, James Sandlin and sons, several Freemans, Mr. Samuel Hill, Hiram Bentley, father of Judge John S. and Oliver, David Shaw, A. B. Garey, Frank Sims, Rev. Mr. Sterns, Asa Edwards, John K. Graves, Silas, Simpson, and Patrick Waites, Wash Campbell (tanner for Crumpler), Mr. Hastie and sons, Joseph Dunlap and sons, and Mr. Zeigler. Wm. Arnold, Hugh and Joe Show were on the Pike, above Crumpler's fine home. The community around Concord was for a long time one of the most thrifty in the county, and sustained good schools, and its church congregations were large and intelligent. While not now equal to its former standing, it is still above the average. Here the writer taught school after returning in 1865 from the army. He was pastor of Concord when he entered the army in 1862.

It would hardly be right not to say more of A. B. Gary and Frank Sims than to mention their names. Gary was the father of Jere Gary, the young merchant of Nixburg, partner with Gus Morgan. Gary was a man of superior mind, and so was his wife a woman of fine mind, and one of earths best Christians. They had but two children, Jerre and the wife of Frank Sims. Jerre was a young man of splendid personal appearance, tall, erect, well proportioned, black hair and beard, bright sparkling dark eyes that flashed with intelligence. He was gifted with finest social qualities, and was invaluable in gatherings of young or old, for he had the faculty of keeping up life and vivacity anywhere, and seemed to have no trouble in maintaining a conversation with several at once. His death was from typhoid fever. Large was the circle that felt it had sustained a personal loss in his death. His mother was a benediction to all brought in contact with her, and Mrs. Sims, the daughter and sister, was a fair copy of the mother. Frank Sims was a very thrifty, liberal, public spirited man, who sought to help rather than be helped. The children of Sims and wife, sons and daughters partake largely of the noble characteristics of this noble ancestry. Colonel Austin, who lived about Nixburg and Concord, was also a man of fine qualities, and his wife was a lovely Christian character. Their children were a source of pleasure to their parents and acquaintances because of the fine qualities inherited and cultivated in them. Colonel Austin died suddenly, without warning, as did his noble son, Judge Austin, recently in Wetumpka. Another son, Richard Austin, still lives in the neighborhood. Their daughters, the wives of Hon. J. C. Maxwell of Alexander and Dr. Walker of Waxahatchie, Texas, are women of most lovable character. Jones Stephens and Stephen Jackson were both energetic, consecrated Christians, who always bore a full share in all efforts for the betterment of the community, and the progress of religion, and each had fine help in their families. Simeon Penton later became a pillar of the community.

ROCKFORD

This brings us to Rockford, the center of the county, and the last neighborhood to be noticed in this sketch. In 1835, by act of the legislature the county seat was removed from Lexington to this place. After reaching the top of the hills north of Hatchemadega Creek the old home of the Shaws stood. Then for about a mile and a half south, to more than three miles north of Rockford, the Turnpike, which runs through Rockford, passes over a level firm road on the ridge, originally covered with a fine pine forest. The first house on this level stretch of land was that of a Mr. Nesbitt, a relative of the prominent family of that name in Georgia. He raised some fine fruit on his farm. Just above him, one mile below Rockford, Daniel McDaniel lived. He was an early settler and lived for some years after the war here, being for many years a constable and justice of the peace. Mr. Haynie became the owner after his death, and has lived there ever since. The first house after this was the home of Col. J. R. Powell, in the lower edge of the village. This was for years the leading hotel of the place, and the stage stand for the line of coaching running to Abbington, Va. Besides the main building, there was a row of two room cottages extending northward along the street. Here most of the lawyers, officers of the court, and prominent visitors made their homes while in attendance upon court, and were well cared for by the cultivated mother of Colonel Powell and his queenly sisters. Here Colonel Powell's father, and his brother-in-law, Joseph Phelan, died. The place has been owned for a long time by Henry (Dick) Pond, a son of Judge Ebenezer Pond. He has been a leader of the Republican party in Coosa.

Dr. John S. McDonald bought the first lot sold in the place, and spent the remainder of his life here, dying January 10th, 1868. He raised several sons, Thos. S., George, now of Montgomery, William, Albert, James and David, and daughters, Mrs. Cabiness, Mrs. Casey (afterwards Mrs. Manning), and Mrs. Bunt. Mr. John S. Cabiness and Mr. Macajah Casey (whose father was a Revolutionary pensioner till after 1840) were both here while the Indians occupied the country. Among others early here were W. W. Morris, Robert W. Martin, Richard Plunket, Robert A. Coker, first sheriff, Thomas Dunlap, a blacksmith, Abram, William and John Chancellor, Henry W. Cox, John Horton, James A. Pollard, Sr. and Jr., Robert, Cleveland, and Thomas Welch. All these were for a good while residents, and well known, some of whom are more extensively noticed elsewhere in these pages. Horton was a mill owner, a bar-room owner, a merchant, and ran a bakery. Judge Pond married, as a second wife, his widow. James A. Pollard, Sr., lived to near ninety years of age, and never

needed the aid of glasses for seeing. Later Judge Pond came as
Judge of the County court, and lived about the place until his
death, when nearing ninety years of age. Like Pollard, his eyesight never failed. He raised three sons, Larkin, Joseph, and
Henry, and two daughters, Mrs. Frances Lee and Mrs. Cynthia
McLain. Washington Wilson came in the later thirties, and
raised a family of daughters. R. M. Cherry, a lawyer, also made
his home here and in Wetumpka. T. T. Wall also lived here for
awhile. James Carroll, the dresser of deer and sheep skins, was
with the first comers, and his son, Henry, was for a long time a
blacksmith here. Among those who might be regarded as second
in their location around Rockford were William and Solomon Lee
and their sons, Wm. and Robert, came about the same time, and
were merchants. John A. Graham, for years circuit clerk and
lawyer, and Dr. Archibald, his brother, were of this class, as also
Joshua Kilpatrick, who became the successor of Mr. Horton as
the baker of ginger-cakes, and maker of beer. Kilpatrick's cakes
and beer were long known for their peculiar excellency, which
made the mouths of boys and girls water for a taste of them, nor
were they neglected by those of riper years.

Joshua's marriage was quite an event, and, as told by George
McDonald, the boy fiddler, of the occasion, represents some of
the primitive social habits of those days. It was in 1852. Kilpatrick was to marry the daughter of Middleton Coker, two miles
or more west of Rockford. McDonald reached Coker's before
light, and found quite a gathering of neighbors, both men and
women, already assembled. Soon the men started with dogs and
guns for a hunt, while some remained to have the barbecue pits
ready when the hunters returned. The ladies had in some quilts,
and surrounding the frames, they worked faithfully to have the
quilts out in due time. By eleven o'clock the hunters returned
with several deer, a number of turkeys, squirrels, possums, and
birds, which were soon on the sticks over the barbecue pits, such
as were to be prepared in that way. By the middle of the afternoon or before the feast was ready and spread upon improvised
tables, and with the heartiness begotten of much exercise, the late
hour of the meal, and the prevailing good humor of the crowd,
the meal was long lingered over and enjoyed. A little after dark

the bride and groom were married, and congratulations and good wishes were for awhile the order of the day. Then the rooms were cleared of obstructing furniture, and the fiddlers began. There were several fiddlers present, who by turns furnished the music which inspired the dancers. The two best fiddlers were George McDonald, the neatly dressed town boy, and Jonathan Hardegree, with suit of grey home-made jeans, coat cut with dress style of claw-hammer tail. The dress of the party varied from home-made jeans, linen duster, to stylish tailor suits. The dancing and feasting continued all night, with the best of humor and good will, everybody the equal of everyone else socially. With the dawning light of another day the party broke up.

Miss Nancy Logan was one of those early at Rockford, and lived a noted and esteemed woman about the place most of her life. She was a sister of John and Alexander Logan, and Mrs. McDaniel. Still a little later came Judge I. W. Suttle, W. T. Stubblefield, Simon P. and William Shaffer, John A. Suttle, W. D. Walden, A. G. Hallmark, John S. Bentley, Dr. James L. Gilder, George E. Brewer, Nipper and John Tepel, Nathan Hines, Thomas Johnson, Isom Lee, Thomas Fargason, W. H. Womble, and Jno. A. Suttle. Many of these men had sons who took their places later, and some of whom are still among the leading men there, especially is this true of Suttle, McDonald, and Bentley. John Sears and George McEwen came a few years before the war, and built a good mill where Hatchett crosses the Turnpike. Judge McMillan came near the same time.

Since the war, among those who have lived at Rockford, and who have been valuable as citizens, have been J. C. Maxwell, now banker at Alexander City, T. J. Pennington, Felix Smith, John Parker, Washington Smith, Dr. Peddie and son John, whose wife was Georgia Farguson, Evander Jones, Dr. Julius Jones, W. T. Johnson, Lewis E. Parsons, Jr., Zach Sims, Messrs. Batson, Saml. Calfee, John Ward, Mr. Ledbetter, Mr. McEwen, Joseph Holby, Sheriff Cason, Dr. Alfred Massey, Joel Gullege, Henry Norred, Roberts Watts, and Lewis McAlister. Wm. Spigener also moved from Buyckville with his sons, and for some years lived here.

Rockford has usually kept up good schools and churches, and has been noted for the hospitality and public spirit of its people. For many years its Masonic lodge, constituted in 1850, was very large, having a membership reaching from seven miles below to as many miles above the place.

The resident lawyers of Rockford were John A. Graham, a very courteous gentleman, who was for many years Circuit Clerk; Col. R. M. Cherry, a good lawyer, an intelligent and pleasant man, who divided his residence, after the death of his wife, between Wetumpka and Rockford; Henry W. Vox, who was a resident lawyer of the place from a very early day until his death in battle during the Confederate war; E. R. Vernon, who was a good lawyer, a genial gentleman, and a good Christian, but of such delicate health that he died at an early age, leaving one son, Robert Vernon. His wife was a Miss Cleveland, sister of Robert.

Since the war, Felix Smith, well known both in legal and political circles, has been a resident of Rockford, and reared a family highly esteemed wherever known. He was in the Confederate service, though little more than a boy, and yet such were his soldierly qualities that he was entrusted at times with important duties. Once he was sent with dispatches of importance, then not seventeen years old, from the east to the west side of the Mississippi River, then in possession of the Federals. His way of reaching the destination of the papers, was to find some unguarded place, cross in a bateau, swimming his horse beside the boat. The duty was faithfully done, carrying dispatches from commanders on each side of the great river safely. He is still here. Evander Jones has also been a resident lawyer, and a very influential citizen, ever since soon after the war. He is a son of Calvin Jones, long a man prominent in the county. His brother, Dr. Julius Jones, came about the same time, and has ever since had a large practice as a physician. They both married daughters of Thomas S. McDonald, Miss Carrie, and Miss Mattie, and each have been with their mother, most highly esteemed, not only in Rockford, but largely in the county and elsewhere.

Lewis E. Parsons, Jr., son of Governor Parsons, Jessee Edwards, son of Dr. Edwards of Central, and John H. Parker (noticed elsewhere) all came near the same time, and had some prominence here during their stay.

The merchants of Rockford at this time are George B. Mc Donald, George W. Batson, John K. McEwen, J. W. Ledbetter & Co., W. D. Burchard, and Pond Bros.

George McDonald is a son of Thos. S. McDonald. He has recently built him a good home on the lot of his grandfather, Dr. J. S. McDonald, the first lot sold in Rockford. He, his mother, and sister, Mrs. E. and J. Jones, all have very desirable homes. Mrs. McDonald lives in the old home of John A. Graham, but it has been much enlarged and improved.

George W. Batson has been long a successful business man here. John McEwen has grown up from childhood in this community, being a son of George McEwen, and a grandson of John Sears. McEwen, by his steadiness, tact, and uprightness, has secured a good property, has a fine stone edifice in which to transact business, and a large commodious residence where William Womble once had his home. He has traveled a good deal, and is fond of gathering novelties.

J. W. Ledbetter has only been in business a short time, but has been one of Rockford's most prominent citizens since soon after the War Between the States. He is an upright, conscientious Christian, doing well his duty in church as well as State. He has had no children, but his has been a home for some child needing care all these years, so that eight children, now grown, look to him and his excellent wife as father and mother.

W. D. and Burchard Pond are sons of Dick Pond, grandsons of Ebenezer Pond and Wm. A. Wilson, born and raised in Rockford. The post-office for Rockford is in their store. They are highly esteemed, and are prospering. The family home is the old J. R. Powell residence, so long the leading hotel, prior to the war.

J. P. Batson was long a very successful merchant at Rockford, but of recent years has retired from mercantile, and entered the banking life, having a branch both at Sylacauga and Rockford. He has accumulated a good fortune.

A quarter of a century or more ago, D. L. McAlister began running a saw-mill started by T. S. McDonald. He afterward became owner, and he and his sons have continued it, adding from time to time, till it is now a combination of grist-mill, and gin as well. They have done a good business, and secured good property through their industry and good management. The family are loved and held in high esteem in the community. They own good homes and other good real estate, both in the town and country. The father and mother are both dead now, and sleep near the Baptist church of which they were both active and useful members. She was a Miss Radford, of the family that came in Indian times, and whose members have been prominent in county affairs all these years.

The old school-house used as the Masonic Institute of the long ago, has been greatly improved and beautified. Rockford has had a good school since in the forties. Robert McPheters, Sr., is now the principal. He has been a teacher in the county for near a score of years, and is a fine instructor.

The court-house underwent repairs in 1906, at a cost of near $20,000, which has added much to its beauty, also its convenience, comfort, and safety. The court room is a most excellent one.

Its first cemetery was on a hill east of town, and a good many are buried there. But after the Baptist church was constituted, Ned Hanrick of Montgomery gave a lot to the church as a burying ground. The first burial was the little son of Dr. Gilder, in 1856. Now much ground is covered, and hundreds sleep beneath the soil here, awaiting the resurrection trumpet. Among its dead are Judge Suttle, Dr. Jno. S. McDonald and wife, Judge Bentley and wives and daughters, and T. S. McDonald, whose lives have marked so large and important a place in the history of Rockford.

The fine trees surrounding the church with such good shades were little bushes when the house was built.

Northwest toward Hatchett, from an early date several families of Millers owned farms, and these are still owned by their posterity. Near them was Mr. John Jacks, whose sons, Isaac and Sam, were a long time after him still in the county. Somewhat in the same section, but lower down the creek were the Hardegrees, Parishes, Williams Chancellor, and Wm. Bridges. Judge Pond once owned a good farm and a small mill west of Rockford, and not far from there has lived from the first a family of Hatchetts, and not far off other families of old settlers, the Dennises, Lees, and Woods.

CHAPTER V

OFFICERS OF COOSA COUNTY
SENATORS

1837 Daniel E. Watrous, Shelby and Coosa
1840 Dixon H. Lewis, Autauga and Coosa
1843 William L. Yancey, Autauga and Coosa
1844 Sampson W. Harris, Autauga and Coosa
1847 Seth P. Storrs, Autauga and Coosa
1849 Seth P. Storrs, Autauga and Coosa
1853 James R. Powell, Coosa
1855 James R. Powell, Coosa
1857 Daniel Crawford, Coosa
1859 George E. Brewer, Coosa
1861-2 George E. Brewer, Coosa
1863 William Garrett, Coosa
1865 William Garrett, Coosa
1867 Reconstruction——No election
1868 Thomas Lambert, Coosa and Elmore
1870 Thomas Lambert, Coosa and Elmore
1872 C. S. G. Doster, Coosa and Elmore
1874 A. J. Terrell, Coosa and Tallapoosa
1876 W. Levi Johnson, Coosa and Tallapoosa
1878 W. Levi Johnson, Coosa and Tallapoosa
1880 G. R. Banks, Coosa and Tallapoosa
1882 W. P. Oden, Coosa and Elmore
1884 Jefferson Falkner, Coosa and Elmore
1886 Jefferson Falkner, Coosa and Elmore
1888 John H. Parker, Coosa and Elmore
1890 John H. Parker, Coosa and Elmore
1892 Albert T. Goodwin, Coosa and Elmore
1894 Albert T. Goodwin, Coosa and Elmore
1896 Richard S. Nolan, Coosa and Tallapoosa
1898 P. O. Stevens, Coosa and Tallapoosa
1900 W. R. Oliver, Coosa and Tallapoosa
1903 W. L. Lancaster, Coosa and Elmore

REPRESENTATIVES

1837   W. W. Morris
1838   W. W. Morris
1839   Ambrose B. Dawson
1840   W. W. Morris
1841   William L. Yancey
1842   Anderson H. Kendrick
1843   Howell Rose
1844   Howell Rose
1845   Howell Rose and James R. Powell
1847   Samuel Spigener and Daniel Crawford
1849   A. H. Kendrick and Frederick F. Foscue
1851   Henry W. Cox and Neil S. Graham
1853   William Garrett and James H. Weaver
1855   George Taylor and N. S. Graham
1857   George E. Brewer, Evan Colffee and A. H. Smith
1859   A. H. Smith, Calvin Humphries and W. D. Walden
1861   Allen Maxwell, David W. Bozeman and Albert Crumpler
1863   Thomas U. T. McCain, E. S. C. Parker and James Vanzandt
1865   T. U. T. McCain, John Edwards and James Vanzandt
1868   James Vanzandt
1870   W. Levi Johnson
1872   W. Levi Johnson
1873   Daniel Crawford
1874   W. L. Johnson
1875   Robert H. Gullege
1876   Robert H. Gullege
1877   John B. Kelley
1879   Daniel J. Thompson
1881   Richard S. Nolan
1883   John H. Porter
1885   John A. Suttle
1887   J. N. Nabors
1889   William C. Brown
1891   Richard S. Nolan

1893 R. S. Nolan
1895 H. R. Robbins
1897 J. H. Porter
1899 J. H. Porter
1901 J. H. Porter
1903 John Johnson

DELEGATES TO CONSTITUTIONAL CONVENTION

1861 George Taylor, Albert Crumpler and John B. Leonard
1865 Daniel Crawford, C. M. Cabot and William A. Wilson
1867 James F. Hurst
1875 William Garrett
1901 J. C. Maxwell, Senatorial Dist. John H. Porter

JUDGES OF COUNTY AND PROBATE COURTS

1834 Aug. 20th, Robert W. Martin, Judge of County Court
1837 Oct. 20th, Ambrose B. Dawson, Judge of County
      Court (*)
1837 Dec. 8th, Ebenezer Pond, Judge of County Court
1848 Aug., Isaac W. Suttle, Judge of County Court
1850 May, Isaac W. Suttle, Judge of Probate
1856 May, Archibald A. McMillan, Judge of Probate (**)
1862 May, Archibald A. McMillan, Judge of Probate
1867 Thomas H. Fargason, appointed Judge of Probate
      (***)
1874 Aug., John S. Bentley elected Judge of Probate
1880 Aug., John S. Bentley elected Judge of Probate
1886 Aug., John S. Bentley elected Judge of Probate (****)
1892 Jan., Archibald D. Bentley appointed Judge of
      Probate
1892 Aug., John C. Penton elected, and died Judge of
      Probate
1894 Aug., A. D. Bentley, appointed Judge of Probate
1898 Aug., J. A. Crawford, appointed Judge of Probate

(*) Dawson resigned to take seat in legislature—Pond appointed
(**) Removed by reconstruction
(***) Appointed by Federals
(****) J. S. Bentley died

CLERKS OF THE COUNTY COURT

1833   April 15, George W. Jones
1834   March 12, Alfred C. Mahan
1837   Dec. 9, Robert W. Cleveland
1845   Aug. 12, Isaac W. Suttle
1848   Aug. 12, Albert G. Hallmark

The office was abolished upon the establishment of the Probate Judgeship, and the duties of both the county judge and clerk combined with additional duties. This displaced Hallmark.

CLERKS OF THE CIRCUIT COURT

1833   April 15, Thomas R. Coker
1834   March 12, James P. Daniel
1837   Oct. 23, T. W. Hatchett
1841   Sept. 11, William S. Caldwell
1845   Aug. 12, John A. Graham; held to 1853
1853-62   Aug., William T. Stubblefield (°)
1863   March, Joseph Taylor appointed
1864   Aug., John S. Bentley elected
1865   Aug., John S. Bentley appointed by L. E. Parsons
1866-74   Nov., John S. Bentley elected
1874-91   Washington L. Smith, died
1891-2   G. R. S. Smith
1892-1904 William T. Johnson
1894   W. E. Bailey

SHERIFFS

1833   April 15th, A. R. Coker
1837   Feb. 22nd, James E. M. Logan, died 1839
1839   Alexander Smith appointed to vacancy
1840   Feb. 27th, William J. Campbell, died March 27th, 1842
1842   April 10th, Alexander Smith appointed to vacancy
1842   August, James R. Powell

1845	August, Jas. H. Weaver, resigned Dec. 2nd, 1847
1847	Dec., A. G. Hallmark appointed to vacancy
1848	August, Thomas T. Wall
1851	August, Stephen A. Pearce
1854	August, William A. Wilson
1857	August, T. T. Wall
1860	August, Ellis Logan
1863	August, Jessee M. Wilson
1866	August, Fred Allen
1868	Jan. 27th, William C. Lackey, Federal appointment
1871-4	August, Robert H. Gulledge
1874-7	August, Joseph Pond
1877-81	August, J. T. Thompson
1881-5	August, H. R. Robbins
1885-9	August, Saml. R. Calfee
1889-93	August, J. D. Hull
1893-7	August, J. T. Cason
1897-1901	August, W. R. Walker
1901-7	August, T. J. Tippet
1907	August, W. R. Walker

JUSTICES OF THE PEACE AND CONSTABLES

Only a few of the first will be given, as it would require too much space for a full list. The first Justices were commissioned September 29th, 1834. They were Robert W. Cleveland, Solomon Robbins, Archibald Downing, Thompson Coker, John A. Chapman, and Charles Williams. In October of the same year there were added John S. Galby, Lynne Cloud, John D. Wilson. In the spring of 1835, E. T. Heard, Robert W. Martin, Benjamin Robinson, and Thomas S. McGowan were appointed. In 1836, Johnson Byars and Washington Barton were made Justices. In 1837, Solomon Robbins and Thompson Coker resigned, and in the same year Solomon Wood, John Looney, Richard Steward, William Richards, Isaac W. Suttle, William R. Moore, and John Lightfoot were made Justices.

No constables appear on the record until 1835, when the names of the following appear as such, viz: T. H. Heard, Hillary

Williams, James M. Logan, John D. McCassail, and John Logan.
In 1836, there were added to this list Clinton King, Moses Ray,
Nimrod Morris, Caleb Boaman, William Hannon, R. F. Cleveland, and John S. McDonald.   There were a few constables that
for a number of years served especially about court time.   The
writer recollects one of these who had a stentorian voice, whose
business was to assist the sheriff in keeping order in the court
room.   He would watch and the least disturbance would call out
with that deep, harsh voice, "Keep less silence thar."

The first Notaries Public appointed in the county were J. P.
Daniel and M. D. Simpson.

COUNTY SUPERINTENDENTS OF EDUCATION

1856	May, George E. Brewer, resigned Nov. 1857
1857	Nov., Rev. Elbert Smith appointed
1858-60	May, Rev. Elbert Smith elected
1860-2	May, T. W. Fitzgerald
1862-4	May, John C. Humphries
1864-6	May, Oliver C. Bentley
1866-8	May, R. P. Mackey
1868-70	May, Dr. Jacob McLendon
1870	Matthew Moore; he died and Henry Pond filled the vacancy
1872-4	T. J. Pennington
1874-6	John P. Hannon
1876-92	T. J. Pennington
1892-4	B. C. Hammons
1894-6	John F. Vardeman
1896-8	W. P. Fulmer
1898-1900	John F. Vardeman
1900-8	John H. Johnson

A satisfactory list of tax assessors, tax collectors, and county
treasurers could not be had.   They are therefore omitted, much
to the regret of the writer.

Among the early holders of these offices the name of Captain
Loyal, an uncle of Mrs. Col. Austin, may be mentioned as a very

efficient tax assessor, who was kept in office for a long time. A Mr. Burgess was collector. He lived near where Kellyton now stands. Sometime in the forties when he had collected some thousands of dollars, he was last seen near Sockapatoy in the afternoon. He was robbed and killed but no clue to the deed could be found. A few days afterward his horse and buggy were found unattended near Kington, of Autauga.

William Connaway, who lived near the "Half Acre," and owned a mill, was for a number of years tax collector. Once while holding several thousand dollars of collected taxes, he was robbed in his home. But the perpetrators were soon discovered, and most of the money recovered. He was closely related to the family of Connaways near and around Poplar Springs. Was familiarly known as "Uncle Billy."

EARLY CUSTOMS OF INTEREST

In the early days of the settlement of Coosa it was the custom for neighbors to be very helpful to each other, and to convert these seasons of help into occasions of social pleasure.

The country settled rapidly and houses were needed. At first there were no saw mills, and for sometime but few, so that sawed lumber could not be gotten at all, or only by long and expensive hauls. The consequence was that log houses were the rule. To 1850 frame houses were scarce. Sometimes at first dirt floors, or those made of puncheons from split logs, hewed to some degree of smoothness, were not uncommon. The first benches for school houses and churches were not unfrequently made of like puncheons, with large augur holes bored into them with the proper slant, so that when the legs, cut from saplings, were driven into the holes, the seats would be steady. There were no back rests.

Houses, of course, varied in size from the single room log hut, to the large two storied houses made of large hewn logs, with verandas or awnings. The most common, however, for the average man who looked after comfort and not too much expense, was what was called the two room or double log house, with a hall of ten or twelve feet between. The rooms were usually from 18 to 20 feet square. The walls were made of skinned poles five or six inches through, or logs of ten or twelve inches split in two in the center. After the walls were raised the split side, which was inward, was hewed comparatively smooth, and the outside likewise well skelped with the broadaxe. The cracks were usually lined with long boards rived from good splitting timber, and drawn to smoothness with the drawing knife, sometimes if the house was desired to be very tight the cracks were chinked on the outside with split pieces of timber, and this daubed with mortar. These houses usually had shed rooms in the rear of the main rooms, thus making four rooms to the house, and if more rooms were needed, two sheds on the front some less than the main rooms, so as to have a sort of open court in front of the hallway. These sheds were made either of poles, or boards rived in long strips. The houses were covered with two or three feet boards rived out of blocks of these lengths sawed from good splitting trees.

There were generally built in the back yard, some distance from the main building, separate houses for cook and dining rooms, smoke or meat houses, store room, and dairy. Stables, cribs, and barns were made in like manner, near by, but with less care usually to appearance.

When the logs for a house were cut and put on the ground near where the house was to be built, the neighbors were invited to come to the house raising on a specified day. They would assemble by seven or eight o'clock and after the sills had been properly placed on their pillars of sawed lightwood blocks, or of rocks, four men, skillful with an axe, were chosen as corner men, and each took possession of a corner. If the house was double, eight corner men were required. The other men brought the logs and hoisted them to the corner men who would proceed at once to cutting a notch so as to fit the log below after the first had been fitted to the sill, so as to keep the wall both perpendicular and steady.   Often a good fit would be secured at the first cutting.   If not, the corner men turned the log up, and re-modeled the notch until a fit was secured.   These men had for scaffolding on which to stand while cutting and fitting these notches only the cracks between the logs, or standing on top of the turned up log or pole.   This required steady nerve, skillful handling of axes, and a good and quick eye as to what notch was required.   A constant run of social chat, hunting feats, stirring incidents, interesting exploits, or political matters made the time pass pleasantly and more like a good-natured social gathering than the hard work it was.

The hour of noon arriving, the men would sit down to a good dinner, about the best the hostess could get up with her own cooks if she owned or hired them, if none were had, some of the neighbor women would come in and help get up the dinner and supper, for usually both meals were eaten on such occasions.   If a quilting was had by the women in connection the men were waited on by the ladies around the long improvised table made gay with jest, joke or lively talk.   Then the ladies would eat while the men rested, smoked, chewed their tobacco and cracked their jokes.

Usually by night the house would be raised and the rafters (commonly of skinned poles) were properly set upon the plates, as the flattened top log was called.   Another bountiful meal for supper was eaten and then all would break off for home, unless a party had been decided on in connection with the house rais-ing, in which the younger members of the families would come in and share in the social function.   If the "raising" was not com-pleted they would come back next day and finish up.

LOG ROLLINGS AND QUILTINGS

Another occasion for help and social gatherings came in with "log-rollings" every spring.   The farmer would cut up the timber that had fallen in his fields through the year, and in his freshly cleared land called "the new-ground," and make him some "hand-sticks," about five feet long, made of tough hickory saplings usually, with the bark taken off, and the stick tapered at each end with the drawing knife so as to make it easy to grasp with the hand, and the sticks were seasoned so as to prevent too much springiness.

When all was ready the neighbors were invited a few days before so as to give opportunity to arrange business at home for leaving, on a certain day the "log-rolling" was appointed to be. They would gather early at the house of the one whose logs were to be rolled, and proceeding to the field, would pair off on the way as to who were to share the same handstick, for there was to be one at each end. In pairing they would try to snatch as well as possible in strength and skill. But if a weaker man fell to the lot of a stronger, the stronger would give the weaker more of the hand-stick, and balance his strength by additional leverage. Where the logs were not heavy they would divide into parties about equal to a reasonable effort in moving the logs, so that heaps would be going up at the same time. But when heavy logs were reached they would double up so as to be able to move the logs. The hand-sticks would be gotten under the log, about equally distant from each end of the stick, and as many sticks would be required for an equal number of men on each side to pick the log up on the sticks and carry to where a heap was to be made for burning by piling a number of logs together. When the sticks were properly placed, at a given signal, each man stooped over with the end of his stick firmly grasped, all would rise together, lifting the log to a heighth so the men could walk standing straight as he carried his burden. Men would exert themselves to the utmost when carrying heavy logs to step firmly and regularly without wavering or wobbling, for a failure on the part of one might bring the log down and hurt someone or move and be a strain to all. No one liked to have his knucks ground into the dirt as it was called, when he could not bring up his end of the stick, or stumble and thereby imperil all, or have to cry out for a rest, and thus renew the heavy strain of a second lift. There was a laudable ambition to be called "a good hand at the end of a stick."

Much pleasant talk would usually be going on when not under a heavy strain, and the best of cheer marked these occasions. A common custom was to have a supply of whiskey at log rollings, house raisings, corn shuckings, and harvestings, and about twice before dinner, twice after dinner a moderate dram be taken, and just before eating a more hearty one. Popular sentiment had not arrayed itself against taking a dram, and most of people thought it right and healthy to take an occasional drink. On these public occasions it was thought quite the thing and needful to keep the nerves stimplated. A good and bountiful dinner and supper were always expected and enjoyed on these occasions.

At the log-rollings it was common for the wife to have a quilting at the same time, and so the men and women of the neighborhood were together and while the men were rolling logs some of the women would be around the quilting frames, while others prepared the noonday and evening feasts. Often at night the young people came in for a party, and went through the dance or plays. Those were days of good neighborship, pleasant friendships, and strong attachments growing out of these frequent social gatherings.

HARVESTING

When the small grain, wheat and oats ripened there was another coming together of the neighbors for harvesting the grain, beginning with the one whose grain was first ready. As on the other occasions they were early on the ground. The company would divide out, several of the best cradlers taking the scythes or cradles. Each of these was followed by one or more binders, and these again by others who would bring the bundles or sheaves into heaps of a dozen or more which would be shocked up and capped to turn the water. So when evening came all was ready for the grain to stand shocked in the field till time for hauling and threshing.

The writer remembers when no threshing machines were in the country. The wheat or oats were piled in a great pyramid in a barn if there was one large enough, or if not in an open place prepared for it. At the base of this pyramid there was a thick layer of bundles around it, and several horses or mules were driven around and around on this layer until it was supposed as much of the grain was trodden from the heads as was practicable. This trodden straw was gathered off and thrown outside, and another layer of bundles put down and so on until the whole had been trodden out.

To keep it clean, pans on handles were in the hands of parties to catch the droppings from the horses before it should fall among the grain. Others were on the center pile to throw down as new layers were required, and others had charge of the horses to keep them going, or lead off as occasion required. When a sufficient quantity of the grain was trodden out so as to require removal it was taken up from the floor and put in a place to await the fanning. Fans came in before threshing machines, but before the fan came in, the winnowing was done, by one standing on an elevated place and lifting the grain and chaff as high as might be, slowly shake it from the vessel, and let the wind blow out the chaff as the wheat or oats fell in a pile below. That process would look now like obtaining clean grain under difficulties. Quiltings sometimes came in with "harvestings."

CORN SHUCKINGS

Another of these social helpful gatherings was in the fall of the year, when the days were getting short and the nights long and the air crisp. The corn would be hauled in long large heaps around the cribs. If the roof was not on hinges so as to be raised or part of the side on hinges, logs near the top were slipped out, and the remaining ones secured from falling. The neighbors were notified that the "corn shucking" would be on a certain night. Several negroes that were experts in "corn songs" were asked to come and tell others to come. It was generally understood that a corn shucking was free to any who wished to come, so that if the familiar sound of a number of negroes singing corn songs at one place was heard, any negro man or boy felt he had a right to go, and they generally went, for they expected two things that appealed strongly to a negro, and that was a good dram and a good supper. As the hands arrived they went at once to the corn pile and began shucking, throwing the husked ears into the crib, and the shucks to the rear. They commenced at the outer edge of the pile of corn, and cleaned up the corn to the ground as they went. There were usually two or more recognized leaders in singing the corn songs, and as they would chant or shout their couplet, all the rest would join in the chorus. There was not poetry or metre to these songs, but there was a thrill from the melody welling up with such earnestness from the singers that it was so inspiring that the hands would fly with rapidity in tearing off the shucks, and the feet kick back the shucks with equal vigor. As a sample of the songs and chorus, the leader would shout out with a ringing tune, "Pull off the shucks, boys, Pull off the shucks," and the crowd would shout out in a ringing chorus, "Round up the corn, boys, Round up the corn." Again he would say, "The nights getting off, boys, the nights getting off," and they would respond, "Round up the corn, boys, round up the corn." Again he would say, "Give me a dram, sir, give me a dram," and they again, "Round up the corn, boys, round up the corn." This singing could be heard on a still night two miles or more.

When the night would be wearing off and still a good deal to shuck the pile would be divided by some mark, and the shuckers divided as near equally as could be done hurriedly. A negro song leader would be chosen for each pile, and this leader would mount up on his pile, cheer up his men, strike up some stirring song, gesticulate violently and sway his body to the music, push corn down to those shucking, and do whatever would stimulate to active work. The interest that would be aroused, and the rapidity with which the shucks would fly would be astonishing. Whichever side shucked out his pile first, would break out into a song of victory, but turn in at once and help finish out the other side.

Most of the song was impromptu, suggested by immediate conditions, except the chorus, which was uniform. When the corn was shucked it was also cribbed, being thrown into the open-ing as the shuck was stripped off. As soon as the pile was fin-ished, the crowd gathered up the shucks in great armfuls, and heaved them into rail pens nearby, that had been built ten or twelve rails high. Some would be in the pens treading down the shucks as they were thrown in, and building the pens higher as needed with rails hauled already near by for the purpose.

When this was done, the leaders would pick up the owner on their shoulders and carry him several times around the house, followed closely by all the others singing some of their most stir-ring songs, and praising him in their songs. After thus carrying him around in triumph, they would enter the hallway with him on their shoulders, and seat him in a chair, and with a shuffling dance around him, go out into the yard. A hearty dram was then given them, and then they were seated to a rich supper around an improvised table. Negroes and whites enjoyed these shuckings very much, and while there was no approximation to social equality, there was the best of feeling mutually among them. The negro did not dream of being familiar, and yet there was nothing like servile fear, but a genuine respect and kindly feeling to the whites.

DIVISIONS OF MEAT

Another custom of those times is worth mentioning as show-ing the friendship and confidence among neighbors in the way of helpfulness. During the summer and fall months when fresh meats could not be kept long at a time, it was customary for four large, or eight small families to form a meat club. One would kill a beef one week and divide into quarters or eighths, as the case demanded. The day of the killing was known, the members of the club would have a representative at the place of killing, and when the division was made, each would carry home his piece. The next week another would kill, and so on till it had been around the club, when it would start round again, and keep it up until the weather became cool. This enabled the families to have fresh meat weekly without the danger of losing, and have a change from vegetables, bacon and poultry.

A PECULIAR RELIGIOUS PHASE

Religious excitement in meetings used to be much greater than now. It was not unfrequent for several to shout in a meeting, and sometimes most would be in tears, if no higher demonstration of excessive interest. At times of revivals there would be a score or more at times shouting at once, and continue until exhausted. From about 1850 to near 1860 there was a prevalence of a sort of trance that was peculiar. It was generally confined to those who shouted. It would usually follow after a long spell of shouting, but not always. Sometimes before the one had been shouting long would develop the trance state. They appeared to become unconscious of surroundings. The body would be rigid. The face pale nearly as if dead, but with a placid sweet expression upon it. If they breathed it was barely perceptible. This would continue sometimes for hours together, but not always so long. Upon arousing they would claim a loss of sense of surroundings, and sweet visions of divine things, and a feeling of great peacefulness.

TAN YARDS

The following tan yards were known by the writer to be in the county. There might have been others.

Baileys', near Mt. Olive
Brooks', near Brooksville
Burgess', near Kellyton
Crumplers', on Swamp Creek
Edwards', above Central Institute
Half Acre, name not known but just
    below the Half Acre
Harris', near Kellyton
Leonards', near Nixburg.

PRIVATE CEMETERIES

The following private cemeteries are in Coosa:

Bradford's, Joseph near the Bradford factory, where part of his family are buried.

Bloomfield's, location unknown.

Foster's and Miller's, near Hatchett Creek, northwest of Rockford. These two families, early settlers, have buried here.

Graham's, John A., in Rockford.

Kelly's, Dr. James, near his old home. He, his brother, the preacher and other members of family buried here.

Marberry's, Leonard, on his plantation near Kellyton. He, wife and others of family buried here.

Maxwell's, Reuben, near Alexander City. He, his wife and sons, Allen, Frank, Willis, and most of his daughters are here.

Murchison's, nine miles southwest of Rockford. He and several sons and daughters and grandchildren are here.

Hutto's, west of Rockford.

COW BELLS

Reference is made elsewhere to a Mr. Ward as a celebrated bell-maker. This will not be understood by people of this day without reference to a custom of belling stock prevailing until after the war.

Cattle were turned upon the range to feed upon the rich pasturage and they would ramble off for some miles. Milch cows were desired at home at night and all other cattle gathered at different times. To facilitate the search for them, bronze bells of far sounding capacity were fastened around their necks by a leather strap. These were also put around the necks of sheep and goats.

When the cattle were desired, someone going into the woods to hunt them would be guided by the ringing of the bell. The bells were of different sounds and of an evening as the stock were brought up a home-like music was produced by the ringing of these bells.

CHAPTER VI

MILITARY RECORD OF COOSA

In the earlier days of the country considerable attention was paid to drilling the militia, consisting of company, battalion, and brigade drills. The interest, however, fell off at the time of the removal of the Indians became more remote. The last brigade drill of the militia remembered by the writer was at Rockford in the summer of 1851, while Governor Chapman was the militia chief of Alabama. Gen. M. L. Bulger was commander of the brigade. The drill took place along the streets, and then to the uncultivated field of Col. J. R. Powell, south of his house. A fence was between the road and field, and sentinels were placed along it to keep out intruders. A broad gap was made in the fence to let the ranks of the military through. After they had entered, the sentinels placed here were instructed to let none pass without the countersign. When the drill was finished and they were ready to be reviewed by the Governor and his staff, as they rode to the opening for entrance, they were stopped by the guard who demanded the countersign. The Governor claimed the right to enter as commander-in-chief but the sentinel held him at bay until the officer of the guard came to his relief.

It will be a matter of some interest to give a list of those who held office in the militia of Coosa, which constituted the 68th Regiment of the 3rd Brigade of the 7th Division. Michael L. Bulger was a major of militia in 1832, but the regular record of the county officers is as follows:

(From Militia Records of the State in the office of T. M. Owen, Director of Archives)

Colonels	When	Colonels	When
Henry C. Towns	May 20, 1834	M. L. Bulger	April 11, 1837
Edward Cullent	May 22, 1839	Thomas Smith	Sept. 15, 1845
John Wright	Sept. 16, 1845	Charles Cox	May 29, 1881
Lt. Colonels	**When**	**Lt. Colonels**	**When**
William Moore	Sept. 16, 1835	Thomas Warren	July 12, 1837
Elijah Smith	Oct. 17, 1839	Rial H. Watkins	Feb. 2, 1841
William Stephens	April 8, 1846	Richard N. C. Shelton	Nov. 1, 1847
N. M. Green	Sept. 9, 1861		
Majors	**When**	**Majors**	**When**
John D. Wilson	Sept. 6, 1835	Michael Peevy	Sept. 1840
Bynum J. Kinney	April 3, 1844	Rora Murchison	Nov. 23, 1845
William Knight	Feb. 21, 1848	James M. Griffin	Aug. 13, 1852
M. J. Speer	Sept. 9, 1861		

Adjutants	When	Adjutants	When
Elijah McLemore	July 5, 1837	William Suttle	Dec. 1, 1842
Henry W. Cox	Oct. 7, 1847	Henry Hoffman	Feb. 11, 1862

Quartermasters	When	Quartermasters	When
Isacah Wilson	July 5, 1837	George J. McKenzie	Oct. 7, 1847
Carey Cox	Feb. 11, 1862		

Paymasters	When	Paymasters	When
Jesse Hickman	July 5, 1837	John M. Patterson	July 5, 1837
Adam Harrell	July 24, 1839	Reuben A. Mitchell	Feb. 7, 1847
Williams Cousins	Feb. 11, 1862		

Ensigns	When	Ensigns	When
Andrew Hameran	Sept. 29, 1834	William Nix	Sept. 29, 1834
William Price	Sept. 29, 1837	John B. Dorset	Sept. 29, 1837
William W. Welch	Oct. 11, 1837	Joel Butter	Oct. 11, 1837
John Cone	Nov. 27, 1837		

Surgeons	When	Surgeons	When
Dr. William Lee	May 22, 1839	Dr. Jas. P. Montgomery	Dec. 20, 1850
Dr. Neil H. Baker	July	Dr. M. G. Moore	Feb. 11, 1862

Captains	When	Captains	When
Squire Cloud	Sept. 29, 1834	Eecom B. Bonner	Sept. 29, 1834
John D. Wilson	Sept. 29, 1834	Charles Williams	Sept. 29, 1834
Fouch Cleveland	Sept. 6, 1835	Miles Ragsdale	Sept. 6, 1835
William J. Campbell	Feb. 14, 1836	Henry B. Judge	Sept. 29, 1837
James E. Lee	Sept. 29, 1837	Michael Peevy	Oct. 11, 1837
Davis Campbell	Oct. 11, 1837	Elijah Smith	Nov. 27, 1837
O. P. Hackett	April 10, 1838	Marion Eubank	June 27, 1838
Phillep Jackson	July 27, 1838	John C. Bulger	April 24, 1839
William J. Couch	June 21, 1839	Elias Logan	June 24, 1839
Zachariah Nash	July 26, 1839	John Walls	July 26, 1839
Jordan Van	Sept. 18, 1840	Thomas Morgan	Sept. 18, 1840
E. M. Beck	Sept. 18, 1840	Thomas F. Lorne	Sept. 18, 1840
John Corbett	Dec. 1, 1842	John Clisby	Dec. 1, 1842
Obed Parish	Sept. 3, 1845	William Knight	Feb. 20, 1846
Isaac Bird	March 26, 1846	Sion Kirkland	April 8, 1846
William M. Allen	April 8, 1846	John Chapman	July 8, 1846
Wiley Bailey	Sept. 15, 1846	A. J. D. Sexton	Nov. 19, 1846
R. F. Pollard	Jan. 7, 1847	Absolom T. Davis	March 15, 1847
E. S. M. Hodges	April 30, 1847	F. J. Hatton	Jan. 1, 1848
William B. Shelton	Jan. 18, 1848	W. W. Fowler	March 13, 1849
James M. Plunket	April 8, 1848	James Carden	April 15, 1848
George W. Spivey	June 10, 1848	Robert Traylor	March 15, 1849
William S. Varner	Nov. 17, 1849	M. W. Hall	March 17, 1849
William Flemming	Jan. 9, 1851	John A. Pylant	June 15, 1853
John B. Hubbard	Feb. 11, 1862	Yound D. Harrington	Feb. 11, 1862
J. P. Rawls	Feb. 11, 1862	N. J. Lewis	Feb. 11, 1862
James L. Jeter	Feb. 11, 1862		

Lieutenants	When	Lieutenants	When
George Melton	Sept. 29, 1834	George Lowery	Sept. 29, 1834
Elijah McKenzie	Sept. 29, 1834	William Smith	Sept. 29, 1834
James Watley	Sept. 29, 1837	George W. Cooper	Oct. 17, 1837
James Miller	Oct. 11, 1837	Henry Burgess	Nov. 27, 1837
L. Woodruff	April 10, 1838	Kinion Hodge	June 27, 1838
Joseph A. Hayden	July 27, 1838	John Chancellor (2)	July 27, 1838
William Deason	July 26, 1839	Renza Lewis (2)	July 26, 1839
Duncan Talleran (2)	July 26, 1839	C. J. Brannan (2)	April 24, 1839
William Y. Stanley (2)	June 24, 1839	Richard White (2)	June 24, 1839
John Chancellor	June 24, 1839	David Smith	Sept. 18, 1840
Matt. Carne (2)	Sept. 18, 1840	Lorenzo Woodruff (2)	Oct. 18, 1840
Josiah Choice (3)	Oct. 1, 1840	Kenchen Worrell (2)	Dec. 1, 1842
Silas Rollin	Sept. 3, 1845	James Kirkpatrick (2)	Sept. 3, 1845
William E. Robinson	July 8, 1846	Benjamin Kinney (2)	July 8, 1846
John D. Inabennett	Aug. 17, 1846	Evan A. McKenzie (2)	Aug. 17, 1846

Lieutenants	When	Lieutenants	When
William Driver, Jr.	Sept. 15, 1846	James Shivers	Oct. 5, 1846
Thomas G. Crawford (2)	Oct. 5, 1846	Eenjamin Cummings	July 27, 1847
William Morrison (2)	April 9, 1847	Wiley Fowler (2)	July 21, 1847
F. W. Parrish (2)	July 21, 1847	Felix G. Simmons	July 1, 1848
R. C. Shorter (2)	Jan. 1, 1848	Joseph Rogers (2)	March 13, 1849
John Sanford (Cornet)	March 13, 1849	Neil O. Graham	March 13, 1849
Henry Bird	Nov. 17, 1849	David C. Shaw (2)	Nov. 17, 1849
B. D. Harrison	Dec. 28, 1850	James B. Morris (2)	Dec. 28, 1850
T. J. Vardeman	June 15, 1853	William Massey (2)	June 15, 1853
C. F. Enslen	Feb. 11, 1862	V. Frankfurter (2)	Feb. 11, 1862
William Townsend	Feb. 11, 1862	K. A. Townsend (2)	Feb. 11, 1862
A. H. Callaway	Feb. 11, 1862	M. G. Cousins (2)	Feb. 11, 1862
J. Downs	Feb. 11, 1862	Joseph Cardwell (2)	Feb. 11, 1862
W. C. Franklin	Feb. 11, 1862	L. W. Jinks (2)	Feb. 11, 1862
W. Roberts	March 6, 1862		

(From Militia Records in Archives of State)

THE WAR RECORD OF COOSA

Coosa has a war record of which her people need not be ashamed. The first military movement in view of real warfare began in connection with the disturbance about Indian hostilities in the early part of 1836. A hostile feeling appeared among the Indians growing out of the violation of the treaty stipulations on the part of the whites, and crookedness on the part of some of the whites in trading with the Indians, especially in lands. Threats were made and widespread discontent was among them, and hostilities were feared by the whites. This state of affairs existing, there was a meeting held by the citizens of East Wetumpka, February 4th, 1836, with a view to the formation of a volunteer company. Col. T. W. Flemming was made chairman, and Dr. T. E. Evans, secretary. The meeting proceeded to the election of officers for the company, and W. J. Campbell was elected captain; H. C. McClung, first lieutenant; A. B. Flemming, second, and —————— Cooper, ensign.

A committee on by-laws was appointed consisting of W. J. Campbell, H. C. McClung, A. B. Flemming, W. T. Childs, and Dr. J. Folk; and Campbell, Flemming, Evans, and Folk were appointed to procure arms, the purpose being to form a company of light artillery. A committee to agree upon suitable uniforms was composed of Mr. Lyon, Mr. Topping, and W. J. Couch.

August 5th, 1836, a letter was written by Isaac Lyon, in behalf of the company, to Governor Clay, asking for a field piece,

60 muskets, and 60 swords for equipment. He informed the Governor that the arms then on hand, about forty muskets, were procured by the individual effort of Captain Campbell in Mobile, and might be called for at any time. He further informed him it was a light artillery company, consequently the need of a field piece, and they wanted to serve either on foot or as mounted infantry, therefore the need of both guns and swords. He urged the claim because the company had been organized more than six months, and had been received and sent to Florida against the Indians, and the company had so discharged its duties there as to entitle it to the consideration asked. He further urged that it was the only regular volunteer company between the Coosa and Tallapoosa rivers.

(From original manuscript papers in State Archives)

Mr. Yancey's paper in May, 1839, speaks in complimentary terms of the service of this company in Florida. The Company is frequently alluded to by the Wetumpka papers for its material aid in different celebrations. Campbell, the captain of the company, was made sheriff of Coosa, and died in May, 1839, at Rockford. The company was reofficered June 21st, 1839, by making W. J. Couch, captain; B. C. Yancey, 1st Lt.; Elias H. Neal, 2nd Lt., and Lorenzo Woodruff, 3rd Lt. The company was called the "Wetumpka Borderers." This was the first company from Coosa in actual service.

The next one to see service was one organized by John A. Chapman, June 7th, 1836, by authority of Gov. C. C. Clay. It did three months patrol service among the Creek Indians. John A. Chapman was captain; A. Harrell, lieutenant, and J. A. Hamilton, ensign. No other names appear on the papers filed. The company sought pay from the United States for the service rendered, but General Jessup declined to pay until he was informed that they were organized by proper authority and assigned to duty. Governor Clay was written to about it, September 9th, 1836, whereupon he wrote to General Jessup informing him the company was raised by his authority, and the claim was good.

(From "Original Papers" in State Archives)

May 13th, 1836, a committee consisting of S. Gallagher, L. J.
Bradford, T. Johnson, A. Crenshaw, E. Burrows, and William T.
A. Houghton communicated to Governor Clay that on a report
which had reached Wetumpka of some serious hostile acts of the
Indians about Tallassee, a party had gone from Wetumpka to in-
quire into it. It proved not to be true as to Tallassee, but it was
reported that at Catlin's store, fourteen miles above, that two
wagoners, one white, the other a negro, had been killed, and that
Catlin only escaped by fleeing on a pony without saddle or bridle.
That several families from the neighborhood had forsaken their
homes, and had come to Wetumpka. That the men of the neighborhood had built a block-house, and that sixteen mounted men
and ten or eleven footmen had gone to give aid, taking half the
arms in Wetumpka. They appealed to the Governor to send
them arms. They also said that the chiefs admitted the hostile
feeling of the young men.

(From "Original Papers" in Archives of the State)

John J. Word of East Wetumpka, wrote a letter to Governor
Bagby, May 7th, 1838, stating that having understood that he, as
Governor, had issued a call for volunteers for the defense of the
Cherokee part of Alabama, notified the Governor that he, thereupon, had formed a company of eighty men, ready and anxious
at anytime to serve as foot or mounted infantry as soon as authority should come from him.

("Manuscript Papers" in Archives of State)

This shows the spirit animating the early settlers to defend
their homes, or help the people anywhere in danger. There is
nothing among these papers in the Archives to show that the company of Word was accepted by the Governor.

MEXICAN WAR

Texas was a part of Mexico until 1836 when it declared its
independence of and separation from Mexico, establishing a government of its own. Mexico refused to acknowledge its independence for sometime, but it was acknowledged by the United States

and other powers. Mexico differed from Texas as to its boundary also. Bitter feelings existed between the people of the two countries. In the issue of *The Argus* of March 22nd, 1842, is an account of the invasion of Texas by Ariosta with 14,000 troops, and that San Antonio, Goliad, and Victoria had been taken without resistance. General Burleson was said to have gotten together about 1,200 volunteers, and it was supposed that 4,000 Texans were hurrying from different parts to meet the invaders. The papers of March 30th contained a thrilling account of the invasion of Texas by Santa Anna with an army of 21,000 invading from two points. The counties of Texas were hurrying forward their quotas of troops. President Houston says in his proclamation, "War will not cease to be waged against Mexico, nor will we lay our arms aside until we have secured the recognition of our independence. We invoke the God of Armies." In a May issue there is in the paper a contradition of the report that Texas had been invaded from Mexico, but that strong feelings of hostility existed and that volunteers were hurrying to Texas from the United States. In 1845, Texas applied for admission into the Union, and was received. Texas claimed the Rio Grande as her western boundary, Mexico denied it, and sent an armed force into the disputed territory. Texas had been received as extending to the river, and when Mexico entered, it was an invasion of what was then a part of the United States, and she sent forward troops to protect her people. This led to the war between the United States and Mexico, which resulted in the defeat of the latter, and large acquisition of territory from her by the former. The war lasted from December, 1846, to February, 1848, and it was no trouble to enlist men for it.

In May, 1846, a company called "The Coosa Volunteers" was organized at Wetumpka, as shown by a letter of May 20th, 1846, on file in Archives of the State, from Bennett S. Griffin, who had been elected captain of it. It had been organized under the proclamation of Gov. Joshua L. Martin, issued May 10th, 1846. Captain Griffin, in his letter, styled his organization as a company of "Riflemen." The names of the other officers or men are not given in the letter nor has any further record of them been found.

Henry W. Cox of Rockford raised a company for the Mexican war, that was mustered in, June 2nd, 1846, for six months, and became Co. B. of the 1st Regiment of Alabama Volunteers, under Col. Jones M. Withers of Mobile. The officers were H. W. Cox, captain; Levi G. Boswell, 1st Lt.; James S. Oliver, 2nd Lt.; Charles G. Cargill, 1st Sergt.; Henry A. Livingston, 2nd Sergt.; William T. Stubblefield, 3rd Sergt.; Overton Hitchcock, 4th Sergt.; William A. McDonald, 1st Corpl.; William W. Patrick, 2nd Corpl., Richard H. C. Shelton, 3rd Corpl.; Kention Marberry, 4th Corpl. No further record of the company is available. These were the only companies from the county known to have been in that war, but there were doubtless others of the county in other commands, and it is more than probable that some were in Capt. Rush Elmore's Company that went from Autauga in 1847 as the company was started near Wetumpka. John Q. Loomis, afterward a prominent citizen of the county, was 1st Sergt. in Captain Barr's Co. A., 1st Battalion, Alabama Vol., commanded by Lt. Col. J. J. Seibles, mustered into service November 25th, 1847.

(Archives of the State)

This shows the spirit of patriotism animating the Coosians which raised two companies when only fifteen were asked for from the State.

THE CONFEDERATE WAR

The next war was the fearful struggle between the United States and the Confederate States of America. Feeling had long been engendered, and was growing in bitterness between the States of the North and the South on the subject of African slavery. Slaves were once held in all the States of the Union, but it was not profitable in those north, and they had gradually sold them until most of the slaves were confined to the Southern States where their labor was profitable. After getting rid of their slaves by sale to the South, a sentiment sprang up among the people of the North that slavery was wrong. The question was agitated until a political party was formed to prevent the extension of slavery into any territory where not already established, and to oppose the admission into the Union of any slave State. There was much strife over the admission of Missouri in 1820 because it held slaves. A compromise was finally agreed upon by which Missouri with slavery was admitted, but that slavery should be forever prohibited in any territory thereafter lying north of 36.30 parallel of latitude, the southern boundary of Missouri. It was accepted unwillingly by the South, for her people felt it to be a wrong to them, for they had paid, to say the least, as much in money and in life for the territory as had the North, and they were therefore joint owners. They claimed that having joint ownership, and slavery being property as much as any other thing was, and so recognized by the common Constitution, that the Southerner should be protected in his slave property in the territories with all the guarantees thrown around other property; and if a majority of the people of a territory were in favor of slavery, and allowed it by her constitution when she came to form herself into a State they should be admitted with slavery. The Mexican war resulted in the acquisition of a large territory, some lying south of 36.30, and some north. When California asked for admission as a state, the contention became strong again as part of it lay south of the dividing line. A compromise was again agreed upon, viz: the admission of California as a free state, but two territories, Kansas and Nebraska, north of 36.30, were organized, protecting slavery in them as territories, and leaving the people thereof free to establish or prohibit slavery as they saw fit when they came to form a State Constitution. This opening the territory to slavery so aroused the anti-slavery sentiment that the "Free Soil Party," afterward called the "Republican" or "Black Republican" party, sprang rapidly into strength, and feelings on both sides became intense. In 1860 this new party was strong enough through the dissensions of the others, to elect a president, Mr. Lincoln, upon a platform opposed to the admission of any more slave states, and to the introduction of slavery into any territory of the United States. This success of a party hostile to the property interests of the South, and that denied them an equal participation in the common property, and that had placed the reins of government in the hands of those pledged to debar the Southern people of the lawful rights guaranteed by the Constitution of the Union, the South claimed that the North had broken the compact by which the Union was formed, and the purposes for which it was formed. Her leaders foresaw the issue to be the final destruction of a property valued at two and a half billions of dollars, for since the guarantees of the Constitution had been so ruthlessly trampled upon to inflict these injuries that the same instrument would be broken whenever in the way of the accomplishment of any fanatical purpose of the party. Their safety appeared to be in a peaceable secession from the old, and a formation of a new union of homogeneous views. Early in 1861 secession had taken place, and a government called the "Confederate States of America" had been formed.

The feeling of war was in the very air in 1860 and the military spirit ran high. "The Wetumpka Light Guard" was a volunteer company already existing. "The Wetumpka Light Dragons" was organized in August, 1860, with Leander Bryant, Captain; R. E. House, 1st Lt.; R. M. Cain, 2nd Lt.; W. S. Cunningham, 3rd Lt.; W. O. Haggerty, 1st Sergt.; N. J. Fogerty, 2nd Sergt.; John W. Bird, 3rd Sergt.; Thomas Ard, 4th Sergt.; W. J. Bailey, 1st Corpl.; J. J. Pogue, 2nd Corpl.; R. Holman, 3rd Corpl.; F. M. Mann, 4th Corpl.; Thomas M. Mason, Surgeon; William S. Sarsnett, Quartermaster; and George L. Mason, Secretary. There were thirty-two privates of the most prominent young men of Wetumpka.

Another company was formed in August, 1860, called the "Central Institute Cavalry," of which Michael Peevy was captain; J. H. Sanders, 1st Lt.; B. J. Peel, 2nd Lt.; W. F. Peevy, 3rd Lt.; David Berritt, 1st Sergt.; J. L. Chappell, 2nd Sergt.; James Howard, 3rd Sergt.; W. A. Florence, 4th Sergt.; B. R. Evans, 1st Corpl.; C. A. Kelly, 2nd Corpl.; F. M. Keith, 3rd Corpl.; Gibson Duncan, 4th Corpl. There were thirty-five privates from among the substantial farmers and young men around Central Institute.

The Wetumpka Light Guards was officered October 30th, 1860, by having John Q. Loomis as Captain; Edward S. Reedy, 1st Lt.; Osceola Kyle, 2nd Lt.; J. C. Mackey, 3rd Lt.; C. C. Tommy, 4th Lt.; O. C. Smith, 1st Sergt.; W. C. Havis, 2nd Sergt.; E. F. Stack, 3rd Sergt.; John P. Shaffer, 4th Sergt.; B. F. Melton, 1st

Corpl.; M. Nick Due, 2nd Corpl.; Thomas S. McDonald, 3rd Corpl.; James M. Smoot, 4th Corpl.; H. H. Robinson, Ensign; E. R. Mitchell, Treasurer; J. M. Smith, Secretary; J. B. Hubbard, Quartermaster. It had among its privates many of the prominent young men of the place. Among those who were for years after the war identified with Wetumpka and its interests were C. F. Enslen, now a wealthy banker of Birmingham; N. W. Green, long Marshal of the place; George Sedberry, a merchant, sheriff, and now Examiner of Public Accounts; Walter J. Taylor, W. S. Seaman, W. H. Alexander, N. B. Williams, Horiatio and Leon Robinson.

When Alabama seceded, Governor Andrew B. Moore ordered the Light Guards, with other volunteer companies, to Mobile and Pensacola to take possession of the forts and other public property in the name of the sovereign States of Alabama and Florida, being within their borders, and rightfully belonging to them. All was taken except Fort Pickens on Santa Rosa Island. The company remained in garrison duty until relieved by other troops later. By a pay-roll for part of April and May, 1861, J. Q. Loomis and O. Kyle still appear as Captain and 2nd Lt. but J. W. Whiting is 1st Lt. and R. W. Goldthwait, 3rd Lt.; Wm. F. Laney is 1st Sergt.; Samuel I. Horton, 2nd Sergt.; John T. Hill, 3rd Sergt:; George F. Buckley, 4th Sergt.; Edward C. Thornhill, 1st Corpl.; George W. Narramore, 2nd Corpl.; John E. Daniel, 3rd Corpl.; and Cornelius W. Cantrell, 4th Corpl. There were sixty-five privates at this time. It was attached to the first regiment of infantry.

Under a call made by Governor Moore for state troops to garrison the forts and for other purposes of defense, Henry W. Cox made up a company that was mustered into service February 28th, 1861, with H. W. Cox, Captain; Charles H. Tiner, 1st Lt.; George W. Hannon, 2nd Lt.; Julius H. Kendrick, 3rd Lt.; John M. Loyal, 1st Sergt.; William D. Leonard, 2nd Sergt.; John M. Lykes, 3rd Sergt.; Caswell J. Sears, 4th Sergt.; Reuben F. Gilder, 1st Corpl.; Joseph T. House, 2nd Corpl.; Joseph C. Gaddis, 3rd Corpl.; and Sinclair M. Suttle, 4th Corpl.; Hampton Burkhalter, drummer. There were seventy privates from different parts of

the county, representing some of its best families. This company
went to Mobile and did garrison duty at Fort Morgan until relieved by Confederate troops in April, 1861, when the company
disbanded, having served the purpose for which it was raised.

THE THIRD ALABAMA REGIMENT

When Lincoln issued his call for 75,000 volunteers with a
view to coercing the Confederate States back into the Union, the
Confederate government called for volunteers to defend her soil
and maintain the government. Volunteers rapidly formed, and
in April, 1861, the 3rd Ala. Regiment was formed with Jones M.
Withers as Colonel; Tenant Lomas, Lt. Colonel, and Cullen A.
Battle, Major. This regiment was noted for its gallantry in the
many battles in which it was engaged, and by its loss of 260 killed
showed that it had taken its place where the enemy were strong.
This was the first regiment that went to Virginia from Alabama,
and the Light Guards of Wetumpka was Company "I" in this
regiment. E. S. Ready was Captain; Osceola Kyle, 1st Lt.; Lewis
H. Hill, 2nd Lt. There were some other changes of officers, and
there were fresh recruits in its ranks but the roll is not at command to consult. Captain Loomis, upon the return of the company after its service as State troops, had been commissioned as
captain of Co. E., 1st Battalion of Artillery, and had resigned his
place with the Light Guards. He was afterwards made Colonel
of the 25th Alabama Regt. and he had John Stout of Coosa as his
adjutant. Captain Reedy was wounded at Seven Pines, and
wounded and captured at Boonsboro. He was promoted to major
and placed on detached service; and was for some time commander of the Camp Watts of Direction at Notasulga. Lieutenant Kyle had resigned in the Light Guards to accept the cap-
taincy of Co. C. in 13th Ala. Regt. Lieutenant Hill became captain of the Guards, but resigned because of health, and B. F. K.
Melton became Captain. The first casualty of the company was
the accidental killing by a sentinel of Lt. Henry Storrs, at Norfolk, early in the war. He was a very promising young man and
his death was felt to be a bereavement to all Wetumpka.

EIGHTH ALABAMA REGIMENT

It had for its first Colonel, John Anthony Winston, and later Hilary A. Herbert. It was the first regiment from Alabama that was enlisted for the war. It was a gallant regiment, and lost, killed and mortally wounded about 300. Company B of this regiment was from Coosa with T. W. W. Davies, Captain; George W. Hannon, 1st Lt.; M. Gibson McWilliams, 2nd Lt.; Louis H. Crumpler, 3rd Lt.; G. T. L. Robinson, 1st Sergt.; J. M. Loyal, 2nd Sergt.; J. W. Canterberry, 3rd Sergt.; A. M. Debardelaban, 4th Sergt.; N. Jester, 5th Sergt.; W. M. Howard, 1st Corpl.; C. M. Maynard, 2nd Corpl.; D. W. Bouring, 3rd Corpl.; A. B. Bailey, 4th Corpl. Captain Davis resigned, March, 1862, to become Major of the 28th Ala., and afterward transferred to the navy. G. W. Hannon became captain and was killed at Gain's Mill, July, 1862. M. G. McWilliams became captain, and died January, 1863, when G. T. L. Robinson became captain. Lieutenant Crumpler resigned the latter part of 1861. J. B. Hannon was promoted to first lieutenant, Maynard and Loyal were both promoted to lieutenants, and killed at Frazier's Farm, 1862, Canterberry was promoted to lieutenant, and died 1862. Debardelaben was promoted to lieutenant in 1864. Captain Davies had been the successful teacher of the Military School of Wetumpka to the time of organizing the company. Some of the officers and privates of his company were students in the school.

From the organization of the company in May, 1861, to January 1st, 1865, it had nine commissioned officers, and 114 enlisted men. Of these, 22 were killed, 58 wounded, 1 died of wound, 23 died of disease, 10 were discharge, 5 transferred, 22 captured, and 1 deserted. The regiment lost about 100 at Williamsburg, 144 at Seven Pines, nearly half at Gain's Mill, and again at Frazier's Farm. It suffered heavily at other of the great Battles of Virginia.

TWELFTH ALABAMA REGIMENT

This regiment was organized at Richmond in July, 1861, with Robert B. Jones of Perry as colonel. It opened the battle of

Seven Pines and captured three lines of the enemy's works by gallant charges, losing 211 killed and wounded in the battle. It did nobly through the war, and lost heavily in killed and wounded.

Company B of this regiment was from Coosa, with Joseph H. Bradford as captain; John C. Goodgame, 1st Lt.; Henry W. Cox, 2nd Lt., and Patrick Thomas, 3rd Lt. Other officers, number of privates, casualties, etc., cannot be given as there are no records on file at Montgomery. This was a twelve months' company, and was being formed when Captain Cox returned from State service, and he united with it. When it was reorganized, after enlistment for the war, Captain Bradford, who was too old for field service, resigned, and Goodgame became captain. He was afterward promoted to major, then to lieutenant colonel. He was on detached service much of the time, especially in enrolling conscripts and catching deserters. After his promotion, Cox became captain, and was killed at Chancellorsville while bravely leading his men. He was succeeded by Patrick Thomas who was killed at the last struggle at Appomattox.

THIRTEENTH ALABAMA REGIMENT

Was organized at Montgomery, July 19th, 1861, with B. D. Fry, colonel; J. C. B. Mitchell, lieutenant colonel; Samuel B. Marks, major. At Chancellorsville it lost nearly half its men on duty. At Gettysburg its colors were planted on the crest of the ridge, where they were torn to pieces, and the regiment suffered very heavily again. Two of its companies were from Coosa, Kyle's and Ellis Logan's. George C. Storrs of Wetumpka was Sergt. Major.

Company C was organized at Wetumpka, July 15th, 1861, with Osceola Kyle, Captain; Walter J. Taylor, 1st Lt.; Bailey A. Bowen, 2nd Lt.; Thomas S. Smith, 3rd Lt.; John C. Humphries, 1st Sergt.; Samuel D. Sandford, 2nd Sergt.; Henry W. Pond, 3rd Sergt.; William A. Freeman, 4th Sergt.; Stephen B. Jackson, 1st Corpl.; John T. Dunlap, 2nd Corpl.; Thomas R. Edwards, 3rd Corpl.; John H. Speed, 4th Corpl. It had in all 106 privates. It was mostly made up of farmers, but there were two lawyers, four mechanics, four teachers, one physician, three merchants, one saddler, and one tanner.

Kyle was promoted to lieutenant colonel of the 46th Ala. Regt. and Walter Taylor became captain until his death by disease July 2nd, 1864. Bowen then was captain till the close of the war. Henry W. Pond was elected 2nd Lieutenant in July, 1862, and was promoted to 1st Lt. William H. Crawford was elected 3rd Lt. in July, 1862, and was promoted to 2nd Lt. Thomas H. Smith was elected captain of a company in Hilliards Legion in May, 1862. Humphries was discharged in December, 1861, and afterwards raised a company of cavalry. The company had to January 1st, 1865, six commissioned officers, and 114 enlisted men. There were killed and died of wounds 17, wounded 27, disabled 12, died of disease 26, discharged 18, deserted 1.

Company H was organized at Mt. Moriah church July 2nd, 1861, with Ellis Logan, captain; Stephen Richard Allison, 1st Lt.; James L. Gilder, 2nd Lt.; Adolphus Wilson, 3rd Lt.; Sinclair M. Suttle, 1st Sergt.; Locuis M. Wilson, 2nd Sergt.; William B. Wilson, 3rd Sergt.; Reuben F. Gilder, 4th Sergt.; William F. Estes, 1st Corpl.; Robert B. Calfee, 2nd Corpl.; Elliott E. Estes, 3rd Corpl.; George S. Gulledge, 4th Corpl. Captain Logan resigned May, 1862, on account of health, and Allison became captain, serving through the war. He was once captured, but was exchanged. James L. Gilder resigned June, 1862. Reuben F. Gilder was made 3rd Lt. December, 1861, and promoted to 1st Lt. June, 1862, and died from wound September 5th, 1864. Thomas S. McDonald was elected 3rd Lt. September, 1862, and was discharged September 10th, 1864, because of wounds received at Chancellorsville. The company had to January, 1865, 7 commissioned officers, 122 enlisted men. There were 9 killed and died of wounds, 26 wounded, 8 disabled, 28 died of disease, 27 discharged, 8 deserted. Most were farmers, but there were 4 merchants, 2 doctors, 1 dentist, 1 lawyer, 1 printer, 5 mechanics, and 2 teachers.

SEVENTEENTH ALABAMA REGIMENT

Was organized at Montgomery in August, 1861, with Thomas H. Watts as colonel, after him R. C. Farris, and later Virgil S. Murphy. It suffered severe losses, especially at Shiloh, Peach Tree Creek, the 28th of July at Atlanta, and at Franklin, Tennessee. Coosa had one company in this regiment, that of Thomas C. Bragg, who had a fine school at Central Institute. The war spirit seized the young men of the school so they were enlisting in the companies being raised. Bragg's patriotism was stirred so that he abandoned the school and raised what became Company D, with Thomas C. Bragg, captain; Dixon S. Thaxton, 1st Lt.; John D. Hester, 2nd Lt.; William D. Haill, 3rd Lt.; Warren R. Rush, 1st Sergt.; Joseph W. Calloway, 2nd Sergt.; John T. Atkins, 3rd Sergt.; Robert M. Holland, 4th Sergt.; Seaborn M. Stewart, 1st Corpl.; Newton A. Storey, 2nd Corpl.; John T. Lauderdale, 3rd Corpl.; W. William Lee, 4th Corpl. There were 67 privates on the first roll. But little can be told of the company, as there are no records on file at Montgomery. Captain Bragg resigned in 1862, and John D. Hester became captain, and remained so through the remainder of the war. The company was composed principally of farmers and young men. The company was mustered into service September 17th, 1861.

EIGHTEENTH ALABAMA REGIMENT

This was organized at Auburn, Alabama, September 4th, 1861, with Edward C. Bullock of Barbour as colonel. He died in the winter, and Eli S. Shorter became colonel. He resigned in the spring of 1862, after the Battle of Shiloh, and James T. Holtzclaw, raised in Coosa, became colonel, and was promoted to Brigadier General for gallantry and efficiency. The regiment did duty about Mobile until ordered to Corinth in March, 1862. It lost heavily at Corinth, having 125 killed and wounded. It aided largely in the capture of Prentis's Brigade. At Chicamauga it lost 22 officers and about 300 men. It participated in the battles from Chattanooga to Atlanta, and from there to Nashville. After this, it was again in service at Mobile. Co. D. of this regiment was from Coosa with Guy Smith as captain. He resigned

and Charles M. Cox became captain. He resigned and W. H.
Hammond was made captain, and was killed at Chicamauga.
George M. Williams became captain. He was wounded at Chicamauga, and captured at Franklin, Tenn. No records on file from
which to gain other facts.

TWENTY-FIFTH ALABAMA REGIMENT

There was no company in this regiment from Coosa, but it
furnished its colonel, John Q. Loomis, a popular and talented
lawyer. He was captain of the Light Guards, and commanded
it during its service for the State at Pensacola. Then he resigned
as its captain, and became captain of Co. E., 1st Battalion of
Artillery. He became colonel of the 25th Alabama Regt., which
was organized at Mobile in December, 1861, by the consolidation of two battalions. Colonel Loomis commanded the brigade
of which the 25th was a part at the Battle of Murfreesboro, in
which engagement the regiment lost 13 killed, 88 wounded, and
13 missing. It lost a good many all the way from Dalton, especially on the 26th of July, 1864, at Atlanta, where it was depleted
nearly one-half. It also lost heavily at Franklin, Tenn. Its adjutant, John Stout, was also from Coosa, a son of Rev. Platt Stout.
He was but little more than a boy in years, but a brave and gallant officer, receiving wounds at Murfreesboro, Atlanta, and
Franklin. After the war he became one of the most prominent
Baptist ministers of South Carolina.

THIRTY-FOURTH ALABAMA REGIMENT

This regiment was organized at Loachapoka, April 15th,
1862, with Julius C. B. Mitchell as colonel. Its first engagement
was at Murfreesboro where it lost heavily. At Chicamauga, Missionary Ridge, and in the campaign from Dalton, it shared in the
glories of that masterly retreat, where the enemy, though con-
stantly advancing, were ever worsted in the battles fought. It
suffered heavy losses, especially on July 22nd and 28th, 1864, at
Atlanta. It was finally consolidated with the 24th and 28th Ala.
Regts. It had three Coosa companies in it. Of Co. A., Thomas

J. Mitchell was captain; R. G. Welch, 1st Lt.; W. Floyd, 2nd Lt.; James Carleton, 3rd Lt.; W. E. Young, 1st Sergt.; B. T. Welch, 2nd Sergt.; James Carleton, 3rd Sergt.; V. R. Duncan, 4th Sergt.; W. Z. Davis, 5th Sergt.; S. A. Steed, 1st Corpl.. J. T. Shepherd, 2nd Corpl.; Samuel Nunnery, 3rd Corpl.; S. G. Welch, 4th Corpl. It had 115 privates, 74 of whom were from Coosa, and most of the others from that part of Montgomery north of the Tallapoosa River. Most were farmers. Captain Mitchell resigned, and R. G. Welch became captain, and commanded through remainder of the war. He was wounded at Chicamauga, but is still living, and vigorous. It is not known how many joined this company in all, as only its first roll has been seen. Its casualties cannot be told for the same reason, and the writer has been unable to get help from survivors. This is true of other companies.

Company B. had John N. Slaughter for captain. He was a physician but devoted himself to teaching. Eason B. Wood was 1st Lt.; W. G. Massey, 2nd Lt.; J. C. Taylor, 3rd Lt.; M. S. Bazemore, 1st Sergt.; A. J. Vanzant, 2nd Sergt.; J. P. Barnett, 3rd Sergt.; J. P. Bazemore, 4th Sergt.; J. W. Burt, 5th Sergt.; C. C. Pate, 1st Corpl.; A. J. Groom, 2nd Corpl.; William L. Collier, 3rd Corpl.; J. M. Callaway, 4th Corpl.; S. G. Adams, drummer; F. M. Robertson, fifer; and 98 privates. It was organized at Montgomery, May 26th, 1862. Captain Slaughter was promoted to major upon the resignation of Major Henry McCoy, and Eason Wood became captain. He was captured at Missionary Ridge, and the command fell to Lieut. M. Lambert. Major Slaughter was wounded at Atlanta. He lives at Goodwater. Captain Wood at Hubbard City, Texas. The particulars of the company cannot be given for inaccessibility to records.

Company C. was from Coosa with James M. Willis, captain; John E. Hannon, 1st Lt.; W. G. Oliver, 2nd Lt.; James D. Wall, 3rd Lt.; George W. Spigener, 1st Sergt.; L. W. Jinks, 2nd Sergt.; J. T. P. Oliver, 3rd Sergt.; J. S. Edwards, 4th Sergt.; A. B. Blocker, 5th Sergt.; A. C. Fargason, 1st Corpl.; R. A. Collier, 2nd Corpl.; W. H. Spigener, 3rd Corpl.; J. B. Jones, 4th Corpl.; and 88 privates on the first roll. Captain Willis resigned, and Lieutenant Oliver became captain. He was wounded at Jonesboro. No records to consult for further statements.

THE FORTY-SIXTH ALABAMA REGIMENT

This was formed at Loachapoka, May, 1862, with M. L. Woods as colonel and Osceola Kyle as the well known gallant Lt. Col. was from Coosa. He was a very fine officer, and had he not been in prison during most of the fighting period, would doubtless have attained to distinction, for he had military talent of a higher order. The regiment was in Tennessee and Kentucky under Kirby Smith, went through the siege of Vicksburg, and was on Lookout Mountain in "The Battle of the Clouds," Missionary Ridge, the campaign from Dalton, and was surrendered in North Carolina. It did its duty well everywhere. At the Battle of Baker's Creek, May 16th, 1863, all its field officers were captured, and kept in prison until near the close of the war. Riggs, its adjutant, was killed at Baker's Creek. From May, 1863, to the surrender, 1865, it was commanded by Capt. Geo. E. Brewer of Co. A. Coosa had two companies in it.

Co. A. was from Coosa with George E. Brewer, captain; Daniel J. Thompson, 1st Lt.; John M. Collins, 2nd Lt.; Thomas J. King, 3rd Lt.; T. R. Harden, 1st Sergt.; J. H. Hearn, 2nd Sergt.; J. M. Devaughn, 3rd Sergt.; Francis M. Finch, 4th Sergt.; Francis M. Corley, 5th Sergt.; Uriah A. Darden, 1st Corpl.; D. G. A. Spigener, 2nd Corpl.; Robert Higgins, 3rd Corpl.; Russell Hand, 4th Corpl. There were enlisted 120 privates. There was 1 preacher, 1 teacher, 2 merchants, 2 blacksmiths, 1 saddler, 3 mechanics, and the rest were farmers. The company was mustered in at Montgomery, February 24th, 1862, and did duty from then at Pensacola until it was evacuated in May, 1862. It united with the 46th Ala. Regt. at Chattanooga the latter part of June, 1862. Captain Brewer was detached from the company in command of the regiment from May, 1863, and the company was commanded by Lieutenant Thompson, an efficient officer. Lieutenant Collins was sometimes detached to command other companies because of his efficiency and was for some months the acting adjutant of the regiment, owing to the disabling wound of A. J. Brooks, ad-

jutant. Lieutenant King died July 23rd, 1862, near Powder
Springs, Tenn. Micajah S. Booth was elected to the vacancy November 13th, 1862. He died at Meridian, Miss., January 4th,
1863, and Sinclair M. Suttle, who had been transferred from the
13th Alabama, was elected 3rd Lt., January 23rd, 1863. J. M.
Devaughn, Aaron Vincent, Wm. M. Johnson, James R. Wilkerson,
and Andrew J. Collins were promoted to sergeants, and J. D.
Kelly, John N. Cooper, James I. Hill, and Richard A. Foster to
corporals for gallantry. The company was formed at Rockford.
This was a splendid company, and though several others had
larger muster rolls, this company usually had the largest number
for duty in the regiment. There were killed and died from
wounds 18, wounded 10, died from disease 33, captured 13, discharged 9, deserted 13, but most of them near the close when
hope was lost. Perryman Maxwell was a fine soldier though
only a boy, and had been on the staff of the regiment, as orderly,
for a good while when killed at Jonesboro.

Company B. was also from Coosa with James R. Cross, captain; Joseph T. House, 1st Lt.; J. P. Bannon, 2nd Lt.; James H.
Willbanks, 3rd Lt.; Pleasant H. Macon, 1st Sergt.; F. R. Green,
2nd Sergt.; R. C. Singleton, 3rd Sergt.; Isaac C. Blake, 4th Sergt.;
J. H. Butler, 5th Sergt.; E. M. Black, 1st Corpl.; W. S. Barrett,
2nd Corpl.; J. E. Scott, 3rd Corpl.; S. D. Bowran, 4th Corpl.
There were 65 privates on the roll when mustered in at Brooksville, Ala., on March 6th, 1862. It was recruited from time to
time until it became a very large company. There are no records
that can be consulted for information. The company was made
up of good soldiers, in the main, and a number of its men could
be relied upon for the most desperate undertakings. Its casualties were heavy, but cannot be stated with definiteness. A. J.
Brooks was detailed from an early period as an orderly on the
commander's staff, and was commissioned as Adjutant after the
Vicksburg surrender, by request of Captain Brewer, commanding
regiment. Lt. Joseph House was detached as acting Adjutant
after Riggs was killed, and was killed himself during the siege of
Vicksburg while so acting. Upon his death, Willbanks became
first lieutenant, and F. R. Green was elected 3rd Lt. Green resigned in the spring of 1864, and W. T. Sears was made a lieuten-

ant. Benjamin F. Hodnett and A. C. Swindell were made sergeants for gallantry. After A. J. Brooks was permanently disabled by wound near Marietta, Lieutenant Willbanks was sometimes detached as Adjutant. A. D. Rope of Company B. and John Lee of Company A. were detached as musicians for the regiment from its early service.

Both these companies were as good as were in the Army, and could be relied upon in times of peril. Lieutenant Collins and A. J. Brooks, with some others whose names are not known now, were among those who volunteered to follow Colonel Pettus in retaking the fort by the railroad at Vicksburg which was captured by the enemy in the memorable general assault of all the lines on the 22nd of May, 1863. When Pettus came up with the reserve forces under his command, this fort was in the hands of the enemy. General Lee ordered it recaptured. None seemed inclined to undertake it. Pettus, after other efforts failed, called for volunteers, when the two named with a few others from the 46th Ala., and a larger number from Wauls, Texas Legion followed the intrepid Pettus, and soon the Stars and Stripes were down, and the Confederate flag was again floating on the rampart.

Of the 47th Ala. Regt., Brewer in his "Alabama" says there was a Coosa Company K. in it, whose captain was J. Fargason. But there are no records on file in Montgomery, and the writer has been unable to learn anything of it. It is presumed to be true, however, as Colonel Brewer, the author, had access to records not now in Montgomery.

FIFTY-THIRD ALABAMA REGIMENT

This was a mounted regiment organized in Montgomery in November, 1862, with Moses W. Hannon as Colonel, and operated with the Army of the Tennessee. There was a Company C. in it from Coosa, of which John C. Humphries was captain; William T. Massingale, 1st Lt.; John W. Hunter, 2nd Lt.; George W. McEwen, 3rd Lt.; Gibson Burkhalter, 1st Sergt.; William P. Ward, 2nd Sergt. The other officers are not known, as there are no records.   Lieutenant Massingale says there were 112 privates, and that the company was organized at Wetumpka in May, 1862.

FIFTY-NINTH ALABAMA REGIMENT

This was formed by the consolidation of the Second and Fourth Battalions of Hilliard's Legion.   The Legion was composed of five battalions, organized by Col. Henry W. Hilliard at Montgomery, in June, 1862.   The Second Battalion had six companies commanded by Col. Boling Hall of Autauga, and Maj. William Stubblefield of Coosa.   They were in East Tennessee and Kentucky, at Chicamauga and Knoxville, but did most of their service in Virginia after the Spring of 1864.

Company C. was from Coosa with Louis Crumpler, captain; Isom L. Lee, 1st Lt.; William R. Davie, 2nd Lt.; Joseph E. Pond, 3rd Lt.; Lewis L. Shaw, 1st Sergt.; William A. Wilson, 2nd Sergt.; James L. McDonald, 3rd Sergt.; Robert Snider, 4th Sergt.; John M. Lee, 5th Sergt.; Sanford L. Kirkpatrick, 1st Corpl.; Wiley Cowart, 2nd Corpl.; Thomas J. Mitchell, 3rd Corpl.; William Sample, 4th Corpl.   There were 104 privates, most of them farmers.   There are no records from which to get its casualties or other particulars.   But the writer remembers that it suffered heavily in deaths from sickness, and in battle, for it fought bravely.   Its captain was only about twenty when he entered the service.   He was a son of Rev. Albert Crumpler, and now lives at Sylacauga.   When Major Huguley was promoted, Crumpler became Major.   Lee had resigned and Lieutenant Davie became captain.   He was a son of Dr. Davie of Buyckville, and a good officer.

Company K. was from Coosa with Wesley D. Walden, captain; Wesley G. Delaney, 1st Lt.; John Burrough, 2nd Lt.; Thomas Hull, 3rd Lt.; Socrates Spigener, 1st Sergt.; William C. McGrady, 2nd Sergt.; J. W. Akins, 3rd Sergt.; John D. Posey, 4th Sergt.; Rufus McSwain, 5th Sergt.; William M. Posey, 1st Corpl.; James M. McGrady, 2nd Corpl.; J. H. Akins, 3rd Corpl.; James Patterson, 4th Corpl.   There were 87 privates on the first roll, most of them farmers.   There are no records from which to get information. Robert H. Gullege went from ranks to a lieutenantcy. Captain Walder was killed at Chickamauga just as he mounted the works of the enemy in a gallant charge by which they were taken. Robert H. Gullege then became captain and commanded through the remainder of the war.

Company A. was mostly from Coosa, with some from Tallapoosa. John H. Porter, captain; Alpheus Goga, 1st Lt.; W. H. Huitt, 2nd Lt.; A. J. Smith, 3rd Lt.; F. M. King, 1st Sergt.; N. H. Benners, 2nd Sergt.; E. J. Carlisle, 3rd Sergt.; W. B. Carlisle, 4th Sergt.; A. A. Collins, 1st Corpl.; G. W. Reeves, 2nd Corpl.; A. C. Honor, 3rd Corpl.; and 52 privates; 17 killed and died from wounds, 24 died of disease, 9 deserted, all after February, 1865. Captain Porter died 1902, in Coosa.

THE SIXTIETH ALABAMA REGIMENT

This was made up of the six companies of the Third Battalion, and four from the First Battalion of Hilliard's Legion. Like the 59th (as Hilliard's Legion), it was in Tennessee and Kentucky, and was in the Battle of Chicamauga, losing heavily. After this, in November they were organized into regiments, and were at Knoxville under Longstreet, and from there to Virginia. John W. A. Sanford was colonel.

Company A. was from Coosa with Thomas H. Smith, captain; John H. Leonard, 1st Lt.; William L. Roberts, 2nd Lt.; William L. Thompson, 3rd Lt.; Matt. Britton, 1st Sergt.; C. R. Hicks, 2nd Sergt.; J. W. Thompson, 3rd Sergt.; D. L. McAlister, 4th Sergt.; R. A. Palmer, 5th Sergt.; W. H. Hales, 1st Corpl.; M. C. Poner, 2nd Corpl.; J. W. Rayfield, 3rd Corpl.; David Hughes, 4th Corpl. There were 64 privates at its organization. There are no records from which to learn further of the company. Captain Smith was the oldest son of Alexander Smith, a promising young lawyer of Wetumpka. He died in 1870. Lieutenant Leonard was a son of John B. Leonard, and now lives at Alexander City. D. L. McAlister is at Rockford in the mill business.

SIXTY-FIRST ALABAMA REGIMENT

This regiment was organized at Pollard in September, 1863, with W. G. Swanson, Colonel, and Lewis H. Hill of Wetumpka, lieutenant colonel. He had been a lieutenant in the Light Guards. It was first a part of Clanton's command, but early in 1864 went to Virginia, and suffered heavy losses.

There was a Coosa Company C. in this regiment with Julius P. Haggerty, captain. He was retired and C. C. Long became captain. Colonel Hill was captured at Petersburg. There are no records of the company to be reached. Haggerty was of the prominent family so long known about Wetumpka.

Brewer's History of Alabama, in its account of the 63rd Ala. Regt., speaks of a company of which J. W. Suttle of Coosa was captain and afterwards became Major of the regiment. But no records are on file, and the writer has no recollection in regard to it. This regiment was on duty about Mobile. George J. Suttle, the youngest son of I. W. Suttle, was at Mobile for a time at the last of the war.

Brewer also in what he says of the 56th Ala. Regt., speaks of Company J. as being from Coosa, and a Mr. Demson as its captain. Records are not on hand, nor can the writer learn anything reliable.

SECOND ALABAMA CAVALRY

Was organized at Montgomery, May 1st, 1862. It was in Farguson's brigade, and participated in the campaigns of the Army of the Tennessee, suffering considerable loss. It hung on the flanks of Sherman's army in its "March to the Sea." It became the escort of President Davis from Greensboro, N. C., to Georgia. It surrendered at Forsyth, Ga., with 450 men.

This had one Coosa Company, G., William P. Ashley, captain; Wm. F. Beckett, 1st Lt.; Jeremiah Busbee, 2nd Lt.; William P. Gaddis, 3rd Lt.; Wm. N. Ward, 1st Sergt.; Wm. Pritchett, 2nd

Sergt.; William Pylant, 3rd Sergt.; Thomas Barnett, 4th Sergt.; D. C. Lauderdale, 5th Sergt.; John Tekell, 1st Corpl.; D. L. Lauderdale, 2nd Corpl.; Willis Shelton, 3rd Corpl.; William H. Thomas, 4th Corpl. There were 66 privates at time of mustering in. No records after this at hand. Captain Ashley wounded at Decatur, Ga.

The 6th Alabama Cavalry, which was organized at Pine Level, Montgomery County, in 1863, had in it one Company, K., partly from Montgomery and partly from Coosa, with Waddy T. Armstrong as captain. No records accessible.

The 7th Alabama Cavalry, which was organized in July, 1863, had for a captain of Company D., Charles P. Storrs of Wetumpka, but as there are no records it is not known if the company was from Coosa.

Ellis Logan, who had resigned as captain of Co. H., 13th Ala., in May, 1862, on account of health, returned to Coosa and resumed his duty as sherfif. In May, 1864, under a special Act providing for the enlistment of such as were exempt from Confederate service, to form companies for home defense, thus supplementing the power of the Confederate forces in the State for protection within the State borders, Ellis Logan raised a company of this kind, of which Logan was captain; Jeremiah Busbee, 1st Lt.; J. L. Bilby, 2nd Lt.; C. B. Henderson, 3rd Lt.; J. P. Earhart, 1st Sergt.; Caleb Bailey, 2nd Sergt.; John C. Bulger, 3rd Sergt.; Jacob Farris, 4th Sergt.; A. T. Stanley, 1st Corpl.; W. F. May, 2nd Corpl.; Taylor Coker, 3rd Corpl.; T. Watt, 4th Corpl. There were 68 privates. This company did some service in South Alabama.

This closes the record of organized forces furnished for Confederate service from Coosa. There was a goodly number of her citizens in organizations from other counties, in different branches of the service. Her men as a rule were as gallant as those from any section of the South, and that is to say the world never produced better fighters, for Southern valor is at no discount.

Under the military history of Coosa it is well to say that at one time since the war Rockford had a good volunteer company. Goodwater also had one, but nothing definite can be said of them, as the writer has failed to elicit information.

HISTORY OF COOSA COUNTY

By Rev. George Evans Brewer

PART II

CHAPTER VII

SCHOOLS AND CHURCHES

It was desired by the writer to have given a fairly full account of the schools and churches of the county, but he has failed in his efforts in this direction, and must be limited to what he can call up from memory, except as to the Missionary Baptist Churches, which can be more fully set forth as the history of that demomination extending to 1895, written by himself, may be consulted.

The first school outside of Wetumpka, about which anything is known, was one at Nixburg, taught first perhaps by a Mr. Nix. From the first a school was kept up here and at times it was flourishing, especially was this true when Jerre Gary in the latter forties gave tone to it. He was followed in 1849-50 by a Mr. Kirkpatrick from Tennessee, who was a good teacher. In 1851, A. G. Brewer, who the year before had a fine school three miles above, took charge of the school at Nixburg, and was very successful, but gave up the school sometime in 1852 to become the editor of *The Christian Telegraph*, a Methodist Protestant paper of Atlanta. For some years the school was held up to a high standard, and reached its climax under Fred Oliver, after the war. The next school was in the Oakchoy neighborhood, started in 1837, taught by a Mr. John Brown. Here the children of J. W. Suttle, George Johnson, Spears, and the Harrells received their first school instruction. This school was broken up by a disturbance growing out of a fight between Eli Harrell and Hezekiah Spears, which originated in children's tales. Next, and soon after,

Charles Bulger, a nephew of M. L. Bulger, began a school rather in the same section, at Pine Grove, where he taught for two years, This neighborhood has usually kept up a good country school. John W. Brewer, a brother of the writer, taught here two years after the war. At an early period not later than 1837, the Scotch people had a school at the Carolina Church settlement. At Malcolm Smith's, on Hatcheesofka, there was a good school at an early date. From about 1840, schools were had in most neighborhoods where there were children enough to form one. It would be tedious and unprofitable to undertake to name all these. Only those most noted will be spoken of. For some years good teachers were employed for the school in the neighborhood of Reuben Jordan. This school had a wealthy patronage.

About Sockapatoy and Bradford's Factory schools were maintained and for some years Dr. John N. Slaughter had a very flourishing one called "Washington Academy." Rockford kept up a good school from about 1851, called the "Alabama Masonic Institute." Before this time John Hannon, Thomas Crawford, William Lee, and J. S. Bentley are remembered as teachers. A. L. Chapman gave the school a start such as it had not before had. He was followed by Geo. E. Brewer, and he in turn by S. B. Brewer. Others are not remembered well enough to state particulars, until after the war, when a Mr. Mackey revived the school. He was followed by T. J. Pennington, who for several years kept the school up well, until retiring to his farm and county superintendency. Since then the school has had several fine teachers. Good schools were also kept up at Equality and in the neighborhood of Joseph and Monroe Parker.

Jasper McAdory taught several successful schools, the last at Hanover. At its close he bought the farm of John A. Pylant and quit the school room. Mt. Olive usually kept up a good school. At Buyckville a good school was kept up for a good series of years, in fact, hardly ever without one. Among its earlier teachers were Conrad Wall, William Holtzclaw, George E. Brewer, and Major Isaac Hall. Later Fred Oliver there, as wherever he taught, had a very large school. Its present teacher, who has been there several years, is Samuel Bentley. A good school was usually maintained at Antioch Church, especially in the days of the Rogers. Concord was another neighborhood that usually employed good teachers. John and William Hannon and John Hunter were for years good teachers who taught in different parts of the county. But the ranking school of the county was the Central Institute, a Baptist high school, located on the Plank Road, twelve miles north of Wetumpka. It was instituted and fostered by the Central Baptist Association from 1854 to 1860, when it was sold to Prof. Thomas C. Bragg, who for several years maintained its high standard. The building was a good, well arranged two-story brick structure. There was also a good female academy under Mr. Walkley kept up here, contemporaneous with the Institute, which was a male institution. After the establishment of the Public School System of Alabama in 1856, there has been a steady improvement in the schools of the county. In more recent years, since Goodwater has become a place of mercantile importance, it has had a good graded school to dispense learning among its young. At one time while Capt. John H. Clisby lived in the Weogufka country they had a good school there, taught by Thomas Crawford, a smart man and in some respects a rare genius.

Among the schools of note, but of brief existence, was an academic one established by Rev. McAlpine, a Presbyterian minister, at Pine Flat, near the fine home of John A. Graham. He was followed by Rev. A. G. Brewer in 1850. It was consolidated with the Nixburg school, in 1851.

The exact dates of the organization of the first churches cannot be given, but it was as early as 1834 that Smyrna, near Goodwater, was constituted. It is believed to be the oldest church of the county outside of Wetumpka. The Baptists were all united that this time, and the agitation on missions was just beginning. A convention is said to have been held with this church in 1835, and an association formed, but its name has not been preserved. In the split that came some year later, Smyrna went with the anti-mission party, who call themselves "Primitive Baptists." It has so remained, and still exists at the old location. There is a large cemetery attached.

Bethel is thought to have been constituted not long after and still remains located in the edge of Brooksville. It also went with the Primitives. There is a large cemetery here.

Antioch west of Nixburg was constituted about the time of the other two. The Association is said to have met with it in 1837, when the feeling upon missions produced so much confusion, that Luke Haynie, a preacher among them, induced a dissolution. The church dissolved some years later. No other association was formed until 1845, when the Central came into existence, and later the Primitives formed the Wetumpka Association.

Near this some time Shiloh was formed, some three miles north of Nixburg, and had a number of prominent families connected with it for some years. The first session of the Central Association was held and it was formed here in 1845. The strife on the mission question had grown in intensity, until fellowship was destroyed, and a separation became necessary. Some churches as bodies were for missions, some for anti-missions; some were divided, and mutually withdrew from each other, the majority holding the property and church records, the others either forming new churches, or going to some neighboring church of affinity. Even families divided, husbands and wives, and parents and children not infrequently going with different factions. William Salter and James P. Goggan remained with the missionaries, their wives went with the others. A preacher of the missionary once came to Goggans' seeking lodging, and made the plea to the madam saying, "I am on the Lord's business." She replied, "If the Lord has put His business in your hands I think he has made a very poor choice."

James F. Edens was a member, minister, and for a time pastor of Shiloh, but went with the Primitives. John Bates then became pastor and after him Benj. H. Wilson. He called the meeting in October 1845 with Shiloh church that resulted in the formation of the Central Association which became by far the most influential and numerous religious body in the county. Joseph Hill was a minister in Shiloh, who died a few years back having passed more than a hundred years of life, and last year

Stephen D. Ray died over ninety who was in the constitution of the church. Obadiah Moore and David Radford were ministers, once members. The church has not been so strong since the war as before, and the population changed so that thirty years or more ago it changed its location, going several miles north. There was a large cemetery at the old location, and a good many of Coosa's prominent citizens are buried there.

Those who took sides with the Primitives from Shiloh went into the organization of Fish Pond, which took its name from the Indian town. This has continued its existence, and has been a strong church. There has been kept up an annual singing by Mr. Albert Holloway for about fifty-eight years, on the first Sunday in May. It is the most noted gathering in all this region of country. The people come for miles in all directions, and bring their baskets of dinner, spending the day in singing, eating, and social enjoyment. The cemetery here is large.

Mount Carmel was also one of the early churches, and sided with the Primitives. But little is known of it.

Friendship church was in existence in 1846. It was between Sockapatoy and Bradford's, and once had a strong membership, but it was depleted by death and removals, until it dissolved in 1870. Patrick McKinney, Wm. Corbet, and Saml. Gray, with their families, were among its last members.

Harmony was constituted about 1846 or 1847 in the eastern part of the county, several miles from Brooksville. For a long time John H. Colley, one of its members, was its pastor. He died at an advanced age just a few years since, and is buried in its cemetery. A few years back the church was moved nearer Brooksville.

Good Hope church was in the southeastern part of the county, eight miles west of Tallassee. It was a good strong church, in a pretty part of the county, and had a good membership. Five entered the ministry from its membership, Benj. Timmerman, Y. D. Harrington, Joseph Norton, Calvin Swindall, and O. C. Swindall. Others have been ordained since the church was cut off into Elmore. There is a well kept cemetery attached. In 1871 and for two or more years, it had four deacons over eighty years old, Mr. Fielder, Norton, Timmerman, and Chas. Gregory.

Union church was one of the very early churches, and was in the constitution of the Association. It was located a mile above Central, until after the Central Institute had been established, when it was moved down to the village. This was a good church with a strong membership before the establishments of the school. Afterward it was very strong, so many persons of means and influence going there to educate their families. It once had seven ordained ministers members of it, Joseph Bankston, James Russell, Platt Stout, James Jeter, A. T. Holmes, B. T. Smith, and Bright Skipper. Joseph Bozeman, who died a few years since, the popular and beloved pastor of the first Baptist church at Meridian, began his religious life here. There are two cemeteries belonging to this church.

Mt. Gilead, several miles northeast of Central, was another one of the early churches. It is Primitive, and located in a pretty place. It has never been a strong church. It has a cemetery.

The time when Concord was constituted is not known. It joined the Central Association in 1848, but it existed before that time. It was for a series of years one of the strong churches intellectually, financially, and numerically; and though it has lost in these particulars, it is still a good church. Sterling Speer was ordained here, and was a young growing minister in power, when cut off by death. The cemetery is large.

Salem joined the association in 1848, but the writer is of opinion it had an earlier existence. It was not far from Hatchett Creek, and between Rockford and Weogufka. It was never a strong church, but had some fine members.

Poplar Springs was constituted in 1848, and grew rapidly, so that in a few years it had a larger membership than any other in the Association. Meetings of wonderful power used to be held, such as the writer has seldom seen elsewhere. For several years a number of the members had temporary houses built, and had meetings just after the order of Camp meetings. They usually had able pastors, until an unfortunate disturbance led to a split in the church which has never been entirely healed. Many of its influential members moved away and died. Rev. J. R. Steely, Hardy Jones, and J. M. Butler were members. The cemetery is large.

Mt. Zion was established about 1849, about eight miles northeast of Wetumpka. It was a pretty belt of pine land. Rev. Joel Nichols and Robert Stewart were members. Nichols was baptized at Old Elam Church, near Montgomery, in 1824. The church went down soon after the war.

There was, for a time from 1849, a Missionary Baptist church called Bethel, but its location and history are unknown to the writer.

Antioch church was constituted in 1849, about 12 miles nearly north of Wetumpka. It still exists, and has been a good church, and once had a strong membership in the days of the Rogers, Lawsons, Holifields, and Holtzclaws. There is a well-kept cemetery here.

Weogufka was one of the early constituted churches, being nearly as old as the white settlement, but did not join the Central Association from the Mulberry until 1849. It was a strong church for a number of years, but became weakened by the death and removal of a number of the Taylors, Calfees, Mooneys, Lindseys, Hughes, Calloways, and Thompsons. It is on Weogufka Creek not far from where the Rockford and Marble Valley road crosses it. Its cemetery is large.

In 1850 three new Baptist churches were constituted, Rockford, Shady Grove, and Bethesda. Rockford church never had a large membership at any time, but it was always an active, progressive body, and exerted a strong and good influence in the Association. It has sent into the ministry Geo. O. Brewer, J. P.

Shaffer, and Chas. Bentley. Shady Grove was five miles below Rockford, to the west of the Turnpike. Though a good church, it was never a strong one. Bethesda was constituted in 1849, near Brooksville, and is still in good condition. Rev. Darius Martin, who has been clerk of the Association so long, joined here, a boy, was set apart to the ministry, and has served it as pastor a number of years. Catt Smith was a member here and was perhaps ordained here. There is a large cemetery here; Rockford, Bethesda, and Shady Grove each have cemeteries.

Paint Creek and Providence were organized in 1851, and that year united with the Association. Paint Creek was near the creek of the same name, in the northwestern part of the county, and only maintained an existence for about six years. Providence is in what is now the southwestern part of the county, then the western, and not far from the Coosa River, on the River Road. There is a cemetery here, in which some of the very early settlers are buried.

Mt. Olive was constituted in 1852, and the name of the church has been placed upon the neighborhood and post office. This has been a good church from the start, and has had no lapses such as often mark the history of churches. W. C. Brown has been a leading member and deacon since soon after its organization. Rev. J. W. Fulmer has been a minister in her membership about thirty-five years. The cemetery is large.

Mt. Zion was a few miles from where Eclectic now is, and for some years was a right flourishing church, but it finally dissolved, and went into other neighboring churches. A few years after the war another church was constituted nearby, called Antioch No. 2. But it has since been absorbed by Eclectic.

Union Springs joined the Central Association in 1853 from the Mulberry. It was constituted in the early settlement of the country, not far from Mable Valley. It is in a good country, and has been a strong church during most of its existence. The neighborhood and church were right much disturbed just after the war by what was known as Shermanism, originated by Mr. Sherman, a sort of religious fanatic, who claimed to possess wonder working power, and denounced right earnestly the existing order of things in the churches.

In 1855, in the present limits of Goodwater, a church called Spring Hill was constituted, and continued a few years, but never became strong enough to build a good house or keep up the organization. After Goodwater became a place of business in 1883 a church was constituted that has become a good church, with a good building, costing several thousand dollars.

In 1857, about six miles below Sylacauga, Bethany church was formed, and did right well for a time. At the close of the war, political differences caused a rupture ending in the split of the church. Those who were of the Republican sentiment held the house, but the others organized what has since been known as Macedonia, a very good, though weak church. Bethany did not survive long.

In 1858, a church was constituted near Travelers Rest, on the Trace, called Sardis, but it never became a church of strength. There was one constituted at Mt. Moriah, some four miles below Weogufka church, on the same creek. While it has kept up its organization it never became a church of much power, and for a good many years has been a member of an Association organized in opposition to progressive church work.

Lebanon church was constituted in 1859, below Buyckville on the Trace, on a beautiful site, surrounded by a pretty country. It has been a prosperous church, though never very strong. Within the past few years a trouble arose among them, leading finally to a split, each party claiming to be the church. This, of course, is a bar to the progress of either.

Southwest from Rockford, about nine miles east of the Jackson Trace, there was a church established named Wayside. While never very strong, it was able to maintain a fairly vigorous life from just before the opening of the war until within some years past it has become stronger.

No churches were constituted during the progress of the war, but in the summer of 1865, Olive Branch, a little below Shady Grove, westward, was organized, but it never became strong, being too much circumscribed in territory.   There was another a few miles east of Union Springs, in the northern part of the county, called Holly Springs, but neither did it every accomplish much.

Hatchett Creek church began its existence in 1868, near the mouth of that large creek.   It never became a church of strength.

Four Baptist churches of the Primitive order have already been named among those early constituted in the county, viz.: Smyrna, Fish Pond, Mt. Gilead, and Bethel.   There were others constituted at a later date, but the time, and other facts have not been obtained.   There is a church of this order below Buyckville a few miles, which was in existence in the fifties.   Swamp Creek is a church near the creek of the same name, between the Turnpike and Trace, that had an existence as early as the fifties.   It is not nor has it been very strong.   Mt. Pleasant is another in the neighborhood of McAdory's, but its history is unknown.   Pleasant Hill, about Bazemore's Crossroads, had an existence probably in the forties or earlier, as Foscue and the Bazemores were members, but they were early in the country.   Marble Valley likely had an early origin, but the writer has only known of it since about the opening of the war.   Liberty Hill, on the Smith's Ferry road 3½ miles west of Rockford, was constituted sometime after the war, probably not more than twenty-five years ago.   If there are others in the county they are unknown to the writer.   This denomination is not very strong in the county, but numbered among its members a good many very valuable citizens.

The M. E. Church, South, is the next most numerous and influential denomination to the Missionary Baptists in the county, but the writer, after soliciting several of its people to give information, whom we thought could and would, has failed to get what he desired, for it was his wish to have given briefly a statement of the churches of the different denominations, and their location, as he has of the Baptists.   He searched the "History of Methodism," by West, for it, and failed there.   So he can only give such as is recollected by him. Some of the first comers who knew Rev. Mr. Willis, say that as early as 1835 he came as a missionary of the Methodists and labored in Oakchoy and Nixbury neighborhoods, and succeeded in forming the church at Nixburg, and at Jordan's. He was a relative of the Suttles on the maternal side.

It is presumed that the first M. E. Church was the one at Nixburg. This existed perhaps as early as 1834 or 1835. It was later made a church of the Methodist Protestant denomination, by its leading members adopting the tenets of that body. It was for a good while a strong church of that order, and was the leading church at Nixburg. There is a large cemetery there in which sleep a number of those who figured in the early settlement of Coosa. Camp meetings were held at Nixburg for a few years about 1850, and before.

A few miles southwest of Nixburg there was a good strong church that was called Ebenezer, but often spoken of as Ellis Chapel, from two prominent members familiarly called "Uncles Ben and Nathan Ellis." This has always been noted for its congregations. There is a large cemetery there.

In the neighborhood of Reuben Jordan and the Spiveys, between Nixburg and Elkahatchie, there was an M. E. Church established about 1837 or 1838, called Wesley Chapel. This was a good strong church. In 1847 a Camp Ground was established here, and continued seven years. It is claimed there were 48 conversions the first meeting. Willis gathered this body together. (History of Methodism, p. 675.)

The writer attended a meeting here in 1850.

Still farther northeast, later, there was and is another church with a good membership, in the neighborhood of Mr. William Rogers. This is close to the county line.

There is another church near where Shiloh now stands, about 8½ miles east of Rockford, but this church has been organized probably since the war. About half way between that and Rockford there is another called Mt. Pisgah, on the Rockford and Kellyton road, as is the one just before named. This church has been noted for good meetings and congregations. There was an M. P. Church near here, once with a large membership.

A Methodist church existed from an early date about Socka-patoy and Bradford which had a membership in which there was both property and culture. It is thought, but not known, that a church of this order was near where Goodwater now is. One is there now.

The first church at Rockford was a Methodist church, begun about 1839. It held sway until 1850, but from then the Baptists took the lead. They have, however, always kept up their existence.

At Hanover from an early period they have had a church with a good membership called Andrew Chapel. There is another up in the Mt. Olive neighborhood, and one built in the latter fifties between Hanover and Rockford, called Sears' Chapel for John Sears, the noted Millwright. At each of these churches there is a cemetery. A large stone shaft marks the resting place of Sears, the leading spirit.

There is a Methodist church also not far from the Weogufka church, but its name or date is not known. There is also one in Marble Valley, and one in the neighborhood of Stewartville.

There was a church below Traveler's Rest probably called Lykes Chapel, where John Lykes had his membership, and another in the neighborhood of Varners, nearer the river. Still lower down, in the neighborhood of the Olivers, Knights, Hannons, and Whetstones, there was another with a well-to-do membership. About a mile east of Buyckville there was a chapel, but it was never strong.

Between Buyckville and Mr. Humphries there was a Chapel that for a series of years was a strong body called Providence

Church. Here Mr. Humphries had his membership. Aboue this, not far from the Turnpike, was the Speers Chapel. In the Mur chison neighborhood there was an old church, still perhaps existing, but the name not known.

At Brooksville there is a Methodist church, which was among the early places of worship in the county, though never very strong. There was a Methodist church remembered near Dr. Edwards, above Central, and one now in Eclectic, that had been there long before Eclectic was thought of, when that was a part of Coosa. Eli and Fletcher Williams and Kidd and Whetstone were members. Another near the Plank Road, to which McCain, Thornton, and the Rev. Barney Elliott belonged, existed for years before the war. These are all that are remembered, but there were probably others. The following facts are obtained from the "History of Methodism," viz.:

The first circuit rider sent to Coosa Circuit was Rev. James P. McGehee, for 1839, the year the circuit was created; 1841, Rev. George W. R. Smith; 1842-43, Revs. Jesse Ellis and Edward W. Barr; 1844, Theophilus Moody and J. W. Ellis; 1845, John Hunter and William Ira Powers. The writer remembers that John Hunter and James Towles were on the circuit in 1854 or 1855.

The Methodist Protestants had churches as remembered by the writer, one at Nixburg already spoken of. They also had one at Pine Grove, east of Nixburg a few miles, where the large Nolan family had their reunion in 1902. There was one near Rev. Albert Crumpler's east of Turnpike, called Pleasant Hill, which was for some years a right strong body, where large congregations gathered. There was another at Concord, about 4½ miles east of Rockford. And one 4 or 5 miles north of Nixburg, and Flint Hill, about five miles west of Rockford. There were probably others but are not now remembered. This denomination has not been so strong since the war, for just after it, a large number went into the M. E. South, as much contended for by the Protestants in their organization, had been incorporated into the M. E. System. Most of the talented ministers of the Protestants, and many of its ablest laymen, went over. Rev. Albert Crumpler, A. G. Brewer, James Vanzandt, David Messer, and William Nolan were the principal resident ministers.

Of the Presbyterians, the first church was at Carolina, and for a time it was a strong church, but death and removals finally broke it down. The writer has been told that Alexander Smith deeded the land for the graveyard that was used by them, and has since been used by others. Presbyterians in our section have not been given to occupying the country like Baptists and Methodists. The Presbyterians have another church above Sockapatoy called Webster, that had a pretty good membership, and still continues, unless the church at Goodwater has absorbed it.

There was a church also between Weogufka and Marble Valley that was kept up for some time from as early as the fifties. It may still be in existence. Later there was another established at what was called Pine Flat, three miles above Nixburg. This was named McAlpine, and yet exists. There is a cemetery there. If there were other Presbyterian churches in the county the writer has not been able to learn, except the small organizations of Cumberlands at Nixburg, Sockapatoy, and Rockford, kept up by Jonathun Mitchell for a number of years. He was a very earnest consecrated man.

It is not known by the writer whether the "Christians or Campbellites" ever succeeded in establishing any churches in the county or not, or others than those named. It would have been much more satisfactory to have given a better view of the churches than has been given, for their influence has had much to do with changing the drinking and rowdy habits that prevailed in so many places for many years. Most crossroads, and many other places had their drinking shops, and Saturdays and public days had much that was bacchanalian about them. The improvement went on gradually, until the temperance agitation from about 1848 to 1854 gave it a rapid forward movement. By 1856 the crossroads doggeries, as they were called, were mostly gone. Since the war there has not been anything like the old practices of drunken rowdyism that prevailed earlier.

CHAPTER VIII

TIMES OF POLITICAL EXCITEMENT

Coosa seems to have had no representative in the Legislature before 1837, but the writer has failed to learn any reason therefor. It would be a pleasure to give a sketch of each race about which interest gathered, if facts could be obtained, but in absence thereof must be content with such as can be had.

In 1837 and 1838, W. W. Morris was elected without opposition and without excitement to the House of Representatives. The elections and terms of office then were annual. The senator for that time was Daniel E. Watrous of Shelby. In 1839 some interest sprang up, for there were three candidates for the House, W. W. Morris standing for re-election, and Ambrose B. Dawson, another lawyer, opposed him. They were both Democrats. Samuel S. Graham was a candidate for a while, but in a letter came down, claiming he had been persecuted, and that of a religious nature. Dawson was elected by a small majority. J. W. Campbell was elected sheriff, and was opposed by M. B. Casey and Iver D. Patterson.

In 1840, judging by the silence of the papers (and there was one for each party in the county), there was not much excitement. W. W. Morris and A. B. Dawson were candidates again, and for the first time a Whig candidate ran as such. This was A. R. Coker. Morris was elected, receiving 364 votes, while Dawson had only 173, and Coker 258.

In 1841, Lewis Kennedy, Dr. John H. Thomas, William S. Kyle, Dr. H. N. Norris, and William L. Yancey were all candidates for the House. The papers do not indicate that there were any special issue, party or otherwise. Yancey was a Democrat, and the writer knows Kyle was a Whig. Two of the candidates, Thomas and Norris, received no vote. Kennedy received 155 votes, Kyle 95, and Yancey 596. Henry W. Cox was a candidate for Circuit Clerk at this election, but failed.

There was a good deal of interest in the election of 1843, especially in the senatorial race. W. L. Yancey and W. W. Morris opposed each other. The issue between them, both being Democrats, was on the question of "white basis." Those known as the white basis advocates, favored laying off the Congressional districts according to the free white population that would entitle to a representative. The "mixed basis" claimed that the districts should be laid off on the basis governing the congressional representation, which was the white population and four-fifths of the slaves. Morris claimed that as the representation in Congress had that for a basis, it was right to form the districts accordingly. The other side claimed that would give the rich white men in places where the slave population was large an undue share of political power, having his own and four-fifths more. Yancey was elected to the Senate over Morris for Coosa and Autauga. Howell Rose, Henry W. Cox, and Elijah Smith ran for the House. Rose was elected, but Smith ran close to him.

In 1844, Yancey resigned as senator, and ran against Daniel E. Watrous for Congress, and was elected, and Howell Rose was re-elected to the House. If there was opposition or any excitement, it is not known.

The election of 1845 was without excitement so far as known, the interest centering in the election of men who might use influence in the removal of the capital from Tuscaloosa to Wetumpka. This was the first time Coosa was entitled to two representatives. Howell Rose was again chosen, and Col. James R. Powell was his associate.

In 1847 there was no excitement, and if the Whigs had any candidate in the field it is now not remembered, and Capt. Samuel Spigener and Daniel Crawford were chosen to represent the county in this first session to be held in Montgomery.

In 1849 there was more interest, as the Whigs had candidates in the persons of George Johnson and A. B. Nicholson for the House, against A. H. Kendrick and Fred F. Foscue. Isaac W. Suttle was also Whig candidate for Judge of the County Court.

George Johnson only missed election by one or two votes, and Suttle was elected Judge. While Kendrick and Foscue were in attendance at the Legislature, the new capitol building was burned. In this race Wm. S. Kyle was the Whig candidate against Seth P. Storrs for the Senate. N. S. Graham, B. B. Moore, and D. W. Bozeman also ran for the House.

There was quite an interest taken in an election in the Spring of 1850. The Legislature changed the law so as to do away with the County Court, and substituted the Probate Court. This threw J. W. Suttle out of his judgeship, so he became a candidate for Probate Judge, and was opposed by Capt. Samuel Spigener. It was a closely contested race, but Suttle won.

The feeling ran high in 1851. The excitement on the slavery question had been freshly aroused by the admission of California as a free State, and by the change in regard to territories. Those who strongly contended for Southern interests were called "Fire-eaters," and the others were denominated "Unionists." Neil S. Graham and Henry W. Cox were the Democratic Fire-eating candidates, and George Johnson was a Whig Unionist, but his associate is forgotten. Public speakings occurred over the county, and each side was anxious to win. But again Johnson was beaten by only a vote or two. Hawk Dawson was a candidate for sheriff in this race but was beaten. It is thought that A. B. Nicholson ran in this race again for the House.

In 1853 James R. Powell ran for the Senate, and Col. William Garrett and James Weaver for the House. There was a Methodist preacher named Smith and William Knight of Nixburg who ran also, but it is not now remembered whether they ran as Whigs, or simply on a temperance issue. They were opposed to the Sons of Temperance and other temperance organizations. Quite an excitement on the subject prevailed for a year or two. The two named were leaders, and made the issue prominent, as an effort to interfere with the rights of the people in attempting to put down whiskey. The others were not champions of the temperance side, and so ignored the issue. The three first named were elected. Garrett was elected Speaker of the House.

In 1855 there was much interest, for Knownothingism was in flower. In the early part of the year a large percentage of the people had united with the secret political order known as "Know-Nothings." The main feature of their platform was opposition to foreigners and Catholics for office, and the party's name was "The American Party," but received the popular title of "Know-Nothings" from the answer to be given to all questions prying into it, "I don't know." Joseph H. Bradford and another whose name I do not remember were its candidates for the House, and a full ticket was in the field for all the offices. In the opening, it looked as though the new party would have a walkover, as the lodges were numerous, and the members obligated to support the candidates put out by them. But before the election, most of the Democrats had withdrawn from the lodges, and had rallied to the support of Neil S. Graham and George Taylor, who were elected over their opponents. A good many Whigs did not go into the new party, and voted with the Democrats from then on, as the Whigs as a party may be said to have largely abandoned the field from then, except in the struggle for a new rally under the Bell and Everett ticket in 1860. Bradford took his defeat hardly.

The race of 1857 was a very exciting one because of a breach in the Democratic ranks. Conventions and caucuses had not yet become a rule for getting out candidates by political parties. But there were leaders who were trying to make them so, and who, in such as had been held, were manipulating in the interest of themselves. Geo. E. Brewer, then County Superintendent, had been active in getting the Democrats to leave the lodges, and return to the old party, was in the beat meeting for Rockford, by far the strongest Democratic beat in the county. He offered in the beat meeting resolutions acquiescing in the Convention which had been called, but instructing the delegates at the Convention to oppose future calls of Conventions except in extreme cases where party principles were imperiled. He argued that to make them habitual would subvert the fundamental idea of popular elections, and really place affairs in the hands of a few manipulators, as was already in evidence from what had transpired. While the resolutions were in harmony with the sentiments of the most of the meeting, it was thought best not to so instruct the delegates, as the Convention might conclude that Rockford proposed to dictate because of her strength. Brewer was sent as one of the delegates from the beat. He was honest in his opinion, and the history of events since the system has been adopted, has proved the position true.

When the Convention met, before the organization was perfected, one of these leaders announced that he had heard such resolutions had been offered, and the author was there as a delegate. He made an impassioned speech, denouncing the sentiment as being wrong, and that those who held such views should not be allowed a seat. Brewer replied to it, and said if the senti-ment of the speaker was that of the body they need not refuse him a seat, for he quit the Know-Nothings because they required the voter to submit his private judgment and right under our government into the hands of others. He held the franchise a sacred trust in the hands of the citizen, to be safely guarded for the good of his own and coming generations. Failing to get a repudiation of the utterances of the one attacking, Brewer retired from the meeting before it began to work. After withdrawing he felt that if the matter stopped there he would be misunderstood—that he had nothing to expect from those dominating—and being ambitious to play a part in the future politics of the county, he announced himself, the same day, as a candidate for the House, and afterward published appointments for every beat, and challenged the nominees for a discussion, which was accepted. He felt that in such discussion he could make the people see the correctness of his views, and whether he won the election or not, he would win a respect for his opinions, and not be politically dead. The result justified his judgment. Soon other candidates came out until there was a full ticket. The nominees were Daniel Crawford for Senate (he was not opposed), Alexander Smith, Evan Calfee, and William M. Barnes for the House; opposed by Geo. E. Brewer, William Adkins, and Rev. Robert Stewart. T. T. Wall was the nominee for sheriff, and was opposed by David S. Griffin on the independent ticket. The race started with a high degree of interest, and waxed warmer and warmer as the campaign continued. The fight was made mainly at Brewer and Griffin. Brewer's presumption, a boy opposing the county convention, and its nominees among the most substantial citizens, was preposterous. But such was the vigor of his attacks on their position, and the strength of the defense of his own, that his opponents soon learned their mistake as to having a walk-over. The people turned out enmass to the speakings, many going from one to another for days together. By the election fever heat had been reached. Smith and Calfee were elected by the nominees, but Brewer beat Barnes. Griffin and Wall tied in the popular vote, and Wilson, the sheriff, had to give the casting vote. It was regarded as doubtful for a time which would get it, but he finally gave it to Wall. Griffin contested on the ground of illegal votes for Wall, but Wall gained in the trial.

Brewer's seat in the Legislature was contested in the House on the ground of ineligibility, being County Superintendent at the time of election. His defense was that the Superintendent of Education for a county was not an office under the State as contemplated by the Constitution, but a municipal regulation of the county. The Judiciary Committee of the House, to which the case was referred, divided, the majority, with Judge Jones of Mobile as chairman, reported in agreement with Mr. Brewer's claim; but the minority, with Judge Martin of Talladega as leader, took the position that it was an office under the purview of the Constitution, and that Brewer was not entitled to a seat. The discussion in the House on the two reports was a masterly one on both sides. When the vote was taken the majority report was adopted by a vote of 47 to 40. This gave Brewer his seat.

The interest in the election of 1857 did not die out with the election, but was kept alive until the next, in 1859, when the most exciting race was had that has ever occurred in the county; and is yet remembered well by even the boys and girls of that day. It is still talked of after nearly fifty years have passed. Not only were the feelings of the men enlisted, but the ladies, the children, and even many of the negroes took a deep interest, and were declared partisans of one side or the other. When the Convention met there was a large concourse besides the members and candidates. In classifying the senators in the last session, Mr. Crawford drew the short term, so that a senator was to be elected as well as

members of the House. Garrett was nominated for the Senate.
He had been several times clerk of the House when a young man,
was Secretary of State twelve years, and was Speaker of the House
in 1853, and was regarded a very strong man. Alexander Smith,
Calvin Humphries, and Wesley D. Walden were nominated for
the House. After the nomination, some of the leading men of the
Convention were talking to Mr. Brewer, and said rather exult-
antly to him, "Well, you will be apt to try for the Senate this time,
and we have nominated the man that can beat you." He replied,
"It had not been my intention to run for the Senate this time, but
did you say you had nominated Colonel Garrett with the intention of beating me?" They replied, "Yes." "Well, he shall have
the opportunity, then. I now announce myself for the Senate,"
said he. Announcement for speaking all over the country were
made, and Colonel Garrett was invited to meet Mr. Brewer in
discussion. He accepted, and at most places large crowds assembled, and many went from place to place. Everybody took
sides. The interest reached into the border counties and even beyond. The friends of Colonel Garrett could not bear for him to
be beaten by a stripling, and every effort was put forth not only
by those of the county, but men of influence from other counties
came over to help, and even J. L. M. Curry, candidate for Congress, threw a part of each speech he made in the county into the
scale in Garrett's favor. But in spite of all the odds against,
Brewer defeated him. There were running for the House on the
ticket with Mr. Brewer, Capt. Samuel Spigener, Wm. S. Sarsenett, and T. U. T. McCain. These were beaten by a small majority. Any citizen of the time will say there was never so much
interest before or after. The children at school were for either
Brewer or Garrett, and many were the discussions among them
as to the merits and prospects of their favorites.

The Montgomery Mail had a cut made of a floating United
States flag of large size, with a booming cannon firing a victori-
ous salute. It was made with the full expectation that Hon.
Thomas Judge would defeat Hon. David C. Clopton for Congress
in the Third Congressional District. But Clopton won. Hooper
hoisted his cut over the election of Mr. Brewer, saying substan-
tially: "This cut was prepared in the confident expectation that

the Hon. Thomas J. Judge would win the race over the Hon. David C. Clopton but this expectation has failed, to our disappointment, and it cannot be used for the purpose originally intended. But the next most important race in the State to that of the Third District, was the senatorial one in Coosa between Mr. Brewer and Colonel Garrett, and we gladly use it to announce the success of Mr. Brewer."

When the Legislature met, Mr. Brewer's seat was again contested, as he was not twenty-seven years old at the time of the election, and the Constitution required that a senator should be twenty-seven years of age. Brewer's defense was, that though not of the required age at the time of the election, he reached it before taking the oath of office, which made him a senator. The election was only one of the steps toward it, taking the oath and being seated made him a senator. He held his seat.

The election for delegates to the Convention of January 1861, was attended with much interest, for while all were Southern in feeling, and believed the South seriously wronged already by what had been done, and to be worse wronged when the sentiments of the now dominant Republican party should take shape by its enactments, there was a feeling on the part of many that *secession* was not the remedy for the evil, and especially separate State action. Almost all believed in the right to secede, but some thought that cooperation on the part of the slaveholding States should be secured before taking action. These were called the "Cooperating Party." Others believer that each State had a right to secede from the Union, which was a voluntary compact among the States of the Union upon the terms set forth in the Constitution, and that each State had separately agreed to these terms when they entered the Union, and that a dissolution could only be had by separate State action, as a State for itself should decide if the terms of the compact had been violated, an that cooperation *must follow such separate action.* The matter was earnestly and gravely discussed, the advocates of cooperation claiming that though the right for separate action existed, the policy was not good. The cooperationists succeeded in electing John B. Leonard, Albert Crumpler, and George Taylor. When the vote on the ordinance of secession was reached each of these delegates voted for it.

With the exception of the election in 1874, when the Democrats rescued the State from the "Carpet Bag" dominion, the elections from this time passed off quietly, or at least with no more than the usual interest awakened by personal preferences, until the campaigns when the question of supremacy of the Democratic or Populistic parties was being decided. Feelings became very strongly enlisted, and for several elections it surpassed any others except those mentioned in which Mr. Brewer was before the people.

CHAPTER IX

MEN OF SPECIAL NOTE IN COOSA

Coosa has contributed a number of men who have figured more or less conspicuously in public affairs, some of whom took rank among the leading men of our country. It is therefore right that a chapter should be devoted to their memory, that they and their deeds be not forgotten, and that the citizens of the county may feel a just pride in those who have added lustre to her name. About the nativity of some of these nothing is known, and not much else except the part taken by them in public life, and therefore not much can be said. Where more is known more will be briefly said. Most of them were known personally by the writer, but he acknowledges very cheerfully that he is indebted to Brewer's "Alabama," Garrett's "Reminiscences of Public Men in Alabama," and "Memorial Record of Alabama" for information about many of them. They will be spoken of in the order in which they came before the public, rather than alphabetically, since this course will keep men and the events in which they had a part better before the mind of the reader.

HOWELL ROSE

Pursuing this plan, Howell Rose naturally takes precedence. He was a native of North Carolina, where he was born in 1791, but was early brought to Putnam County, Georgia, by his parents. He came to Alabama in 1816, settling just west of Wetumpka in Autauga County. In 1819 he was elected to the Senate as a member of the first Legislature that convened in the State after its admission into the Union. He held the place three years, but then retired from public life, devoting himself to business so successfully that he became very wealthy. He removed to Coosa in 1834, and was the most wealthy citizen of the county and among those of the State. He settled about four miles above Wetumpka, near the Indian town of Little Tallassee. He started life poor, but his wife brought him some property, but the most of his great estate of land, slaves, and money were the outcome of his industry and management. His estate (after the freedom of his slaves, the loss and depreciation of the war) at his death was estimated at $400,000.00.

In 1843 the people induced him to offer for the House, and he was elected. Yancey was in the Senate at the time. Rose continued in the House through 1843-44-45, making a vigorous effort to have the capitol removed from Tuscaloosa to Wetumpka. For a while there was strong hopes of success, but Montgomery secured the prize. After this, though feeling interest and taking an active part in a private way in politics, he was no more before the public for office. In his person he was tall, of a large, well proportioned frame, and had a commanding appearance. He was a man of strong mind, firm convictions, indomitable will, and earnest in his likes and dislikes. He was brusque in speech, uttering his thoughts without much regard to whether it would please or offend the hearer. He was devoid of policy which shapes itself to the thoughts of others. When once offended he was almost implacable. Mr. Thompson, a fine artist of Wetumpka, painted, by agreement, a splendid full length portrait of Rose standing by the side of a horse he had ridden in the chase. One hand was on the horse's withers, holding the bridle reins. The other held the gun, the butt of which rested on the ground. There laid at his feet a fine stag just killed, the blood oozing from the hole where the ball had entered; and around him a pack of panting hounds, watching the victim they had chased to his death. The painting was good, the scene natural, and the finish of the picture was that peculiarly bright tone which characterized Thompson's paintings. Before the painting was completed Thompson had done something that offended Rose, and he refused to take the picture. Suit was brought, but he fought the case from court to court. When judgment went against him of course payment had to be made, but he would not then have the picture, and a good while afterward the writer saw it in the studio.

Some people depredated much on a large body of woodland lying some miles above Wetumpka, hauling pine off of it to their homes and to Wetumpka for sale. He ran ditches around it for miles where it was exposed, to protect his pine. Still some would trespass. Going along the road one day he met a lad with a wagon load of lightwood that he was satisfied had been taken from his premises. He deliberately set fire to the load, and let it and the wagon burn down. For this he was sued, and heavy damages obtained, but he seemed satisfied as he had his revenge.

He was a large money lender but asked only eight per cent interest. In the fall of 1865, a small band of Federal soldiers who had heard of his wealth, and that he probably had a good sum of gold, went to his house and demanded it. He refused to gratify their demand. They broke open all places where they supposed it might be concealed, and tore up his hearths in the hope of finding it. Failing, they threatened to kill him if he did not give them the money or reveal its hiding place. He replied they could not shorten his days much. They hung him for a while, and let him down, asking if he would not tell them now. His reply was, "I have it, but would see you in hell before I would tell you." They hung him up the third time, and had nearly finished him, and likely would have done so, had not Major Ed Ready and some others from Wetumpka come to the rescue just then. When the squad of Federals left Wetumpka these men suspected the squad was after some mischief, and as soon as they could procure horses and weapons they followed, coming in time to save Colonel Rose's life. The Wetumpkians were discovered by the Federals time enough to mount and start from the house of Colonel Rose. Ready and his crowd followed, by the soldiers made through the woods to the river and passed over amid the fire of the pursuers, but only one of the gang was killed. Rose died not a great while after this, leaving a widow. He had no children. He gave the Ft. Jackson plantation to Col. Liddon Saxon, Benjamin Trimble, and W. T. Hatchett as compensation for being executors of his will.

W. W. MORRIS

The next in point of time was W. W. Morris. He was a native of Tennessee, and came perhaps with Joseph Bradford from there to Alabama in 1834 or 1835. He was a lawyer, and such was his ability in his profession that he soon took the lead and held it for several years. He was the first County Judge, and representative the county had in the House, which was in 1837. He then lived in Wetumpka. But after his return from Tusca-loosa, he moved to Rockford. He was very popular and was re-turned to the House in 1838. In 1839, A. B. Dawson defeated him by a few votes, but in 1840 he beat Dawson by a large ma-jority. In 1841 he ran before the Legislature for solicitor of the Eighth Judicial Circuit, but was beaten by Sampson W. Harris. In 1843 he and William L. Yancey ran for the Senate on the white and mixed basis issue. Yancey defeated him. In 1845 he ran before the Legislature for Chancellor of the Middle Division. Again he was opposed by a fellow county man, Wiley W. Mason, and was again beaten. These successive defeats chagrined him, and he moved to Texas, where he soon secured a good practice, and after some years became a popular judge in his adopted State. His religious connection is not known.

SAMPSON W. HARRIS

Sampson W. Harris, a son of Stephen Harris of Eatonton, Georgia, and a graduate of the University of Georgia, came to Coosa in 1836, and settled at New Georgia, having his law office in Wetumpka. He was a man of good medium height and size, of vrey graceful and engaging manners, personally attractive, a good lawyer, and fine speaker. In 1841 he was elected over Mr. Morris as solicitor for the circuit, which he resigned in 1844 to run for the Senate from the District composed of Coosa and Au-tauga, and was elected. In 1847 he ran for Congress from the District—was elected, and impressed himself upon the Congress even in his first session. In 1849 he was re-elected, defeating John S. Hunter. In 1851, William S. Mudd of Jefferson opposed Mr. Harris for Congress, but like his other opponents went down in defeat. Harris was of the "fire-eating" party. The writer re-members a pun he made on the name of his opponent in one of his speeches, when he cautioned them saying: "Fellow-citizens, I plead with you to be careful lest my opponent should throw *Mudd in your eyes.*" In 1853 he was again elected over S. D. J. Moore of Lowndes. In 1855 Hon. William B. Martin of Benton was the Know-Nothing candidate against Mr. Harris, but his good fortune adhered to him, and he was again elected. He died before his term expired in Washington in the spring of 1857, greatly to the regret not only of Coosa and his District, but generally for he was widely known, and was a favorite with all who knew him. After his death his family removed to LaGrange, Ga. Col. Sampson W. Harris of the 6th Ga. Regt., in the Confederate Army was a son. He was a member of the Presbyterian Church.

A. B. DAWSON

He was a native of Georgia, and came to Wetumpka in its early settlement, opening there a law office. When Wiley W. Mason came to the place later he former a partnership with Dawson, thus making a strong law firm. He was made Judge of the county court in 1837 but resigned it in 1837. In 1839 he ran against W. W. Morris for the House of Representatives, and won by a small majority. But in 1840 he and Morris were again competitors for the House, but Morris won by a small majority this time. Information of him is limited, but it is probable he returned to Georgia. He was a man of culture and pleasing address. His brother, John A. Dawson, became one of the most eloquent and popular Baptist preachers of western Georgia and east Alabama.

WILEY W. MASON

Another man who rose to prominence in the early history of Coosa was Wiley W. Mason, another native of Georgia, and graduate of her University. He came to Wetumpka in 1838, and became a law partner of A. B. Dawson. He rose rapidly in his profession, and in 1845 was elected Chancellor of the Middle Chancery Division over J. B. Clark of Greene, and W. W. Morris of Coosa. He bought a farm in the Elkahatchie neighborhood, and lived upon it a few years. He was the first clerk of the Central Baptist Association. In 1852 he moved to Macon County while still Chancellor. He was a prominent member of the Baptist church, and was at times elected as President of the Alabama Baptist State Convention. He was one of the representatives of Macon County in 1861, and was made Speaker of the House. He was a pleasant genial man, easy to approach, of good ability as a lawyer, and a pleasant speaker. His Fourth of July oration at the celebration in Wetumpka in 1839 was said by *The Argus* to have been quite eloquent. He died at Tuskegee in 1870, much loved for his warm and generous heart, and affable manners.

EBENEZER POND

Ebenezer Pond, a native of Vermont, 1799, May 3rd. He first came to Richmond, Va., then to Columbia, S. C., and then with M. L. Bulger came early to Alabama from Georgia after a short stay in Macon, and lived about Montgomery from about 1823 or '24 to 1835, when he came to Wetumpka. He had a brother, Isaac Pond, who preceded him to Wetumpka, and was a man of prominence in the place for a good while. Ebenezer Pond was married to Caroline Cleveland by Judge B. Bibb near the Haggerty neighborhood, in the upper part of Montgomery County. Was postmaster at Wetumpka. Upon the resignation of Dawson as judge of the County Court, he was appointed to fill the vacancy December 8th, 1837, and continued in the office until 1848. Upon being made judge he moved to Rockford, and made that his home until his death on June 3, 1878, when he was nearing his ninetieth year. His first wife was a daughter of Larkin Cleveland, by whom he had three sons, Larkin, Joseph, and Henry (commonly known as Dick), and two daughters, Frances who married Isom Lee, and was postmistress at Rockford for a number of years, and Cynthia, who married a Mr. McClain of Talladega. The boys made good Confederate soldiers, except Larkin who died before the war. After the war Joseph went west. Henry has continued to live at Rockford. He became a Republican, and has been a leading man in the party in the county.

Judge Pond was remarkable in more respects than one. He was considerably over six feet tall, a large, well-rounded frame, but not fat. He continued erect, and with good action through life. He had a fine grey eye that never failed so as to need glasses, and could read without difficulty to the last. He was a Methodist, and an ardent Mason. He drew people to him by his social nature. He loved fun, and was a practical joker. Neither man

or boy knew when the Judge would have a laugh on him. Some
of his pranks were not enjoyed by the victims, but it was impos-
sible to stay out of humor with him. A boy, standing near, lis-
tening to the Judge tell a story, was likely to have a mouthful of
amber spit on his bare toes. But he would soon be appeased by
the Judge. There was usually a crowd sitting about the stores,
and the Judge was generally one of them. If the day was cold
the group would be around the fire. If he saw one ride up looking cold, he would put the handle end of the iron poker in the
fire, get it hot, and set it up just before the cold man came in.
As usual when one comes to a fire cold, the first thing is to punch
up the fire. The unwary rider would get the hot poker, but it
was dropped before the fire was punched, and a hand rubbing
would be the next performance. Sometimes he would heat an
iron ball, and with protected hands throw it near some person,
with the request to please throw it back. The accommodating
party would pick it up to toss back, but would immediately regret his accommodation. If others paid him back in his own coin
he would take it pleasantly. Once after the war the Judge was
on a visit to Montgomery. Walking up the street nicely dressed,
and with a shining pair of boots on, George McDonald, whose
feet had been practiced on by the Judge, was standing on the
sidewalk, and just as the Judge came near, he spit on his boots.
The Judge turned and asked what he meant. George replied,
"Just paying back old scores." He then told the Judge who he
was, for from boyhood he had outgrown the Judge's memory,
and they had a good laugh over it while George was having his
boots put in good order again.

He generally had something to say to every passing boy.
One morning Tom McDonald was late, and hurrying on to school
with a bird in his hand, just taken from his trap. As he passed
the Judge, he asked, "Tom, what kind of bird is that?" Tom answered as he walked on, "A Joree." On coming to the school
house he did not notice that the school was in session, and turned
the bird loose in the schoolroom. It, of course, flew about ex-
citedly, and the children became almost equally excited, and
studies were neglected for the time. The teacher, John Hannon,
gave Tom a flogging for interrupting the school. In going back

from school, as he passed where the Judge and others were, the Judge called out, "Tom, what did you do with your Joree?" Tom quickly responded, "Swapped it off for a *thrasher.*"

Late in life he married a second time, a widow Horton, who had been the wife of John Horton, the Rockford merchant and owner of a mill and farm on Swamp Creek. There were no children by this marriage.

It would not be fair to leave out of the history of Coosa a negro belonging to Judge Pond, known as "Uncle Frank." He was given to Mrs. Pond by her father, Larkin Cleveland, and was one of the negroes bought from Redmouth, the Indian. He was a good negro, and in giving him to his daughter, Mr. Cleveland requested that Frank should never be sold out of the family. He was a prominent figure about Rockford until his death, which occurred after the war. He was intelligent, and spoke both the Indian and English language, and was therefore used in the early days of the county very much as an interpreter. It was interesting to talk to him about the Indians and their habits, which he retained to some extent, and his talk was much sought after by the whites. But he did not seem spoiled by the notice given him. He was popular with the boys because of the bows and arrows, and blow-guns, of Indian fashion, that he made for them. The blow-guns were made of large canes, about six feet long, well seasoned, with the pith of the joints burned out smoothly. The arrows were of strips of cane heated while green so as to be twisted and made tough. The end was sharpened, and the other end was muffled with cat-tail or some other feathery substance, that filled the barrel of the gun so as to catch the air blown into it, the propelling force which drove the arrow to the mark. These arrows were very hard after cooling, and the points would penetrate almost like metal points. Birds, squirrels, and other game could be killed with them, when used by an expert.

BENJAMIN C. YANCEY

Among those well entitled to be remembered as distinguished among Coosians, was B. C. Yancey. He was born in South

Carolina in 1817. His father was the Hon. B. C. Yancey of Abbeville, and he was a brother of the distinguished W. L. Yancey. He was a graduate of the University of Georgia, and a lawyer. He came to Cahaba in 1837, and was made a master of the Chancery District, by Chancellor Crenshaw. He came to Wetumpka in May 1839, and with W. L. Yancey became proprietor and editor of *The Wetumpka Argus*. He largely controlled the editorial department until August 19th, 1840, when he withdrew from the paper, and returned to South Carolina. He represented Edgefield in the Legislature several times. In 1851 he returned to Alabama, settling in Cherokee, which he reprsented in the Senate in 1855, of which he was made president. In 1856 he went to Atlanta, and remained a citizen of Georgia until his death.

(Brewer, page 168)

Brewer says, "In 1858 President Buchanan made Mr. Yancey minister resident to the Argentine Confederation, and he was there during the war in which an effort was made to coerce Buenos Ayres, one of the states, to adopt the new constitution. The decree of death issued by the Parana government against all captains who should take foreign vessels into the ports of Buenos Ayres, was resisted by Mr. Yancey as an infringement of treaty rights, and he ordered the naval force of the United States on the coast to his aid. The representatives of other powers concurred in his protest, and President Urquiza did not attempt to enforce his meditated barbarity. Soon after, however, he was selected by the contending States as the arbiter of their differences, and President Urquiza's message to Congress, after Mr. Yancey left the country, contained this compliment: 'All Argentines owe the young American minister a debt of gratitude they cannot repay.'" After his return further service abroad was offered him, but he declined. He was tall, large, well formed, dignified and graceful in carriage, and of pleasant address. The writer remembers the admiration he felt for his commanding appearance, and the graces of his oratory when he delivered the address before the school of which the writer was a member at Bethany Academy, in Edgefield, in 1844. Rev. A. G. Brewer and George Galphin, a grandson of the distinguished George Galphin of South

Carolina, were the principals of the school. It was a public exhi-
bition of the school, and a barbecue, at which there was a large
gathering.

William Lowndes Yancey

W. L. Yancey can easily be said, without disparagement to
others, to have been the most distinguished resident Coosa ever
had, and but few countries have ever produced a man of more
note. As an orator he had no superiors, and but few equals. An
audience before him was swayed like a field of waving grain before the breeze. He was a son of Hon. B. C. Yancey of South
Carolina, born while his mother was on a visit to her parents at
the Shoals of Ogeechee, Georgia, August 10th, 1814. The family
were of Welch origin, and oratory seemed inheritable with them,
for several of the family, in different States, have been distinguished for it. W. L. was well educated, a Presbyterian, and
came to Alabama in 1836, settling as a planter in Dallas County.
He also edited a paper at Cahaba. In 1839, he and his brother,
B. C., bought *The Wetumpka Argus and Sentinel,* and continued
its publication under the name of *The Wetumpka Argus.* After
August 1840, W. L., having moved to Wetumpka, and B. C., having returned to South Carolina, took the entire charge of the paper. Owing to the loss of a number of slaves, killed by drinking
water from a spring that had been poisoned, he disposed of the
paper in 1842, and gave himself more fully to the practice of law
to rebuild his financial losses. He formed a partnership with
Sampson W. Harris. This made a strong firm, and commanded
a large practice. His editorials had made such a political reputation for him, that his services were demanded by the public.
He was yet unknown as a speaker. He ran against W. W. Morris
for the House, in 1841, and was elected. In a speech before the
House on the banking question he became known elsewhere as
an orator, as he had become known in the canvas at home. In
1843 he was elected from the senatorial district of Coosa and
Autauga over W. W. Morris, after a rather warm race. W. S.
Kyle was also a candidate. Hon. Dixon H. Lewis resigned his
seat in Congress, and in 1844 Yancey was elected to fill the vacancy, resigning his position as senator. In 1845 he was re-

elected to Congress over Daniel E. Watrous of Shelby. He resigned in 1846, feeling too poor to continue in public life. During his stay in Congress he fought a duel with Mr. Clingman of
North Carolina. Early in life he had killed a Mr. Earle of South
Carolina, but public opinion justified it later as an act of self-
defense. Upon retiring from public life he moved to Montgomery and formed a law partnership with John A. Elmore.

In 1848 he was a member of the National Democratic Convention for the nomination of a president. The Alabama State
Convention had instructed its delegation to withdraw from the
Convention if it failed to adopt certain principles involving the
rights of the Southern States. The Convention failed to adopt
them, and nominated General Lewis Cass, who was himself inim-
ical to them, or at least occupied a questionable attitude toward
them. Yancey and a Mr. Wray withdrew as instructed, and
refused to support Cass. The rest of the delegation retained
their places, and supported the nominee. For this Mr. Yancey
was for some years ostracized by his party. But he was not
anxious for office, and stood by his convictions. In after years
his course was vindicated, and the sentiments for which he was
condemned became prominent in the party creed. From 1856
till his death no one was called on so frequently to speak, and
no speaker ever held firmer grip upon his audience, whether in
sympathy with or opposed to his views. The writer has seen
juries awaken from listless indifference, to an actual leaning forward with open mouths and distended eyes under the spell of
his magic oratory. He has seen vast audiences changed rapidly
from a scowl of displeasure on the face, to the wildest enthusi-
asm, expressed by hundreds of waving hats and handkerchiefs,
while yell after yell would peal forth from surcharged hearts;
then again in a little while almost the whole crowd of stalwart
men would be weeping like friends around the grave of the beloved dead.

Mr. Yancey was at the head of the electoral ticket for Mr.
Buchannan in 1856. There was a feeling widespread during the
session of the Legislature in 1859-60, to give him the place in the
United States Senate, then occupied by Governor Fitzpatrick, but

the election was held off, and so no vote was ever had as between them, as the secession of the State from the Union took place before an election was had.

In 1860 the delegates to the Democratic Convention in Charleston were again instructed to withdraw if guarantees to Southern interests were not inserted in the platform. They were not given, and Yancey was the recognized leader of the large party that withdrew to hold another Convention in Baltimore. The breach was final and the Democrats had two tickets in the field, known as the "Breckenridge" and the "Douglas" tickets. The Whigs had a ticket with Bell of Tennessee at its head, and the Republicans one with Lincoln leading. Never has there been an election that so stirred the hearts of all the people. Yancey was the recognized leader of the Breckenridge forces. He spoke in the leading cities north and south, and captivated the audiences everywhere by his matchless power, and commanded their respect and admiration, even where he failed to convince of the rightfulness of his cause. But it was of no avail. Lincoln was elected. The South felt robbed of her Constitutional guarantees, and must seek them by withdrawal from the broken compact. The result was secession by the Convention in 1861. Mr. Yancey was a delegate from Montgomery, and was made chairman of the committee that reported the ordinance of secession.

When Davis was made President of the Confederate States, he offered Mr. Yancey any position in the gift of the Executive. He chose the mission to Great Britain and France. His efforts were vigorous, but failed to receive an acknowledgement of the Confederate States as an independent nation by European Powers. On his return in 1862, he told his countrymen their only reliance was on themselves. While absent he had been elected to the Confederat Senat, and on his return he took his seat in that body, where he faithfully attempted to carry out his long cherished views of a government administered within the limits of a strict construction of constitutionally granted powers. The results of the war as they developed cast a gloom over him, as over all who loved the South and sympathized in her struggle. But he was saved the humiliation of seeing his beloved country go down in defeat, for he died July 28th, 1863, and is buried in beautiful Oakwood Cemetery at Montgomery, and the spot is marked by a pretty marble shaft. His end came almost simultaneously with the terrible blow of the fall of Vicksburg, and the carnage of Gettysburg, which was the beginning of the end of the terrible struggle. Coosa may well feel proud that it was her privilege to launch Mr. Yancey upon that career which reflected so much credit upon the State and the South.

SETH P. STORRS

While the residence of Seth P. Storrs was on the west side of the river, his office and business were on the east side, and he was more identified with Coosa than Autauga, so that his name rightfully appears as one of Coosa's prominent men. Mr. Storrs was born in Vermont, and was of a family that gave several prominent men to the country, notably the celebrated Dr. Storrs who for so long a time was not only in the front rank of the ministers of New York, but of the world as well. Mr. Storrs came to Covington, Ga., about 1830, and from there to Wetumpka in 1835. He came a lawyer, and from the start was regarded with high esteem for his ability, integrity, and urbanity. He devoted himself to his profession, and accumulated a good property. He could not be called a politician, for he only engaged in political affairs when called by the people to serve them. In 1847 he was elected Senator from the District over Mr. W. S. Kyle, also a prominent lawyer of Wetumpka. He continued to serve until the election in 1853, when he failed to run. He was appointed Judge of the Circuit Court by Gov. Jno. A. Winston in August 1854, But he died at his home in Wetumpka about the first of October 1854, during the session of the Central Association with the church there. The meeting, in its profound respect for him, adjourned as a body and attended the burial, where he now sleeps in Wetumpka's cemetery. Colonel Storrs was never a member of the church, though inclined to the faith of the Presbyterians. He was always highly moral, pure, and chaste, and his deportment would put to the blush that of many who were members. His wife, who was a Miss Bigelo, of Massachusetts, was a member of the Baptist church at Wetumpka from its organization, and one of its most active, liberal, and influential ones, continuing so until her death. Colonel Storrs was of medium height, with some tendency to corpulency. He was always remarkably clean and neat in appearance, with a handsome pleasant face, and his head, though bald, was beautiful, owing to its fine shape, the smoothness of its skin, and perfect freedom from scalp troubles. The rim of hair surrounding the head was heavy, always smooth and even, and a rich silver grey. He was a pleasant and instructive speaker. He left three sons and two daughters, all highly esteemed. Henry was a lieutenant of the Wetumpka Light Guards, and was accidentally killed by a sentinel at Norfolk, Va.; George S. was a major of artillery; and Charles P. was a captain in the 7th Ala. Cavalry, and now resides just below Wetumpka. The daughters were Miss Charlotte, who never married, and Miss Libbie, who married Capt. Thomas Smith of Hilliard's Legion. Both George and Charles made fine reputations as soldiers and officers.

Samuel S. Beman

Another who reflected credit upon his adopted county of Coosa was Samuel S. Beman who began in the county that career which will prevent his name from being forgotten. He was the son of the celebrated Nathan S. Beman of New York, long and widely known in Georgia and Alabama as an educator. He was a half brother of W. L. and B. C. Yancey, whose widowed mother married Nathan Beman. When Samuel was young he was well formed, but by a hurt when he was twelve years old, his body grew but little more in height. He was well educated. In 1843 he came to Wetumpka, and established a law partnership with W. L. Yancey. After Yancey's removal to Montgomery, Beman continued at Wetumpka. In 1844 he took an active part in politics, and his canvass was so brilliant as to give him desirable prominence among the Whigs. In 1846 he was the Whig candidate for Congress, and only failed by 29 votes in the District of being elected over Mr. Cottrell, the Democratic candidate. He added much to his reputation as a stump orator, already brilliant, by his canvass as an elector for General Taylor as President, in 1848. In 1849 he returned to New York where he had been partially reared. He was elected to the Legislature in New York in 1853. A speech in that body in favor of the Fugitive Slave Law ended his prospect for political advancement there. He also delivered temperance lectures in Ohio. In 1856 he moved to Minnesota, and was a member of the first Legislature of the State, in 1857. In 1871 he was elected to the Senate of that State from Winona County. But his sympathy with the South was a barrier to his political advancement in the North. It is freely confessed by all who knew him that his oratorical ability was of a high order. One family gave three distinguished sons to Coosa, and Coosa gave each of them their start in their careers of fame.

James R. Powell

Another remarkable man who had his start in Coosa was Col. James R. Powell. He was a native of Virginia, born in 1814. His father was once wealthy, but lost his property. Powell came to Alabama and taught school for a short time. He had his father and family come to Alabama, and for awhile they kept boarding house in Lowndesboro and Montgomery. In 1836 he came to Wetumpka and commenced contracting for carrying mails. He was successful, and his business grew rapidly. He went later to Rockford, and built a good house, to which he added a long row of two-room cabins stretching along the street, used as sleeping apartments. They were comfortably arranged and furnished. For about twelve years they kept the leading hotel of the place, where the members of the court and bar usually stopped, and that drew the others who liked such association. It was also the feeding place of the many travelers of this popular stage line.

In 1843 Powell was elected sheriff of the county. In 1845 he and Howell Rose were elected to the House in the interest of the removal of the capital to Wetumpka. This was the first time Coosa had two representatives. In 1853 he served in the Senate from Coosa, holding over until 1857. In 1856 he moved to Montgomery where he remained until after the war. During the war he did much transportation for the Confederate government. He had already accumulated a good property, and during the war he invested his Confederate money as it was made in real estate in

Alabama and Mississippi, and became rich. During the winter of 1864 he saved a quantity of ice for which he was offered $40,000, but declined to sell, and gave most of it to the Confederate government to be used in the hospitals.

His foresight, skill, courage in ventures, directed by excellent management, had enabled him from a poor young man, taking small mail contracts, to rise to the ownership and management of long expensive lines of stage coaches, from which he reaped good profit, and fought down strong opposition. These same qualities foresaw much of the possibilities in the Birmingham district, as early as about 1870. He laid out Birmingham on the scale of its prospective greatness, and planned well the foundation for rapid and important growth. He so advertised it at the commencement as to give it almost world-wide notoriety as a place unsurpassed in its possibilities. He seemed to penetrate the future as to its vastness, and worked accordingly. His efforts were successful in bringing rapidly to it the men and means necessary to the fulfillment of his predictions. Through him the Press Association of New York met in Montgomery in 1874, with the Press Association of the State, and he laid before them the facts of the riches treasured around Birmingham, thereby giving general publicity through this and other countries. Because of his devotion he received the soubriquet of "The Duke of Birmingham." He was its first mayor, and stayed at his post during the cholera visit of 1873, to look after the sick. But in 1878, when by invitation he came back from his Mississippi plantation to again run for mayor, he was beaten for the office. He was killed in Mississippi in 1883.

Powell was of rather an imperious disposition, and was not patient under opposition. He was over six feet, erect, with a good form; easy carriage, a sandy complexion, blue eyes, with strongly marked features. While making no claims to oratory, he could express himself well and clearly. He was a good conversationalist, and when he turned occasionally from the tension of business, he enjoyed well social recreation. His father died in Rockford. A younger brother, Addison, died early in his manhood. His mother was a fine specimen of the cultured Virginia matron. His sisters were tall, having fine figures, tastefully dressed, and with handsome intellectual faces, graceful carriage, combined with mental culture and the finish given by extensive travel, they were unusually attractive. One of these sisters, Mary, married Dr. Reese of Selma, and was the mother of Warren Reese, afterward Mayor of Montgomery, and Miss Kate Reese, who married Mr. Burton of Montgomery. Virginia, a queenly looking woman, married Thomas Clark of Talladega, of whom was born Thomas E. Clark. Margaret married James H. Weaver, once sheriff and representative of Coosa, and also Secretary of State. Laura married Joseph Phelan, several times Clerk of the House and Secretary of the Senate. He was also a Minister of the M. E. Church, South. She was an unusually handsome and attractive woman, the mother of two sons, Powell and Sidney. Colonel Powell was a devoted son and brother, giving the major part of his life to the well being, cultivation, enjoyment, and settlement in life of his father's family. After all were grown and cared for, he married a Miss Smyth, who had for some years been a teacher in Mississippi. She was very intelligent, and made him a brilliant wife, by whom there was one daughter, whose education was obtained at the best schools of Europe. Powell was not a member of the church. His wife was an Episcopalian, his mother and sisters Methodists.

James H. Weaver

James H. was the son of William H. Weaver, one of the first and most prominent of the early settlers around Nixburg, who was financially in easy circumstances. James grew to manhood in Coosa, and while yet quite young was elected sheriff in 1845. He was elected to the House from Coosa in 1853. And in 1857 was elected Secretary of State by the Legislature. He discharged his duties well in each place. He married Miss Margaret Powell in 1855. After the war he went to New York, and by some of his dealings there he incurred the displeasure of his Southern friends and never revisited the State.

Joseph D. Phelan

Among the men who had homes in Coosa, and who was well known in his day, was Rev. Jospeh D. Phelan. He was of Irish descent, his father being a native, and his mother was of New England. He grew to manhood in Madison County, Ala. He was elected assistant Clerk of the House from 1838 to 1840, and Clerk from 1842 to 1845. In 1847 he entered the ministry of the Methodist Church, and was regarded as a very good preacher. But feeble health caused him to give up the active work in a few years, preaching from then only occasionally. He was elected Secretary of the Senate in 1853, and held it to the session of 1857. He died at his home in Rockford in 1858. He was a man of good and cultivated mind, pure and lovable in character. His brother, James, was State Printer in 1841. He moved to Mississippi and was there a member of the State Senate, and a Senator in the Confederate Congress. He was regarded as a very fine orator. Another brother, Judge John D. Phelan, was very prominent in Alabama, and presided both on the Circuit and Supreme Benches of Alabama. He married Miss Laura Powell, leaving her a widow with two sons.

Frederick F. Foscue

Rev. Benjamin Foscue was a pioneer settler of Coosa, about Hanover or Weogufka, and was a Primitive Baptist preacher of good property. But he lost a good many of his slaves by cholera, when he was moving from Coosa to Louisiana. Frederick F. came with his father to Coosa, and on reaching his majority became a lawyer. He was a good speaker, a handsome man, and had a popular manner among the people. He was elected, with A. H. Kendrick, to the House in 1849. In 1851 he moved to Marengo County, and represented the county in 1853. After this he went to Texas, and was a member of the Legislature there at the time of secession.

Dr. Nathan Bozeman

Among the men of Coosa who rose to distinction must be numbered Dr. Nathan Bozeman. He was a son of Nathan D. Bozeman, who in the first settlement of the country was just above Nixburg, and in a short time moved about as far below on the Sockapatoy road. There were two brothers older, Col.

Nathaniel Bozeman of Arkansas, and David W. of Coosa. One sister married Col. M. L. Bulger, another John D. Letcher, another Jasper McKinney, and another James Jordan. Nathan read medicine under Dr. James Kelly, the teacher of so many young physicians. He was not thought promising in the outset, but diligently applied himself, having special taste for surgery. He practiced several years in Coosa, and then located in Montgomery. Here he developed his talent as a surgeon, especially in female diseases, and made considerable reputation. In 1859 he went to New Orleans and so added to his reputation as that it had become almost national. In 1866 he went to New York, and in a short while was the most widely known surgeon in the United States, and his reputation extended into Europe, so that at one time there was perhaps not a surgeon in the world more widely known. He became wealthy, and retired from practice. There was a good deal said at one time of his marrying the widow of Commodore Vanderbilt. His family were Baptists, but the writer does not know that he was.

John G. Graham

Whille John G. Graham took no active part in political affairs publicly, yet he was known well in the county and beyond. He came with his father, Archibald Graham, from North Carolina in 1820, first settling in Autauga. He moved into Coosa not long after its settlement, and, being a man of means, bought a large body of land about three miles above Nixburg, upon which he built what was one of the best and prettiest houses of the county. His attention was given to his farm and educating his family until he leased the Penitentiary. He gave his sons and daughters good educations. He was a man of fine personal appearance, courtly in his manners, always well dressed, and his bearing was that of the perfect gentleman. He had a daughter who married Maj. Boling Hall, who lived for some years at the Graham home, after Mr. Graham went to Wetumpka. He had two sons, Neil and Malcolm, who became prominent men. He was a Presbyterian.

William Graham

Another son of Archibald Graham, was William, who also came with his father to Alabama from North Carolina, in 1820. He settled in Montgomery and became a merchant. After serving some years as Judge of the County court of Montgomery, he moved to Coosa in 1841, and farmed. In 1847 he was elected State Treasurer, holding the office ten years, and then retired to his farm near Prattville, where he died in 1859. He was taller than his brother, John G., but his body was not so well rounded. He was, however, a man of good appearance and pleasant address, and was loved for his probity and many good qualities. He was a Presbyterian.

Samuel S. Graham

Though he never held office except for a time that of Assistant State Geologist, yet Samuel S. Graham, son of Archibald, and brother of John G. and William, holds a place among men of note in Coosa. He came to it in its early settlement, making his home near Sockapatoy. His wife was a daughter of Rev. William Rice of Lowndes. He was inclined religiously to the Presbyterians. He was known by everybody in the county, and by nearly all public men of the period, for he was often at courts, the sessions of the Legislature, and where talent was gathered within his reach. He was well educated, and was a walking encyclopedia. His knowledge took in many things, and what he learned he retained, and it was put away so orderly in his mind that he could command it at will. He was very eccentric, and was as well known for his eccentricities as for his learning; but with all he was a kind and genial man. It was a pleasure for him to impart information to any one desiring it. He was a noted pedestrian, and walked more than he rode, though he had horses at his command in plenty. Not unfrequently he would foot it to Rockford, Wetumpka, or Montgomery. He was a candidate for the House in 1841, but came out of the race before the election. He continued to take long walks until his death a few years back.

NEIL S. GRAHAM

Neil Smith Graham was a native of North Carolina, born in 1818, son of John G. Graham. He came at two years of age to Alabama with his father, reaching his majority in Coosa. He was a Presbyterian, and educated at Princeton. He read law under S. P. Storrs, and opened a law office at Wetumpka in 1841. He soon took a good position at the bar. In 1851 he and Henry W. Cox were the candidates of the "Fire-eating" Democratic Party, as it was then locally called, and was elected. He proved an able debater, an attractive stump-speaker. Again in 1855, in the days of Knownothingism, he and George Taylor were elected to the House. In 1856, he moved to Tuskegee to practice his profession. For a number of years he was Chancellor of the Middle Division of Alabama, and died in office a few years since. He was a man of fine personal appearance, dignified, but pleasant and approachable.

MALCOLM D. GRAHAM

Another son of John G. Graham, who became even more distinguished than his brother, N. S., was Malcolm D., born in Autauga in 1826, but was principally raised in Coosa. He had his college course at Transylvania University. He entered the practice of law at Wetumpka in 1850. He was elected Clerk of the House over A. B. Clitherall in 1853. He moved to Texas in 1854, and it was not long until he was in the Senate in that State. He was elected Attorney General in 1858. He was an elector on the Breckenridge ticket in 1860. He went to the army as colonel in 1861. In 1862 he was elected to the Confederate Congress. He could not practice law in Texas under Reconstruction without special pardon, so in 1866 he came to Montgomery, where he successfully practiced till his death. He was a man whose appearance would command attention anywhere. He was honored and loved by all who knew him for his noble qualities of head and heart. He too was a Presbyterian.

COL. THOMAS WILLIAMS

Though the history of Col. Thomas Williams properly belongs to Elmore, yet so much of his life belonged to Coosa that his name will be remembered as belonging to it. His father was the Rev. John D. Williams of Virginia, who came to Wetumpka in 1834, and was long well and favorably known in affairs, financial, religious, political, of the county. He brought ample means with him, but by his ventures in business, when the crash came in 1837 and the following years, he lost the bulk of his property. His sons, Thomas and Robert, therefore failed of the educational advantages that would otherwise have been theirs. But they rose above all their disadvantages to become men of means and influence. Robert became a physician and planter. Thomas was born in Virginia in 1825. He became a successful lawyer and planter. He died at Mt. Meigs. He had accumulated several good fortunes, lost them, but with each loss, by pluck and energy, would succeed again, until the last, a few years since. He attended strictly to his legal and private business, until in an exigency of the party in 1878 without his knowledge, or preconcerted arrangement of friends, in the deep hours of night, he was nominated for Congress from his District. Several times before his friends had tried to get him to accept office, but he would not be persuaded. The committee appointed to wait on him from the Convention, went to his house at the late hour, and aroused him from bed to tell him he was the choice of the party to bear their banner. He tried to decline, but they would take no refusal. He proved a very attractive stump speaker, and beat his opponent, Major Henry McCoy, badly. He was successively re-elected several times. He was a warm-hearted, generous man, of popular address, and always made friends where he went. For a number of years he has been one of the Trustees of the A. P. I., at Auburn, until his recent death, 1903. Though his parents and brothers and sisters were Baptists, he united with the Methodist church. His mother was a saintly woman, beloved by all who knew her. She was baptized when the earth was covered with snow. When her marriage occurred, again a mantle of snow was upon the ground; and she used to express the wish that it might be so when she was buried. Her wish was gratified, for she was laid away during a large snow early in 1880, when she had reached about her ninetieth year.

Col. William Garrett

Among the men of distinction whose homes have been in Coosa, Col. William Garrett is well entitled to take rank among them. His father was a Methodist minister of East Tennessee, and Col. Garrett was also a member of the Methodist church. He was born in 1809, and came from East Tennessee to Alabama in 1833, first settling in Benton. He was elected Assistant Clerk of the House in 1837. The next year, 1838, he was elected Clerk of the House, and re-elected in 1839 and 1840. At the session of 1840 he ran for Secretary of State and was elected. He was continued in this office for twelve years, till 1852, in which year he moved to Coosa. Here he looked after his farm and aided in establishing a good school, called Washington Academy, near Sockapatoy. In 1853 he and James H. Weaver were elected to the House, of which Col. Garrett was made Speaker. In 1859 he was candidate for the Senate, but was defeated by George E. Brewer after the most heated and hardly contested election ever held in Coosa. The race was close, Garrett receiving 1,128 votes, and Brewer 1,175. Brewer was in the army, and not a candidate in 1863. Col. Garrett was elected to the Senate over Capt. Leander Bryant. The ending of the war ended the claim of Col. Garrett to the office, but under the new Constitution, Garrett ran again and defeated Col. R. H. Smoot for the Senate. He was made chairman of the Committee on Finance and Taxation. He was a member of the Constitutional Convention in 1875.

During the Provisional Government of Alabama after the close of the war, in which Hon. Lewis E. Parsons of Talladega was made the Provisional Governor by President Johnson, Parsons appointed Col. Garrett Secretary of State. He resigned September 2nd, 1865, owing to some charges preferred against him, for receiving fees. for preparing applications for pardons, thereby giving precedence to some out of their regular place. The rest of his life he devoted to preparing his valuable work "Reminiscences of Public Men of Alabama," published in 1872.

Col. Garrett was of full medium height, with quite a tendency to corpulency. He was a good conversationalist, possessing a good fund of anecdotes. He was a fairly good speaker, but his fort was in his ability to manage men. He had several sons, but the writer does not know of but two, **Thomas, of Washington, D. C.,** and Elmore, of Anniston, Ala., who has been Engrossing Clerk, from 1875 to 1877; was Clerk of the House in 1886; Assistant Secretary of the Senate in 1892-94-96; and Secretary of the Senate in 1900-03. Thomas died at Mt. Meigs,, Montgomery County, 1910.

JOHNSON J. HOOPER

Coosa was for a while the home of Johnson J. Hooper, who lived in Wetumpka, connected as editor with one of its papers. Though not then widely known, he became so afterward. From Wetumpka he went to Dadeville, and then to Lafayette, where he practiced law. His humorous articles in the Dadeville and Lafayette papers gave him considerable notoriety as a humorist, but it remained for the publication of "Simon Suggs" to place the crown of a prince of humorists on his brow. But humor was not his only gift. He was a good lawyer, a clear strong writer, and an able counselor. *The Montgomery Mail,* of which he was for a long while editor, was the leading Whig journal of the State. When the Provisional Congress of the Confederate States was organized at Montgomery he was elected as its Secretary, and went with it to Richmond, where he died in 1862. Hon. William Hooper, a signer of the Declaration of Independence, was a great uncle, and Hon. Archibald Maclain, another patriot of 1876, was a kinsman. On the maternal side he was descended from Bishop Jeremy Taylor, the English divine and poet. Hooper was for some years Solicitor on his Circuit. His intellect was fine and he was open and frank in his nature, and sunshine was ever flashing from his pleasant face and lips.

ISAAC W. SUTTLE

No man was more widely known in Coosa and the adjacent country, nor more highly esteemed than Isaac Willis Suttle, a son of Jessee Suttle whose father is said to have lived to the age of 109 years, being baptized when 108. Jessee Suttle came to Alabama in 1818, settling the first year on the Tallapoosa River, Montgomery County, and made there a crop of corn by cutting down the cane, punching a hole in the soil among the cane roots for the seed. But little cultivation was needed except to keep down the cane sprouts. He then moved into Bibb, where he remained until 1835, when he moved to Coosa, where he was killed May 1836. Two of his sons, Isaac and William, and three daughters, Mrs. Johnson, Howard, and Ray, came to Coosa. John W., another son, remained in Bibb, and was probate judge for eighteen years. Isaac was born in Georgia in 1809, and came with his father to Alabama, marrying in Bibb a Miss Louisa McCary, a native of South Carolina. He moved to Coosa in 1836, and was soon made a justice of the peace. His school advantages were slim, less than a year being spent in the school room. But he was ambitious to know more, and after working in the day, would read and study at night by a pine blaze, until he had made such improvement that it was hard to tell his lack of school training. He was made a county commissioner, and in 1845 Clerk of the County Court. In 1848 he was elected Judge of the County Court. By Act of the session of the Legislature of 1849-50 the offices of Judge and Clerk of the County Court were abolished, and the office of Judge of Probate established. Thus displaced, he became a candidate for Judge of Probate, and was elected over Samuel Spigener. During his term he and the Commissioners did much for the general improvement of county affairs. He was active in getting up a good school for the town, and was very largely instrumental in getting up the organization of the Baptist church, building its house of worship, and meeting its financial wants. He was for many years the Master of the Masonic Lodge when it had a large membership of the best citizens for miles around. In 1856, Archibald A. McMillan defeated him for the Judgeship. He then entered the practice of law in Rockford, continuing there until the formation of Elmore County, when he moved to Wetumpka and formed a partnership with Col. Osceola Kyle. About two or three years before his death in 1884, he had about given up practice, owing to feeble health, and the depression coming upon him in the loss of so many of his family, in a short time. His life companion died in 1871, and from then, in ten years, his youngest son, George, a merchant of

Wetumpka; his two youngest daughters, Frances and Mattie; his eldest daughter, Mrs. Bentley, and a second wife, Mrs. Sallie Long, all died. He died rather suddenly at the home of his son-in-law, Judge John S. Bentley, June 6th, 1884. He was buried with Masonic honors at Rockford, in the cemetery which he secured from Ned Hanrick, a well known large land dealer of Alabama. He sleeps amidst a number of his posterity.

He was over six feet in height, a large, well-formed, portly frame; fair complexion with a fine blue eye, large, well-formed head, adorned with a suit of dark hair. He was very useful, and his counsel much sought after, for none stood higher in the esteem of the people. He was for quite a number of years Moderator of the Central Association of which he had been a leading spirit from its organization.

From 1845 to 1903 his family relatives have occupied a prominent place in the public life of the county. He, a son-in-law, and grandson were Judges for thirty-three years. A son-in-law, nephew, and nephew by marriage have represented the county in the Senate ten years. A son-in-law, three nephews, and one by marriage represented in the House thirteen years. A son-in-law, and nephew by marriage have been County Superintendents for about eighteen years. Nearly every other office has been held by some relative for a longer or shorter period. But three of his immediate family are now living, his oldest son, Sinclair M. Suttle, lives near Rockford; Mrs. Mary A. Gilder, in Carbon Hill; and Mrs. George E. Brewer, in Montgomery.

George Evans Brewer

George E. Brewer will be long remembered in Coosa both as connected with politics and religion, for he figured in both. He was the son of Rev. Aaron G. Brewer and his wife, Martha (Taylor) Brewer, who came from New York to Georgia about 1830. Rev. Aaron Brewer was the son of George Brewer who was descended from a family that came from Holland to New Amsterdam while a Dutch colony. Aaron was in the Constitution of the Methodist Protestant Church, having been a preacher from 1816, and was sent as a missionary of that Conference to Georgia. He preached and taught at various places in Georgia, South Carolina, and Alabama. He taught several years in Coosa, coming to the county in 1849. Two other sons besides George taught in Coosa, John and Samuel.

George E. was born near Covington, Ga., but was carried by his parents to South Carolina a babe, so that Carolina feels to him more like the land of nativity. He came with his father to Alabama in 1847, settling at Robinson Springs. In the fall of 1849 the family moved to Coosa. Here he began life for himself, teaching his first school in 1851. In 1853 and part of 1852 he was associated with his father in publishing *The Christian Telegraph* in Atlanta, but left there to take the school at Rockford in 1854. That winter he married the daughter, Laura A., of Judge Suttle, to whom have been born nine children, six of whom, three sons and three daughters, are still living. He united with the Masonic Lodge and Chapter, and with the Baptist Church all in 1854. He was elected County Superintendent in May 1856, the first year the office was established. He ran for the House independently in 1857, and was elected over Mr. William Barnes, one of the nominees, after a very exciting canvass. Two years after, 1859, he ran against Col. William Garrett, again independently, and defeated him. His seat was contested both times, but he won. His term lasted till 1863. Three sessions of the Legislature were held in the time, the two regular terms, and the called one just following secession.

In February 1862, he led a company to the war, spending the first three months of service at Pensacola, then joining the 46th Ala. Regt. which he commanded for about two years. He was ordained to the ministry in the fall of 1860, and was serving Wetumpka, Poplar Springs, and Concord churches when he went to the army. He was made Adjutant and Inspector General of Alabama by Gov. Robt. M. Patton, upon the death of General Watson, early in 1866. He resigned at the close of the year to return to the ministry, to which he has devoted himself ever since, teaching in connection with it a few years. He made an active canvass of Chambers County once, while pastor of Lafayette church, in behalf of a temperance ticket. He was Clerk of the Central Association for about fourteen years, and Moderator two. He has been Moderator of the Tuskegee and of the Harris Associations, and many times a member of the Alabama Baptist State Convention, and of the Southern Baptist Convention. He represented the American Baptist Publication Society in Alabama two years. Spent two years in missionary work soon after the war, doing much of the work afoot, owing to his misfortunate in the loss of horses, and inability to purchase without incurring debt. In 1900, Governor Samford offered him the appointment of Chaplain of Convicts for the State, which he accepted, and which appointment was renewed by Governor Jelks in 1903 and again in 1905. His eldest son, E. Brewer, is a successful merchant at Woodlawn, Ala., a liberal, useful member, and deacon of First Baptist Church there. He has one son, George, also engaged with his father in business. Samuel O., the second son, is in the mercantile business in Quanah, Texas. He is the father of five children, three of whom are living.

Chas. M., the youngest son, is a Chaplain in the U. S. Army stationed at Ft. Riley, Kansas. He is the father of three children.

The eldest daughter, Mrs. Sallie T. Bradford, is the widow of Henry Bradford, and living at Notasulga, Ala.

The second daughter, Mrs. B. W. Allen, is the wife of a prominent physician of Columbus, Ga.

The youngest daughter, Mamie, married T. M. Espy of Houston County. All these are members of the Baptist Church.

One daughter, who died in childhood, is buried at Rockford, and one son, Geo. F., at Moss Point, Miss.

John Samuel Bentley

John S. Bentley was the son of Hiram and Lavicie Bentley, who came early to Alabama from Georgia, settling in the western part of Chambers, and moving from there in 1844 to Coosa, a few miles west of Nixburg. He was a farmer in easy circumstances, a good citizen, a member of the Baptist church, and much esteemed for his solid virtues. John was born in Georgia, about 1830, reaching his majority in Coosa, and commenced life for himself by teaching. He was a warm advocate of the temperance cause, during the temperance reformation going on from about 1847 to 1854. In 1850 he married Sarah C., the oldest daughter of Judge I. W. Suttle, at Rockford. Both of them joined the Baptist church at Rockford at its organization, 1850. About 1852 he studied medicine, and went into the water-cure practice at Robinson Springs, Dadeville, and Rockford successively. In 1855 he bought and went on a farm just west of Rockford, and added to it from time to time, living upon its until his death. He was a member of the Masonic Lodge and Chapter. Mr. Bentley wrote in the offices about Rockford at different times. He also held several minor offices. When Joseph Taylor resgined the Circuit Clerkship in April 1869, Bentley was appointed to the vacancy, holding till elected Judge of Probate in 1874. He was re-elected in 1880, and again in 1886, and was in office when he died in January 1892. He was faithful to every trust.

No man of Coosa has done more to promote education, religion, morals, and the general good of the County than Judge Bentley, and no man has commanded more of the love and esteem of his fellow citizens. He was helpful even at personal sacrifice. Largely liberal and hospitable, his house for many years was a free hotel, and seldom did his family, for many years, sit down to their meals alone, but with from two to ten or more visitors to share with them. These visitors were not drawn alone by the bountiful repast furnished, but fully as much by the genial welcome and charm of the family circle. It was no wonder that his death was felt to be a public calamity, and was so sincerely mourned. He sleeps with his loved ones, and parents on both sides, in the cemetery of the church of which he and they were so long strong pillars. He had a good helper, especially in later years, in Thomas S. McDonald, and the two did much to make Rockford a desirable place to live or visit. They will live in the hearts of the people for many years to come.

Bentley and his first wife raised six sons and three daughters. William lives on the home farm; Rufus is in Texas; Judge A. D. is a merchant at Rockford; S. M. is a merchant at Troy; Osceola P. is a minister at Vincent; J. Samuel is a teacher at Buyckville. The oldest daughter, Mary, married T. J. Pennington who has been prominent in the county since the close of the war as teacher, County Superintendent, public spirited man, and a Christian gentleman. He and his noble wife, like Judge Bentley, have kept also a free hotel, where a cordial hospitality has been extended to the members who have shared it. He has been a ready helper in every good work. The second daughter, Emma, married William T. Stewman, a teacher and preacher now living at Warm Springs, Talladega. Sadie, the youngest daughter, married Walter Looney, a successful teacher at Hanover. The two older, Mary and Emma, are dead and sleep side by side at the old church they loved. These daughters, like their mother and grandmothers, threw a charm around their home and church lives that will not be forgotten by any who came in touch with them. Their death came before the meridian of life was reached, but they had lived long enough to be esteemed pillars in the church, and whose loss was irreparable.

Judge Bentley married for a second wife Mrs. Elizabeth Phillips, a sister of Mr. Pennington. By this marriage there were no children. She did not long survive the Judge, and also sleeps near the church she loved.

T. J. Pennington

T. J. Pennington is of an old South Carolina family, but he was a native of Georgia, born June 23rd, 1840. He was a member of Co. B., 3rd Ala. Regt., and discharged from a wound received in the Battle of the Wilderness. He received education at Central Institute, taught there, and then at Rockford, where he married Mary L. Bentley in 1869. After teaching several years at Rockford, he began farming on Redmouth branch, on the farm that was the home of Chief Redmouth, and has made a success of it. He was County Superintendent most of the time from 1870 to 1890. After coming to Rockford he joined the Baptist church, was made a deacon, was a long while Superintendent of the Sunday School, and a very useful and influential member of the church. His mother died at his home in 1887. He is a Mason of both the Lodge and Chapter. He farmed here very successfully, raising nearly all home supplies in abundance, consisting of grains, vegetables, fruits, grapes, cattle, hogs, poultry, etc., and was able to feed his numerous guests bountifully upon the productions of his own industry. His home was rarely without company, who enjoyed to the full the genial hospitality of him and his noble wife. They were both very prominent and useful members of the Baptist church and now sleep side by side in its cemetery.

For more than a quarter of a century he was the treasurer of the Central Association. He was once a candidate for State Superintendent of Education, but failed to secure the place. His death was a bereavement to the community. For years, in addition to caring for his immediate family, he also took care of his widowed mother, his sisters, and nephews and nieces. He lived not for himself alone. He married happily a second time, a Miss Fannie Howle, daughter of Governor Howle; and by this marriage had two sons, who, with the mother, survive him. They still own the farm, but reside in Wetumpka.

DANIEL CRAWFORD

Daniel Crawford was a very modest man, yet such was his force of character, he was of such fine practical mind and solid attainments that he was known and honored not only in his county, but also in the State. He discharged the duties imposed on him in the various offices held by him so as to have the hearty approval of his constitutents. He was a native of North Carolina, and came to Alabama about 1833, settling first in Autauga, and was connected in the mill business, below Prattville, with Mr. John McNeil, a wealthy bachelor whose niece Mr. Crawford married. He went to Goldville, Tallapoosa County, about the time of the gold excitement there. He came to Coosa about 1840, and bought a good farm, putting up a fine mill on Jacks Creek which ran through the farm.

In 1847 he and Capt. Samuel Spigener represented the Coun ty in the House, at the first session held at Montgomery. He was nominated over Col. Wm. Garrett for the Senate in 1857, and was elected. In 1865 he was a delegate to the Convention to form a new Constitution after the war. He was again sent to the House in 1871. He was elected State Treasurer of Alabama in 1874, and again in 1876. His death occurred in 1891, and he was mourned by a large circle of friends in and out of the county. His son, William, married a daughter of Alex. Smith, and lived at the Robbins place at Nixburg; A. D. lives on the old home place; and J. D. is now Judge of Probate at Rockford; a daughter, Miss Jeannette, married J. E. Billups; and Miss Ellen first married Mr. Mathew Moore, and then Col. W. P. Shapard of Opelika.

ALEXANDER SMITH

Among the well known men of Coosa was Alexander Smith. He was of Scotch descent, a native of North Carolina, born about the latter part of the eightenth century. He came with quite a number of others of Scotch descent from the old North State and settled in the Wewoka neighborhood early in 1834. The county and church was called Carolina for a long time. They formed a thrifty settlement, and soon organized a Presbyterian church of which he was an Elder. Smith lived here until after the death of his McMillan wife in 1842. After this he married a daughter of Solomon Robbins, and bought the Larkin Cleveland farm at Nixburg. Here he farmed and traded in stock, during the most of his after life. He was twice appointed to fill vacancies in the office of sheriff. He did not seek office until 1857, when he was one of the candidates elected to the House in that exciting canvass. He was in the still more exciting race of 1859 re-elected to the House.

He was a man of medium size, florid complexion, blue eyes, and quick and energetic in action. He traded much in cattle, and when between seventy and eighty years old could ride through the woods with the rapadity of a young man, and could mount and dismount with nimbleness. He was a good and public spirited citizen, and highly esteemed for his noble qualities as friend and neighbor, and for his open manliness. He had a large family of sons and daughters. The following history is contributed by one of his daughters.

History of the Smith Family

Three of whom were among the early settlers of Coosa County, Alabama—Alexander, Daniel, and Lauchlin. Their great grandfather, John Smith, with two children, Malcom and Janet, came over from Scotland about 1736 (their mother, Margaret Gilchrist, having died on the voyage), and settled with other Scotch families along the Cape Fear and in Cumberland County, North Carolina. From "Sketches of N.C.," we find that in 1765, in the organization of Longstreet Presbyterian Church, that Malcom Smith was a ruling elder, and from that same church, in Cumberland County, these three brothers brought letters when they came to Alabama in 1834.

Malcom Smith married a Mrs. McKasick, formerly Miss Peterson. From this marriage were six sons—John, Malcom, Patrick, Duncan, Neill, and Daniel (and two daughters).

Daniel was the father of the three brothers who settled in Coosa County, and two other sons, Neill and Archibald, who moved to Wilcox County, Alabama, about the same time.

Perhaps it is well to mention here, that Janet Smith, the sister who came over from Scotland with her brother, Malcom (grandfather of the three brothers of whom we are writing), and daughter of John Smith, was married to a McNeill, and was known in the Revolutionary history of North Carolina as "Jennie Band," and was noted for her daring and bravery in time of war. She has many descendants, among whom are the McNeills and McKays, who still point with pride to the memory of their illustrious ancestor, "Jennie Band."

Daniel Smith was the father of the three brothers who came to Alabama about 1834 and settled in Coosa County, forming a neighborhood known as "Wewoka," name taken from the location, between the two creeks, "Big" and "Little Wewoka." These brothers, with others—Grahams, McWilliams, etc.—formed a colony, who organized another Presbyterian church, which they called "Carolina Church."

Daniel Smith's wife, mother of the sons of whom we are writing, was Anna McKay. They had in family thirteen in number. Among them were Archibald and Neill, who moved to Wilcox County, Alabama, and Alexander, Daniel, and Lauchlin, who came to Coosa County. Daniel was Sheriff of Coosa County when he died in 1842 (I think). After his death, Alexander was appointed by Governor Fitzpatrick (I think) to fill his unexpired term. In politics they were Democrats. Alexander afterwards was a member of the Legislature of Alabama for one or two terms. (His father, Col. Daniel Smith, had filled the same place in North Carolina.)

Daniel Smith's family moved with Lauchlin and family, and other Graham relatives to Jackson Parish, Louisiana, in 1852. (Their wives were Jane and Flora Graham, daughters of John P. Graham, a man noted for his integrity and consecrated Christian character. I think he died about 1846. His remains rest in the cemetery of Carolina Church, near the banks of "Little Wewoka," where no sound breaks the rest—and a requiem is sung by the gentle wind, as it moans among the pines that stand like sentinels around this city of the dead.)

Lauchlin with a little colony of Scotch Presbyterians settled in Louisiana about 1852—organized another church, calling it "Alabama." He soon died, followed by deaths of his wife and daughter. From his family still survives a son of some prominence, Judge Newton Smith—he lost an arm in the Civil War—has held places of trust in church and state in Louisiana. Judge Evander M. Graham, a grandson of John P. Graham above spoken of, still lives at Ruston, La.—is also a man of note, and highly esteemed. His father was also an early settler in Coosa County. Alexander Smith's first wife was Catherine McNeill, married and died in Carolina, leaving an infant daughter, Margaret, who after she was grown, married John H. Townsend, who moved about 1853 from Coosa County to Talladega Springs, his last wife being

Mrs. Graham, formerly Miss McMillan, sister to the second wife
of Alexander Smith and both sisters of Archibald, who in later
years was twice elected Judge of Probate of Coosa County. He,
with his widowed mother, came from North Carolina with the
colony of Scotch Presbyterians, who settled in Wewoka neighborhood. Judge A. A. McMillan moved to Waxahatchie, Ellis County, Texas, about January 1869. Died at the age of 73, leaving
several daughters and two sons—one, Neill McMillan, for some
time cashier of a bank in Dallas—and at this time has a lucrative
position in the Union Trust Co. in St. Louis, Mo.

Alexander Smith's second wife, Catherine McMillan, died in
1842, leaving four children. Thomas H. Smith, afterwards a lawyer at Wetumpka, where, after the Civil War, he married a daughter of Col. Seth P. Storrs. She died after a short married life,
and he survived her less than two years—died January 1869. Malcolm died in Richmond, Va., during the Civil War—in 1861 (was
also a lawyer). Lovedy Ann, only daughter by second marriage,
married J. B. Lennard, son of John B. Lennard, Sr., who was a
member of the Secession Convention at Montgomery, Ala. Of
their four sons and one daughter, their eldest, Alexander Smith
Lennard (named for his grandfather), is the sole survivor. His
parents still live, and mourn the loss of three noble sons (Thomas,
Joseph, and John)—all grown and unmarried, who died in rapid
succession, in the last six years. The parents live with their surviving son, whose wife was a Miss Kendrick, daughter of Julius
Kendrick—her mother, Miss Turner of Lowndes County; both
parents died in Lowndes County. A. S. Lennard has three children—two sons and a daughter. They all live together at Alexander City, Ala.

John A. Smith, youngest son of Alexander Smith by his second marriage, is still living near Nixburg—is a successful planter,
and an elder in the Presbyterian church—"McAlpine" quite near
—named in honor of Rev. Robert E. McAlpine, who over 50 years
ago preached at Carolina Church and taught at an Academy a
few hundred yards from the spot on which now stands this
church. In the cemetery are graves of many who once worshipped there.

John H. Smith's wife, formerly a Miss Lennard, died a year ago last September (1903), one month after the loss of a promising son, Dr. Joseph M. Smith, then practicing at Sylacauga, Ala., only 24 years of age. Other sons, Lennard, John, and William, still live. Dr. Malcolm Smith at Prattville, Ala., is also a son.

The wife of Judge James A. Crawford, son of Hon. Daniel Crawford, is his eldest daughter; Mrs. S. H. Thomas, another daughter, lives quite near him; Mayme, his youngest daughter, still is unmarried. William is attending a Dental College in Atlanta, Ga. Lennard, J. H. Smith's eldest son, married a Miss Smith of Louisiana, niece of Hon. Felix Smith at Rockford, Ala. They have several children. Dr. Malcolm Smith at Prattville married a daughter of Mr. Morgan Smith of Autaugaville and they have two children.

J. H. Smith, Jr., is unmarried—lives at the homestad and loves the farmer's life—is a great comfort to his father.

Alex Smith's last wife was a Miss Jane Robbins. She survived him about 30 years. He died at Talladega Springs, whither he had gone for health, August 29th, 1871, in his 78th year. She died 17th of November 1901 at the house at Nixburg, Coosa County, Ala. Left one son, Lauchlin, whose wife was a Mrs. Moore, formerly a Miss Kendrick—her mother was Miss Mary A. Lennard, daughter of Major Lennard. They, with his single sister, Miss Janet, lived at the homestead at Nixburg, Ala. Mary, the eldest daughter by thsi last marriage (of Alex Smith and Jane Robbins) married William H. Crawford, oldest son of Daniel Crawford and his wife, Annie McNeill. Alice, a third daughter, was the first wife of John H. Parker, a lawyer, who died a few years ago at Wetumpka. After his first wife's death (who left three sons) Mr. Parker married Moselle Crawford, oldest daughter of W. H. and Mary Smith Crawford. His first wife, Alice, was the third daughter of Alex Smith by last marriage. One of her sons lives at Montgomery, another is at the University of Alabama, the youngest at school near home.

Mary Smith and William Crawford have two sons in Louisiana—one, Alexander, the other, Daniel, both named for their grandfathers. Alex is married—one son, William H., Jr., is at home with his parents and sisters.

Another daughter of Alex Smith, by his last marriage, is Anna Bell, the widow of Prof. A. H. Hunter, who died a few years ago, in Elmore County, having three sons and two daughters.

Libbie Storrs Smith, youngest daughter of Alex Smith, married Prof. W. M. Bross, at the time, Professor of Mathematics at Marion College, Ala. While Principal of Public Schools at Talladega in 1899 his health gave way. After suffering for a year or more he desided to go to the western part of Texas—Ken County— where he died, with lung trouble, in a few months. His wife, with her two little children, came back to the old home, bringing his dead body with her.

Lauchlin R., the only son by last marriage of Alex Smith, lived a bachelor—did not marry until after his mother's death— lives at the homestead—his single sister, Janette, living with him.

(Another Branch of the Smith Family)

Malcolm Smith, cousin to Alexander, Daniel, and others, lived eight miles above Wetumpka, in what was then Coosa County—now Elmore. He was the son of Neill Smith, a grandson of John Smith, who came from Scotland. I think he first moved from North Carolina, several years before his cousins, Alex, Daniel, etc.—and spent a few years in Autauga County. Before Alex Smith came to live, he made a visit, to look at the country, and was sick for several weeks at his cousin Malcolm's house—sick so long, and so low, that they did not tell him of his first wife's death, which occurred at the time. On reaching Fayetteville, N. C., 20 miles from home, he met a neighbor who shocked him by telling of his loss.

Malcolm Smith, I suppose about the time of the others' coming, came to Coosa County—was a member of Carolina Church. After many years, he moved to Autauga again—was a man of wealth and prominence—reared a large family—Alfred Y. Smith and Mac A. Smith the only sons, now living. (To get exact dates in regard to this branch of the Smith family, I will refer you to Col. A. Y. Smith of Prattville, Ala.)

The large farm owned by Malcolm Smith, on Hatcheesofka Creek, where he lived until his removal to Autauga near Prattville, and where he maintained the good school in the early days of the county, became the property of his son, Neill Smith, who with his excellent wife, if not still living in the old homestead, did live there until recently, at quite an advanced age. There is a tract of two thousand acres of unbroken native forest of fine pine timber still on the place lying along Hatcheesofka Creek. There is not, perhaps, so large a body of pine in all this section of the State.

(1904—Prepared by a daughter of Alexander Smith—Mrs. J. B. L.)

WILLIAM TOWNSEND

Mr. Townsend and his father, Samuel Townsend, came from Madison, Ga., to Montgomery County, Ala., about 1812, settling north of the Tallapoosa River, and near it. He was born near Madison, Ga., in 1789. He married Miss Sarah Zimmerman, who was born in 1794 and died in 1859.

During the forties both Wm. and Samuel Townsend moved near Nixburg, buying the farm and tanyard of Albert Crumpler. Here the father, Samuel, died in 1847, being about one hundred years old. About 1851, Wm. Townsend moved to the lower part of Coosa, and settled on the land leading from Wetumpka to Tallassee. Here he continued to live until his death which occurred when he was about ninety-five. He was a good substantial citizen but never sought office. He owned about 2,600 acres of land, a good negro property, and many cattle, sheep, and hogs. He had twelve children—nine sons and three daughters. His son, Paschal, was born in 1811, and lived most of his life a few miles east of Nixburg. His wife was Sicily Mabry. John was born in 1813, Henry in 1815. He married Mrs. Mary Williams, who was a Dawson and died a few years since near Opelika, Ala. Hiram was born in 1818. Annie was born in 1820 and married Joseph E. Parker. Leonard F. was born in 1822. He went to Wetumpka just before the war and there married Miss Sallie Saxon, daughter of Col. L. P. Saxon. He died at Wetumpka, leaving several children. Eliza was born 1824. She married Maj. J. B. Lennard at Nixburg about 1850. By this marriage there were several children, some of whom are still living, among them the widow of Wm. P. Oden. A granddaughter is Mrs. Ed Jackson of Alexander City.

Mary E. was born 1827, and married Wm. E. D. Moore, a son of Mark E. Moore. Both father and son were long respected and honored citizens of Coosa County, taking an active interest in her affairs. Wm. T. was born in 1829 and married Elinor Howard. Kinchen A. was born 1832, and married Cornelia Howard. He has lived many years near the old home where the father died. Philip A. was born in 1838. He married Miss Weatherall.

None are now living but Wm. and Kinchen, who are with their children in Birmingham. Several of these sons were good soldiers in the Confederate Army.

JUDGE JESSEE M. CARMICHAEL

Judge Jessee M. Carmichael was in boyhood a resident of Coosa, and entitled to a place among those who have added to her fame. His father was Daniel Carmichael of South Carolina, of Scotch descent. The grandfather of Daniel Carmichael came to North Carolina just before the Revolutionary War and served as a soldier in it. The grandfather of Jessee was a soldier in the War of 1812. Jessee's father moved to Coosa in 1842, settling just below Central, near where the Plank Road ran. His father moved to Dale County and became Judge of Probate. Judge Jessee was born in Georgia in 1837. He entered the Confederate Army in April 1862. He lost his right hand in battle, but though one handed he made a success in life. He began the practice of law in 1866 in which he succeeded, as well as being a successful editor. In 1870 he was elected to the House from Dale, and in 1872 to the

Senate. In 1877 was appointed Judge of Probate, holding the office until 1880. In that year he was elected Auditor for the State, and re-elected in 1882. In 1886 he was elected Judge of the 3rd Judicial Circuit, and was re-elected, holding the office until about 1900. Governor Samford appointed him president of the Board of Inspectors of the Penitentiary in 1901, and he was re-appointed by Governor Jelks in 1903. In 1905 he was appointed Auditor by Governor Jelks. In 1876 he was Secretary of the Senate. He has filled all places well. He is a devoutly pious member of the Methodist Church.

Prof. Thomas Coke Bragg

Though not long a resident of Coosa, Prof. Thomas C. Bragg made his influence felt as an educator. He had become well known as such before coming to Coosa from Lowndes. The Baptists had established the Central Institute, a male school of high order. The building cost $9,058. There was difficulty in raising the money to liquidate the debt, and it was sold to Prof. Bragg for $4,025 in 1860. He threw himself with all his might into it, and having the advantage of its becoming well known while in the hands of the Baptists, he was soon well patronized. The war spirit among the young men led a number of them to enlist, and before the close of 1861, Captain Bragg himself led a company to the army. Owing to bad health he resigned in 1862, and returned to his school, suspending for a while in 1865. It was again resumed and continued two years. He then sold, moved to Montgomery and taught there.

Warren S. Reese

Warren S. Reese is entitled to a place among those of Coosa who rose above the common level. He was a son of Dr. Reese of Selma, and a nephew of Col. James R. Powell. When quite a little boy his mother died, leaving him and his sister, Kate, who were taken to the Powell home at Rockford. Here Mr. Reese grew almost to manhood, moving to Montgomery with Powell's family, in 1856. He was a gallant Confederate soldier and captain. His name became widely known by his administration of the mayoralty of Montgomery. It is generally conceded that he was the most progressive mayor the city ever had, and inaugurated that system of public improvements which has added so much to the beauty, attractiveness, and comfort of the city. It was done over the head of strong opposition, though now approved and enjoyed by all. It was during his administration and by his management that the ex-Confederate President, Jefferson Davis, was invited to Montgomery and other Southern cities, when Davis received such an ovation as must have been truly gratifying to the distinguished exile. Reese accompanied him, and may be said to have conducted the triumphal march of the Southern Chief. Afterward he aligned himself with the Republican party, and was at one time its candidate for the United States Senate. He died and is buried in Montgomery. His son of the same name is a resident of Montgomery, and an influential member of the Republican party.

Capt. John H. Clisby

Coosa gave to Montgomery another mayor whose administration for improvement in the city was only second to that of Captain Reese, namely, John H. Clisby. He was a son of Capt. John H. Clisby, Sr., who moved from Montgomery to Coosa in 1842, near where Goodwater is, when John was two years old. Captain Clisby, Sr., lived near Sockapatoy or Goodwater for some years, not far from Stephen D. Hughes, a brother-in-law. He then moved near the Cross Roads in Weogufka. Here John grew to manhood, enlisted as a soldier, and became a Confederate captain. He was brave and true. He became a citizen of Montgomery after the war, and made a mayor whose administration did much for the city. He died in 1902, and the large concourse that attended his burial testified as to the esteem in which he was held.

Edward A. Graham

Edward A. Graham is another mayor given to Montgomery by Coosa. He is the son of Hon. Malcalm Graham, and was born in Wetumpka, 1852. He has been clerk of the City Court; a member of the House; also of the Senate; twice City Recorder;

and in 1889, mayor of the city, declining a renomination. So from these—Reese, Clisby, Graham, and Powell—one must conclude that Coosa is good soil in which to raise City rulers and makers.

REV. BENJAMIN LLOYD

Coosa has also been the home of men who have taken places of distinction in the ministry of the gospel. Rev. Benjamin Lloyd, who came from Chambers County, lived for some years in Coosa. He was a minister of the Primitive Baptist denomination. His early history is unknown to the writer except that he was from South Carolina. He was a man of medium size, and carrying a face that would strike the beholder as denoting intelligence, refinement, and a gentle spirit. He was much above the most of the ministers of that denomination for education. He was compiler and publisher of their "Primitive Hymn Book," which was a good source of revenue to him, and his family, after his death. He moved from Coosa to Butler before the war, and died there. He and his wife had sixteen sons and four daughters. Several of his sons became ministers, most of them Missionary preachers of good standing. The humorous writer so well known in Alabama as "Rufus Sanders" was of his family, a grandson.

REV. JOHN P. SHAFFER

Rev. John P. Shaffer is a minister who spent much of the formative period of his life in Coosa. His father was Simon P. Shaffer, and his mother Martha Shaffer. John was born in Talladega County, but was brought by his father to Coosa when a child, locating on Hatchett Creek, about four miles west of Rockford. After living at the mill built by him for several years, he moved to Rockford, opening a hotel about 1850. This he kept till his death, about 1858. Here John received most of his education, and united with the Baptist Church in 1858. At his father's death he went to clerking in Wetumpka. He went to the war in the 14th Ala. Regt. He was promoted to lieutenant, and was severely wounded, losing part of his foot, and was discharged. He married the widow of his captain, John Bell, who was killed not far from the time Shaffer was wounded. He entered the school room as teacher, and also the ministry, and was a success at both. Through his efforts, mainly the fine collegiate schools at Lineville and Roanoke have both been built. More than twenty years ago he left the school room to give himself entirely to the ministry. He has been a leader in his denomination not only in East Alabama, but in the State, and also in the Southern Baptist Convention. For many years he was a member of the State Board of Missions, and a trustee of the two colleges, Howard and Judson. He is large and commanding in appearance, a fine conversationalist, and exercises wonderful influence over old and young. He has a son and step-son who are Baptist preachers, one of each in mercantile affairs; and his four charming daughters have each married men of prominence in their communities.

John Stout was another Baptist minister who grew from boy to manhood about Central and Wetumpka. His father was the Rev. Platt Stout, who, with his noble wife, was noted for deep piety, refined manners, cultivated tastes, and more than ordinary intellect. Their daughters, Mrs. General McClelland of Talladega, Mrs. Waller of Montgomery, Mrs. Woodruff of Wetumpka, and Mrs. Coker of South Carolina, were noble women, held in highest esteem by all who knew them. Rev. Platt Stout died in Wetumpka in 1867, and is buried there. There was another son, Platt, who married a daughter of Judge Leak of Wetumpka, who was quite deaf, and it was a bar to his progress. Brought up with such environment, it is no wonder, with God's grace in the heart, that John should have become a man among men. He went to the army with one of the Wetumpka companies, and when Colonel Loomis was made Colonel of the 25th Ala., he had John commissioned as his adjutant. He was a good officer and was thrfe times wounded. After the war he went to South Carolina, and there entered the Baptist ministry. He rapidly rose in his calling, and in a little while was recognized as a leading spirit. Before his death there was no minister in South Carolina who commanded more influence, and whose counsels were more sought after and followed than his. He was well known over the Southern Baptist Convention limits, for his zeal and good works. He was, with all this, very modest and unassuming. A few years since he died while attending the Southern Baptist Convention in Texas, in the midst of his still growing strength and usefulness, to the deep grief of the whole denomination. The Baptists of South Carolina have recently contributed $2,500 to erect a mission hospital in China to be called the "John Stout Memorial" erected to his memory.

Rev. James L. Thompson, of Bessemer, was raised in the eastern part of Coosa County. His father died while he was a boy, and he was raised by his mother, near his grandfather's house, Milton Russell, a prominent farmer. Thompson is a man of fine personal appearance, and a most excellent man. He was not possessed of native brilliancy, but by deep piety, consecration, persistent study and effort, has come to the front. He is well known not only in the State, but in the Southern Baptist Convention. For years he has been connected with the State Board of Missions of which he has been both President and Corresponding Secretary. He has also been on the Board of Trustees of the Colleges. He is now pastor at Brundidge.

The two Bentleys, Charles J., of Lanett, and Osceola P., of Vincent, and W. J. D. Upshaw, of Goodwater and Catlin Smith of Texas, were raised in Coosa, united with the Baptist church, and were ordained to the ministry here, and began their life work. They are rapidly forging to the front, and are already extensively known. Lloyd Hastie, longer Moderator of the Central Association than any other man, long held an honored place in the ministry.

Rev. L. M. Wilson of the Methodist church was raised in Marble Valley, and by God's grace and constant application he arose to prominence in his Conference which he maintained to his death, a few years since, near Dadeville. He was a presiding elder many years. He was a success as a farmer also.

Dr. F. M. Law, who recently died in Texas, 1902, lived for a while in Coosa, coming to it from Selma. He married Miss Kate, daughter of Col. Joseph Bradford, in 1851. He returned to Selma, abandoned the practice of medicine to devote himself to the ministry. He went to Texas before the war, and continued his labors among the Baptists there, filling prominent pulpits, and different places of trust and honor in the Texas Baptist Convention. He had been President of the Convention, of its Board of Missions, and trustee of Baylor University. He was a wise, safe, prudent counselor. At his death many tributes appeared in the columns of ₁*The Baptist Standard* from the most eminent preachers of the State, and the denominational papers of the Southern Baptist Convention laid flowers of praise on his grave as they did upon that of John Stout.

Rev. J. H. Colley

This fine old character whose life has been linked with nearly all the years of Coosa's history, came into the county at an early period. He settled a few miles east of Nixburg, living there until his death, only a few years since, when nearing ninety. He was uneducated, and not brilliant, but a solid preacher, which, united to his deep piety and integrity of character, secured the love and confidence of brethren and acquaintances. This was shown by the length of his pastorates running from fifteen to thirty years. He raised a fine family, some of them still in the same community, honored and respected. He was moderator of the Central Association a number of years.

Rev. Joseph Bankston came to Coosa from Troup County, Ga., in the forties. He was then somewhat advanced in years and honors among the Baptists. He had been Moderator for some years of the large Association reaching from West Point to Newnan, Ga. He soon became pastor of several of the strongest churches in Coosa, among them, Shiloh having in its membership men of wealth and prominence, such as Kendrick, Billups, McLemore, Gogans, Ray, Suttle, Wilton, McAlister, and others; and having in its large congregation more wealth and culture than, perhaps any other country church of the county except Elkahatchee. He was a man of fair education, clear thought, considerable gift of oratory, with personal magnetism. He was soon made moderator of the Central Association, which place he held until near his death considerably above eighty years old.

John R. Steely and Rev. Madison Butler, also natives of Georgia, came to Coosa in the forties, settling near Poplar Springs. For about a third of a century, Steely was a well known minister among the Baptists of Coosa and surrounding country. He was not educated, nor was he a man of deep thought, but of profound piety, strong magnetism, and wonderful oratory power, and efficiency in prayer. This made his services acceptable to all. He was very useful in revivals, and the number baptized by him was very large. The same may be said of Madison Butler, for, except in person, their characteristics were similar. Steely was a man of very large frame—Butler only of medium size. Butler was a man of more mental force perhaps than Steely, but the power of prayer and exhortation in each was remarkable. Butler's career was much shorter than Steely's, dying before reaching the meridian of life, while Steely lived to over eighty. Butler baptized a larger number in his few years than any man of his day.

REV. BRIGHT SKIPPER

He came to Coosa about 1849, and was at once called to the church at Elkahatchie. This was, perhaps, the church representing at that time more wealth than any church in the county, having in its membership Reuben Maxwell and his sons, Allen, Frank, and Willis Maxwell; Isaac Smith, Mr. Moon, Seaborn Dread, and William Thomas, Harris McKinney and some of his sons, Lennard Marbry, and others besides them of wealth. The contribution of this church to denominational objects was often as much as all the other churches of the Association. He was also pastor of the church at Antioch, another strong church in wealth, numbers, and influence, having the Rogers, David, Robert, and Joseph; David Lawson, Holtzclaw, Holifield, Black, Dennis, and others. It was here the writer first heard him, in 1851, while teaching in the adjoining neighborhood of Carolina or Wewoka.

He was an uneducated man, having learned to read and write after marriage. He was a fine thinker, naturally logical, with a fine memory, very studious, and possessing the power of stating clearly a thought, and arguing to a logical conclusion. He also possessed in large degree what is called magnetism in a speaker. The

writer has seen, at large gatherings, numbers of intelligent educated men and women sit spell-bound under his sermons, so en-
raptured that bad pronunciation and grammar did not break the
charm of his command. He continued to live in the county until
near the close of the last century. He then went to Texas, where
he died a few years since, advanced in age.

A step-son, Catt Smith, went into the ministry some years
after the war, and about the time that J. L. Thompson, W. J. D.
Upshaw, and Darius Martin did. He soon displayed fine talent
in the ministry, and his services were in constant demand. While
still rising in the scale, and still a young man, he went to Texas,
and soon had a good rank among her ministers.

REV. DARIUS MARTIN

He was a son of Lumkin Martin, an early settler in the county, and whose mother was the eldest daughter of Solomon Robbins, the first white settler, and prominent pioneer. The license
for this marriage was the first one issued in the county or record,
and bears date in 1835. Darius still lives near the place where he
was born, and where he has ever lived. He is now a grandfather,
so that four generations have lived and are working out their des-
tiny on the ground occupied by the Indians with them. While
Martin would not be called a great preacher he is a good one and
above the average—a most excellent, lovable, and pious one, commanding the confidence, esteem, and love of all. He has been
clerk of the Central Association for about a third of a century
which tells that he is a good one.

Rev. Lloyd Hastie was born and reared on Swamp Creek,
not far from the noted tan-yard and mill of Albert Crumpler. He
was ordained by the Concord church about the time of the war.
He was a good soldier in the War Between the States, but from
soon after its close he gave himself to the teaching, preaching, and
farming. He was quite an original character—of an active mind—
and quite a wit. He usually had long pastorates, and was moderator of the Central Association longer than anyone else, about
twenty-five years. He married soon after the war a daughter of

Mr. Jack Looney in the upper part of Coosa. This alliance was quite a help to him as it gave him a good wife and mother for his children; and associated with a family of large influence, his father-in-law being not only an early settler of good property, but one who figured largely in the organization of the county, but in her affairs to the period of its greatest population and power, being a member of its commissioners longer than anyone else. Hastie lived with a daughter after his wife's death. The house recently was burned, and he was burned to death in it. He was much regretted in death.

THE COUSINS

There was a family of Cousins in the vicinity of Eclectic, among whom were two Methodist ministers—one, Bart Cousins, who soon left the ministry and gave himself to the practice of law at Rockford and Wetumpka; the other, A. J. Cousins, became a prominent minister of the denomination, occupying many of the good pulpits of the State, and sometimes filling the office of Presiding Elder. He is still living, and has a daughter, Mrs. Langston Haygood, living in Montgomery.

Wm. Cousins, of this family, has given his life to teaching and has for a number of years been the County Superintendent of Education for Elmore. He is also a Methodist. R. C. Williams, now prominent as a minister, was raised in the same section. He is assigned by the Conference to good pulpits.

W. H. WOMBLE

There lived for years at Rockford, Wm. H. Womble who. moved there from Goldville, Ala. He married a sister of Simon P. Shaffer. He was a prominent member of the Baptist Church, a pure, noble, cultivated gentleman. He moved to Texas, where three of his sons, Wm., John, and Judson, became prominent in business and religious circles. One daughter, Susie, is the wife of Rev. Mr. James Carroll, so long Secretary of both the Board of Missions, and of Education in the State of Texas.

MARK LYNCH

During the fifties Mark Lynch bought the old Wilton place above Nixburg and lived there for some years. He was a Methodist Episcopal South minister of learning, refinement, and talent. A son of his, Clarence, married a daughter of Chas. Cabot. Another son, George, became a Methodist minister and rose rapidly in public esteem. The last known of him by the writer was in Birmingham.

Rev. E. T. Akin was a preacher who came into the county in the forties, and who took good rank, being called to the pastorate of good churches. He was employed by the Association for some years to devote his time to missionary work in the western and mountainous part of Coosa where, in most of it, churches were scarce and weak. He did a good work, and the Association bought him a good farm near Swamp Creek, in the neighborhood known as the Half Acre. He moved about the close of the war to Jasper County in North Alabama.

JUDGE A. A. McMILLAN

He came when a boy with his father and family to Coosa from North Carolina. They were a part of the Scotch colony who settled on Wewoka Creek, constituting the Carolina neighborhood. Several of the family died in the scourge of flux visiting the neighborhood in 1842. He, his brother, Neil, of Camden, Ala., and sister, Mrs. Graham, afterward Mrs. John H. Townsend, survived. He lost one sister, Mrs. Alexander Smith, in the scourge. When he grew up he bought a good farm on Wewoka, near Calvin Humphries, and made a success of farming. In 1856 he defeated Judge Suttle as Probate Judge and moved to Rockford where he lived as one of its most loved and honored citizens until his removal to Texas about 1869. His wife was Miss Scotta, a daughter of Capt. John McKenzie, a native Scotchman. She was a lady of lovely character. She was the mother of several children, who with the parents constituted a handsome and lovely household. The oldest son, William, entered the Confederate army, and was a captain at the close of the war. McMillan and family moved to Waxahatchie, Texas, where he became both planted and banker. He became wealthy. He was a Presbyterian.

Thomas H. Fargasen, who succeeded McMillan by Federal appointment, was of a good family, and had once been a man of some property, and good social standing. He had lost all property and much social standing through dissipation, which soured him in feeling, and made him ally with the Republican party. He made a better judge than was expected. His first wife was a Miss Stanley, and his second was the widow of Robert Cleveland. By his first wife he had two sons, John and David, who became wealthy and prominent merchants in Memphis, Tenn. By his last wife he had a daughter, Miss Georgia, the wife of William Peddie, of Rockford. Judge J. S. Bentley will be noticed elsewhere. His son, Archibald D., who succeeded him by appointment at his death, was defeated at the election in 1892, when the Populists swept the county. But he was virtually the Judge, for J. C. Penton, who was elected, made him clerk, and really turned the business largely over to him. Upon Judge Penton's death, which occurred in 1894, Bentley was appointed to fill out the term. At the succeeding election in 1898, he was defeated in the nomination. This was brought out largely by the plea that the office was continuing too long in one family. His grandfather had been judge for eight years, his father nearly eighteen, and he practically seven years. He is a lawyer graduated from the law school of the University of Alabama. After leaving the office he went into mercantile life. His first wife was Miss Edna, daughter of O. P. Looney. His second is a daughter of Matt. Lawson. He is a Baptist.

J. A. Crawford, who defeated and succeeds him, is a son of the Hon. Daniel Crawford, so long prominent in Coosa affairs. He is inclined to be a Presbyterian. He has made a good officer.

Robert W. Cleveland, the third county clerk in number, but practically the second, was the son of Larkin Cleveland, one of the most prominent men among the first settlers. Robert was himself an active business man at the county's organization. He came into the clerk's office December 9th, 1837, and continued until August 12th, 1845. He was highly esteemed. He died leaving two children, Robert and Caroline. Robert still lives in the county, and Caroline lives at Georgiana, the wife of Clay Parker. His widow married Thomas H. Fargason.

A. G. Hallmark, who succeeded I. W. Suttle, was a man of good education, fine address, and well respected. He was sheriff for a time in the county. He kept the hotel for sometime, and was succeeded in that by Simon P. Shaffer. He moved to Wetumpka in 1854, and after some years to Pensacola. He was a Methodist.

There were several clerks of the Circuit Court about whom not much is known. John A. Graham was elected to the office August 1845, and held it until 1853. He was a lawyer, a nice and courtly gentleman, and related to the Scotch family of Grahams so long prominent not only in Coosa, but in the State. He had a bright son who died while assisting his father in an official position in Washington, D. C., in the later fifties. He also had a brother who lived with him, Dr. Archibald Graham, a good physician, well loved, and a very useful man. He married Fannie Welch. He died at Rockford after the war. He was a Presbyterian.

Graham was succeeded by William T. Stubblefield, who was here among the Indians. Though somewhat dissipated, he was a popular man, and made a good clerk. He was of a very friendly and accommodating disposition. He was removed from office under Reconstruction measures, in 1867, and Joseph Taylor was appointed in his place. Soon after this, Stubblefield moved to Walker County, Ala., where some of his family now are. Stubblefield was elected as a Republican to the Legislature from Walker. He afterward had some position with the Federal Court in Montgomery. His course in later life was not such as his friends would have wished. He was in the Mexican War, and a Major in the Confederate service, in Hilliard's Legion. A good soldier.

Washington L. Smith, who was made clerk in 1880, held the office nearly eleven years, dying in 1891. He was a M. E. Minister, but had been so afflicted with rheumatism as to make it impracticable to continue on the circuit. He was a good man, and good officer. He aided Bentley and McDonald in building up schools and morals. His widow now lives in Montgomery. His children have gone from Coosa. One son, James, married a daughter of Governor Samford, and he is highly esteemed for his pure and upright life. He lives in Mobile.

W. T. Johnson, the present incumbent, was elected in 1892 on the Populist ticket, and has held the office ever since, making a good clerk. He lost a leg in the Confederate army, but it does not keep him from being an active, energetic worker in the discharge of his duties. He is an influential member of the Baptist church, and he takes a great interest in Sunday School work, especially with a class of little ones, who are very fond of him. They stay in his class till age and size require them to be moved to others, but he keeps up his class by recruits from the tots as they come on.

A. R. Coker was the first sheriff of the county and held the office from April 15th, 1833, to February 22nd, 1837. He was here with the first settlers in the county, and was called upon for public service in different ways during his life, because of the esteem in which he was held, and his capacity for business. James E. M. Logan, who succeeded him, died in 1839, and Alexander Smith, spoken of elsewhere, filled out his term. Wm. J. Campbell was elected at the next time, and died after a service of two years and one month. He was a man who filled every place well, and was highly esteemed. The papers spoke of him as being one of the best sheriffs in the State. He had been a prominent citizen of Wetumpka, the captain of her military company, the "Borderers," who escorted his remains from Rockford to Wetumpka, and buried him with military honors. Alexander Smith was appointed to fill out his term. Jas. R. Powell and Jas. H. Weaver, who became sheriffs, are noticed more extensively elsewhere.

T. T. Wall, who succeeded to the office in August 1848, was a young man at the settlement of the country, and with his father, James A. Wall, near Buyckville. He took interest in public life from the first. He was twice sheriff. He was a man calculated to make and hold friends. He was successful in business, and accumulated a good property. He was fortunate enough to hold a good lot of cotton through the war, which sold at the fine prices following the war, putting him in good financial shape again, notwithstanding the loss of his negroes. He lived at different times in different parts of the county. Just after the war he bought the fine old home of John G. Graham above Nixburg on the Plank Road. This had been the home not only of these two, but also of Boling Hall, a son-in-law of Graham, and a prominent citizen of the county. John Goldthwaite, a wealthy citizen of Montgomery, owned and lived here a few years, and died, leaving an only son, who did not long survive his father. Some of Wall's family still own the place. He left several sons, James, whose widow now lives in Wetumpka, a daughter of Jas. K. Oliver; Swep and Dink, and several daughters. The family were Methodists. Stephen A. Pearce, who succeeded him, was a small man, but made an efficient officer. After going out of office, he bought what was known as the "Half Acre," and under him it lost its bad reputation. He died here. He and family were Baptists.

William A. Wilson, who became sheriff in 1854, was in the county at its organization, and from the first had much to do with its public affairs in opening roads, acting as commissioner and in other ways. He bought and opened up several good farms in the county. As he would get them in good condition, he would sell at a good price, and open another. He accumulated a good property. He was a delegate from the county to the Constitutional Convention in 1865, his last public service. He was a small man, but his wife was large and vigorous. They reared a family of fine looking sons and daughters, John, William, Jessee, Adolphus, Lucien, and Hugh. Only one son is living, Hugh, at Fayetteville, Talladega County, and one daughter, Mattie, Mrs. Henry Pond, at Rockford, so far as known to the writer. They were Baptists.

Ellis Logan's father was one of the very early settlers of Coosa in Traveler's Rest beat. Ellis grew to manhood here. He had been deputy sheriff before succeeding to the office. Though not educated he made a good officer. He raised a company for the war, which went to Virginia and did good service. He resigned because of health. He was succeeded in the sherifalty by Ethelred Allen (commonly known as "Dred" Allen). He was a remarkable man. He could neither read nor write, yet was for years a constable, deputy sheriff, and finally sheriff. His papers were always properly executed, and were as safely managed as though he could both read and write. He was shrewd, a good judge of human nature, and fearless in performance of duty. He was strictly honest, and people were not afraid to trust their affairs in his hands. He would gamble, and was usually one of the Court constables at the spring and fall terms, as it gave him a good chance to indulge his propensity for gaming. He had large influence locally in elections, and brought to the support of his favorite candidates a good vote. He was unique in his make-up, and was usually astride a good horse, well caparisoned, and had a good roll of money in his pocket. He lived near the Half Acre.

Samuel R. Calffee, a Baptist, was a son of Evan Calffee, of Weogufka, and a son-in-law of Daniel J. Thompson. Joseph Hull, like Calfee, was of an old family in Coosa, who have lived in it for several generations, as citizens of Traveler's Rest beat. He was a Baptist. They were each sheriffs of the county.

John A. Chapman, who was prominent in the early affairs of the county, and, for some years, a leading commissioner, was the son of Solomon Chapman, who was a soldier in the army of General Jackson in 1813 and 1814. Chapman was not only popular with the whites, but with the Indians also. He was chosen by Chief Redmouth as the executor of his will, the first recorded one in the books of wills for the county. Some of the family are still residents. Their home was south of Sockapatoy.

John Looney, who was longer a commissioner of the county than any other man, was the son of John Looney, a Tennessean in Jackson's army, and who was wounded in the Battle of Talladega by the Indians, from which he never recovered. He was born in Tennessee in June 1805, and was of Scotch-Irish descent. His wife was Miss Cindrella Cooper, of the family of Coopers so long residents of Marble Valley beat, to whom he was married

February 1830. He came to Coosa in 1836, bringing his wife and three little boys, coming in a boat built by himself from Greensport to Fort Williams on the Coosa, and settled the place on which he lived and died May 14th, 1868. He did a good deal of work in opening a channel through the shoals of the Coosa, so that flat boats could transport iron, coal, and cotton to Wetumpka, Montgomery, and Mobile. He often piloted boats down the river. His widow died at the old home, November 18th, 1876. The home is still occupied by O. P. (Dick) Looney, who, like his father, has been many years a commissioner. Looney was an ardent supporter of the Southern cause, and gave four sons to its army. R. F., the oldest, was killed at Atlanta, Ga., July 22nd, 1864; Noah C. and J. J. belonged to Co. B., 34th Ala. Regt., and were captured at Missionary Ridge, and carried to Camp Chase, where J. J. died in February 1865. N. C. died recently at his home near Talladega Springs. O. P. was in Co. B., 12th Ala. Regt., is the only surviving son. There are three daughters still living. One of O. P.'s daughters married Judge A. D. Bentley, another married George McDonald, son of T. S., and both were buried on the same day, at Rockford, in 1900. One son, Walter, married Sadie Bentley, the youngest daughter of Judge John S. The family were Baptists.

Dixon Hall was never a citizen of Coosa, but represented it as senator from it and Autauga from 1840 to 1843. He was of the large and influential family of Halls of Autauga. He was a brother to Col. Boling Hall of Coosa, and like him was a fine looking specimen of humanity, and a man of good culture and mental powers. He moved to Morehouse Parish, Louisiana, in the forties, and was a wealthy and prominent citizen there, near Bastrop.

W. Levi Johnson, who represented the county in the House from 1871 to 1874, and in the Senate from 1877 to 1881, was the oldest son of George Johnson, the builder of the first store in East Wetumpka, and the first mill near Nixburg, and Elizabeth Johnson, a daughter of Jessee Suttle. George Johnson was a Georgian, who first came to Bibb County, and there married Miss Elizabeth Suttle, in 1829. He moved to Wetumpka in 1831, and to the place on Oakchoy, early in 1835, where he died, in 1863. He was

a good mechanic and farmer. A man of good native ability, a
reader of current events, who kept up with the movements of the
times. He was a Whig, and ran twice for the Legislature, first
against Fred Foscue, and last against Neil Graham, but was beat-
en by a very small margin each time. Levi Johnson came to
Coosa a child, and has ever since lived in the county, one of its
successful farmers, an upright, honest and popular man. He
married a daughter of Rev. James E. Edens, by whom he has
reared a family, most of them still in Coosa. He had a brother,
George, who became a lawyer and located at Rockford. He went
to the army, and returned home sick in 1862, dying soon after his
return. Henry, another brother, died in the army in 1863. Isaac,
another brother, is a farmer in Coosa, as is also John, who represented the county in 1903 to 1908. He was the Democratic nominee once before, but was beaten. There was one sister, Martha,
who married William Justice, who, with his father was early here.
Justice lived near the old home until sometime after the war,
when he moved near Eclectic, where he died a few years since.
Dr. Justice of Central is a son. The family were Baptists. The
Doctor was in the Senate in the session of 1911.

Wm. P. Oden, once senator, 1882, from Coosa and Elmore,
was a son of John P. Oden of Talladega (whose second wife was
Miss Catherine Crumpler, a daughter of Albert Crumpler). He
lived for some years at Rockford, practicing law, and then moved
to Wetumpka, and lastly to Childersburg, where he died a few
years since. His wife was Miss Alice, a daughter of Maj. J. B.
Leonard. He was a Baptist.

John H. Parker, who was senator from 188 to 1892, was a son
of Dr. E. S. C. Parker of Nixburg. His mother was a daughter of
Henry Lee, one of Nixburg's first citizens. He married Alice, a
daughter of Alexander Smith. He began the practice of law at
Rockford. Was active in politics. He moved to Wetumpka before his election to the Senate, and continued his practice there
until his death in 1902. He was a member from Elmore of the
Constitutional Convention of 1901.

Richard S. Nolen, who represented Coosa in the House in
1881, and in 1891-93, and in the Senate in 1896 to 1898, was a son

of Abner Nolen, who, with his brother, Stephen Nolen, were early settlers in Coosa. From them have sprung a numerous family. At a reunion of the family held in 1902, at Pine Grove Church, east of Nixburg, there were four hundred and twelve of the descendants of these two brothers present. The Nolens had a competency, but their boys labored on the farm. R. S. married Eliza, a daughter of Williamson Spears, whose wife was a daughter of William Suttle. Spears and his father were early settlers also of Coosa, locating in the Oakchoy neighborhood. Williamson Spears lives now on the place first settled by his father. Nolen profited by his farm experience, and has been successful, accumulating a good property. He has given his family as good educations as the academies of the country could furnish. Some of his sons are physicians, one a lawyer of Alexander City and all business men who have gained fortunes. He had a brother, Rev. W. J. Nolen, a leading minister of the M. P. Church, who has a son, Dr. W. L. Nolen, a physician of Chattanooga, Tenn., who is vice-president of the Tri-State Medical Association. R. S. Nolen went with the Populist party, and by them was elected to the Senate. In 1902, he was a Republican candidate for Conress from the Fifth Congressional District, but was beaten by C. W. Thompson, Democrat. The Nolens were patriotic Southerners, and contributed a good quota to the Confederate cause. They were generally Methodists, and useful citizens. Jack Nolen is a rich banker of Alexander City.

Anderson H. Kendrick, who represented Coosa in the House in 1842 and in 1849, at the time the Capitol building was burned, was a Georgian who came early into the neighborhood of Nixburg. His wife was a widow Smith, who had two daughters, Mrs. Wesley Hall and Mrs. Augustus Morgan, by her first marriage, and to sons, Julius and Anderson Kendrick, by the last. Kendrick was a man of fine property, and his home was a large well furnished one, where a liberal and refined hospitality was extended. He was a man of solid rather than brilliant talents, and was highly esteemed by all who knew him. He and his wife both died at their home near Nixburg. He was a member of Shiloh Baptist Church. His sons, Anderson and Julius, are both dead.

They left children. A daughter of Anderson is wife of Mr. Edward Jackson of Alexander City.

Capt. Samuel Spigener was a brother of Joel and William, all of South Carolina, who came early to Coosa, settling near Buyckville. Captain Samuel obtained his title by running a steamboat in South Carolina. He represented Coosa in the House in 1847, the first session held in Montgomery. He was a pleasant genial man, who easily made friends. He had a pleasant farm with a few slaves who made him a good living, and plenty to enable him to exercise a free and pleasant hospitality. He ran for Judge of Probate against Judge I. W. Suttle, a Whig, as a Democratic candidate in 1850, the inauguration of the probate court system; but Suttle won the race. He was also an independent candidate for the House in 1859, but was beaten. William Sarsenett and T. U. T. McCain were also candidates for the House with Spigener. He had two sons, Samuel and David, who served in Co. A., 46th Ala. Regt. A daughter, Miss Harriett, married Major Isaac Hull, long a teacher in the county, and another, Miss Eliza, married her cousin, Joel Spigener, Jr. He was inclined to the faith of the Universalists.

Henry W. Cox, who was elected to the House in 1851 with Neil S. Graham, came to Rockford at an early period from Bibb with his widowed mother and three maiden sisters, Misses Nancy, Pernetta, and Sarah, and later assumed the care of two nephews. He was a lawyer of substantial attainments in his profession. He never married, but gave all his earnings to the support of the family. He was a good and patriotic citizen. He raised a company in 1846 for the Mexican War. Upon the secession of Alabama in 1861, he at once raised a company of State troops, which was sent to Mobile by Governor Moore. When the Confederate States assumed control, this company returned home. Soon, in connection with Joseph Bradford, he raised a company in the summer of 1861, that went to the Virginia army with him as second lieutenant. Captain Bradford resigned, and Cox became Captain. He was killed gallantly leading his men in the Battle of Chancellorsville. He was an ardent Southerner, and was elected to the House on what was called the "fire-eating" ticket, in the excitement growing out of the admission of California as a free state. The family were Baptists.

Calvin Humphries was from Georgia, born March 6th, 1806. He came to Coosa in the forties, and by the force of his character, soon commanded a good influence. He was a successful farmer, and his business qualifications caused him to be made a commis- sioner, which position he held for a long time. He had a fine farm on the Wewoka Creek, through which the Turnpike ran. He was a tall fine looking man, of pleasant manners, and his hos- pitality cheerfully rendered, made his home a popular visiting place. He was elected to the House in 1859. He lived to a good age, dying on the place so long his home. He raised several sons who were fine specimens of manhood. Several of his sons were in the army, one, John, being the captain of a company of cavalry. Calvin and Dock married two daughters of Frank Sims, one, James, married a daughter of David Lawson, William married a daughter of Green Holifield, and Osceola married a niece of Frank Sims. The old homestead still belongs to the family. He was an active member of the Methodist Church and a licentiate, a member at Providence. He died April 18th, 1890, and is buried at Providence M. E. Church, where sleep a number of his family. He had a daughter who married James Willett, now owner of Likes mill, a good Confederate soldier, as was his brother, Wm. Willett.

W. D. Walden, who was a member of the House in 1859, was a merchant at Nixburg for a number of years, and then trans- ferred his business to Rockford where he continued until his death. His first wife was a daughter of Solomon Robbins, by whom he had one son, Walker, still a citizen of Coosa. His sec- ond wife was Miss Eliza Moore, of Rockford, by whom he had three children, and who went to Texas soon after the war. Wal- den was a good merchant, and made a good property. He made no public speeches, his talent being for business, not oratory. He led a company to the war in June 1862, joining Hilliard's Legion. His company was afterward in the 59th Ala. Regt. He was killed at the Battle of Chickamauga, just as he mounted the enemy's works, in a gallant charge of the regiment at Snodgrass Hill.

MAXWELL FIELD

(The following is contributed by Mr. J. C. Maxwell)

The Maxwells of Coosa County are of Scotch-Irish descent. They trace themselves from Joel Maxwell who was living in Orange County, Va., in 1740 where his son, Thomas Maxwell, was born that year. Thomas married a Miss Henry in Virginia, and with her and his father he came to Elbert County, Georgia, in 1792. Unto Thomas Maxwell and his wife were born two daughters and four sons. One of these was Reuben Maxwell, who married Elizabeth Thornton in 1820, and soon thereafter came to Talbot County, Georgia, where he lived until the winter of 1844-45, when he and his wife and ten children came to Alabama, and bought land on both sides of the line between Coosa and Tallapoosa counties. He built his home, however, on the Tallapoosa side. He was a spirited and thrifty farmer and imbued with the pioneer spirit, and succeeded in amassing a comfortable fortune, and took pride in building one of the best homes then known in the county. He died in May 1861. His venerable wife survived him until May 1883. His ten children were Allen T., Elizabeth, Francis M., Sarah, Clarey A., Willis M., William, Eugenus, Virginia, and Susan M. Of these, only one, Susan M., who is the wife of Capt. W. L. Rowe, of Dadeville, Ala., is living. Allen T., Francis M., Willis M., and Virginia, who was the wife of William M. McKinney, moved into Coosa County early in the '50's.

Allen T. Maxwell, eldest son of Reuben Maxwell, was born November 29th, 1822, in Elbert County, Georgia. In 1842 he was married to Cynthia Susan Carreker, of Talbot County, Ga., she dying July 29th, 1850; he was married a second time to Elizabeth Walker, of Taylor County, Ga., in August 1852. The children of the first marriage were Nancy E., Lovick P., and Jacob C. The children of the second marriage were Allen L., Mittie I., Anna B., Mary V., Leila, and Benjamin F.

Allen T. Maxwell was a man of extraordinary good sense, a successful farmer and a public spirited citizen, taking an active interest in the affairs of State and Church. In 1860 he was elected to the Legislature as a Whig and was, therefore, in politics in the strongest period of Alabama's history. He believed in the preservation of the Union, but when Alabama seceded he threw his whole soul and means into the cause of the Confederacy. The state of his health prevented him from entering actively into the military service, but he wanted to be represented on the field of battle, so he hired a man as a substitute to represent him. After the war he continued his farming operations until his death September 11th, 1881. His second wife, Elizabeth Walker, survived him until January 30th, 1890. Nancy E., his eldest daughter, died in infancy.

Lovick Perryman was a born soldier. The fires of war so stirred his young heart that he ran away and joined the Confederate army before he was quite 14 years old, and he followed the fortunes of Bragg, Johnston, and Hood under the immediate command of Capt. Geo. E. Brewer, Company A of the 46th Alabama Regiment, two and one-half years to lose his life at Jonesboro, Georgia, September 1st, 1864. Those who knew him as a soldier say there was none truer and braver than he.

The following tribute to his memory was written by Capt. George E. Brewer in 1864 who was then commanding the 46th Alabama:

"The subject of this notice, L. P. Maxwell, son of Hon. A. T. Maxwell of Coosa County, died near Jonesboro, Georgia, September 1st, 1864, from a wound in the hips and bowels received at Jonesboro August 31st, 1864. He was a native of Alabama, born October 29th, 1847. He bid fair to win a name among men, had his life been spared. At the age of 14 he entered the service of his country, and to the day of his death showed a devotion to the cause, by word and deed, that should put to the blush many older (and should be) wiser heads. As a private soldier he was never known to flinch from any duty, however hard, or shrink from danger, however great. As orderly for regimental commander, he was always at the post where duty called, whether in camp or on the field; and when bullets filled the air he would carry orders from one point to another on the field of battle, with a coolness and promptitude seldom surpassed. It was while in discharge of his duty as orderly, that he received the wound that ended his career, before he had entered upon manhood, and caused him to yield his life in his seventeenth year, a sacrifice upon the altar of Southern Independence. His memory will long be revered by those who knew him, for his noble qualities of head and heart. In his death his family has lost one of its brightest jewels."

Jacob C. Maxwell, the second son, was born June 10th, 1850. He was fairly well educated and his father purposed that he should be a lawyer; but at the age of 21 he decided that married life on the farm would be more congenial to his nature. So he wooed and won Miss Temple J. Austin, youngest daughter of Col. T. L. Austin of Coosa County, and he was married to her September 7th, 1871. After living twelve years on the farm he moved from Coosa County to Alexander City in Tallapoosa County, where he embarked in the mercantile business with his brother-in-law, E. L. Goggans. He afterwards sold his interest in this business and became Cashier of the Alexander City Bank, which position he now fills. He was a member of the Constitutional Convention of 1901 from the Senatorial District of Coosa and Tallapoosa Counties. He was a good working member and he enjoyed the respect and confidence of the entire body. Being of a public spirit, he has had much to do with the material prosperity of Alexander City, having served her several terms as Alderman and Treasurer. He is regarded as a broad-minded and liberal citizen, ever ready to contribute liberally of his means to those in need, and to any enterprise which has for its object the uplift and betterment of humanity and surrounding conditions. He, with others, promoted the Alexander City Cotton Mills, an industry now in successful operation. He is connected with it as a director and local agent. In politics he has always been a Democrat, and in religion a Baptist. He is the present Moderator of the Central Baptist Association.

Allen Leonidas, the third son, was born in Coosa County, July 25th, 1853. He was married to Mattie L. Adams, of Lee

County, December 24th, 1872, and died March 9th, 1887, leaving his wife and his son and daughter surviving him.

Mittie I., the second daughter, was born in Coosa County, September 7th, 1886. She was married to C. S. Bandy of Lee County, December 3rd, 1872, and again to Geo. F. Walker, of Tallapoosa County, in 1890.

Anna B., the third daughter, died in infancy.

Mary V., the fourth daughter, was born February 29th, 1860. She married W. V. Whatley in 1875 and now lives in Gorman, Texas.

Lela, the fifth daughter, was born July 29th, 1862. Married E. L. Goggans in 1880, and died March 27th, 1889.

Benjamin F., the youngest son, was born December 11th, 1867, and is now living at Alexander City, Ala.

Francis M. Maxwell, second son of Reuben Maxwell, was born in Elbert County, Ga., in 1825. He came to Alabama in 1844 and first settled in Tallapoosa County near his father. He moved to Coosa County early in the fifties. In 1847 he was married to Lucinda Carreker and she dying, he was again married to Alabama Jordan in about 1855. She still survives him, and lives at Kellyton, Alabama.

He, too, was a successful farmer. He was a man remarkable for his good judgment and common sense, his intense piety, his devotion to his family and to any cause he espoused. He was a Deacon in the Baptist Church, and was regarded as the strong pillar of his church, and as the wise counsellor of his pastor. He was charitable in all things, regarding that as the chiefest virtue in good citizenship. He was a good Confederate soldier, always at the post of duty. When death claimed him in December 1891, there went out from us one of the best men that ever lived in the County.

From his first marriage there came Nancy E., wife of E. W. Thomas; Susan Emma, who died about the year 1875, and Jessie M., who died about 1887. A youn man of much promise was lost to the country in his death.

From the marriage with Alabama Jordan were born Reuben J., who died in boyhood; Annie E., who resides at Kellyton, Ala.; William E., Eugene, Francis M., Jr., Cecil K., Charles M., and Sidney. These were worthy sons of a noble sire. Drs. Wm. E. and Cecil K. are successful practitioners of medicine at and near Kellyton, Ala.—men of much learning and skill—an honor to their father and to their profession. Eugene and Charles M. are successful business men in Seattle, Wash. Francis M., Jr., stands high in his profession as a lawyer in Waco, Texas. Otis A. is a teacher in Denison, Texas, and Sidney is a life insurance man in Houston, Texas. All of them are making a success of life in their chosen professions—largely due, no doubt, to early training as well as personal effort.

Willis M. Maxwell, third son of Reuben Maxwell, was born in Talbot County, Georgia, July 7th, 1837, and came with the balance of the family to Alabama in the winter of 1844-45. In 1858 he was married to Martha McKinney, of Coosa County, and moved into Coosa in 1860. The children of his marriage were Reuben M., October 23rd, 1860; Willis M., Jr., October 27th, 1862; Julius P., July 31st, 1864; Minnie E., October 31, 1867; Martha L., October 6th, 1869. He was a man of fair education, splendid physique, and personal address and he commanded the attention and respect of any crowd he entered. He had just started in life when the war came on. But at the call of his country he laid aside the plough and hoe, for he was a farmer, and answered the call by enlsiting in the 47th Ala. Regiment as Lieutenant, where he served with distinction. He was afterward promoted to Quartermaster and, later on, was detailed to raise provisions for the army in the field. The war over, he gathered the remnants of what was left and started life again. He was making splendid headway when, shattered in health, he fell prey to heart trouble and died February 26th, 1871, loved and honored as one of nature's noblemen.

Reuben M., his eldest son, is a good citizen and farmer in Marshall County, Alabama.

Willis M. is in Texas.

Julius P. is a successful farmer and merchant in Pleasant Hill, Dallas County, Alabama. He is in many respects much like his father—in personal appearance, nobility of character, and Chrstian charity.

Minnie E. resides at Alexander City, Alabama, with her mother and sister, Martha L., who is the wife of Hon. Geo. A. Sorrell.

None of the other descendants of Reuben Maxwell ever lived in Coosa County, but the writer of this sketch would feel that it was incomplete without mention of Eugenus Marwell, the youngest son, who early enlisted in the Confederate cause, and belonged to the bodyguard of the great and gallant soldier, Albert Sidney Johnston, who fell at Shiloh. It seems a cruel fate that this young man should have been in the thickest of the fight on that bloody field for days, where he won honors worthy of promotion and came out unscathed, to fall victim to immediate sickness and death. But such is Providence, and there should be no complaint at His workings.

David W. Bozeman came as a child with his father, Nathan Bozeman, to Coosa in its first settlement, and was a farmer having a nice home at Central before the school was located, or the village started. After the Central Institute was located he built the hotel afterward owned by Mrs. Holifield, and kept it, until just before the war when he went to Wetumpka as president of the bank. His father was a man in good circumstances, and all his sons were highly respected men, and his daughters equally so as women. David was a distinguished looking man, and commanded the profound esteem of all who knew him for his uprightness, morality, and fine business sense. Though not a member of the Baptist Church, his leanings were toward them, and he was made a trustee of their Central Institute, to which he was a liberal contributor. In 1861 he was elected to the House. After the war he moved to Texas, and most of his family with him, settling near Waco. William Bozeman, a son, married Miss Sallie, a daughter of John A. Pylant, for many years a very prominent layman among the Baptists.

ALBERT CRUMPLER

Beasant Crumpler, father of Albert Crumpler, came to America soon after the Independence of the United States and settled in Virginia, but soon thereafter removed to Autauga County, Ala., and died there in 1840. His wife, the mother of Albert Crumpler, was Elizabeth Wright, who came from Wales with her parents who were early settlers in Virginia.

Albert had little education, but was a close observer, and read a great deal, and kept well posted on all political questions of the day. He was a tanner by profession. Began in 1830 in Autauga County, Ala., near Prattville, where he first leased a tanyard, and afterwards bought it of Col. Wm. Bibb.

He was a member of the Secession Convention in 1861, and of the State Legislature in 1862.

He was a Democrat and often on some important committee work. For a long time a member of the M. P. Church, later of the M. E. Church, South, and a local minister.

He was a R. A. Mason and Chaplain of Rockford Lodge.

He married Maria Zeigler, near Prattville, Ala., March 9th, 1832. She was a daughter of Nicholas Zeigler and his wife, Catharine, who lived near Prattville. She was of Dutch descent, but from what part of Germany I cannot say.

Albert Crumpler moved to Coosa County in 1836, and settled near Nixburg. In 1843 moved near to Rockford; and in 1867 moved to Childersburg, Talladega County, where he contniued his vocation of tanning leather. His children are Albert J., and wife, Elizabeth Ann; Catherine E., widow of the late John Oden; Lewis Henry, and wife, Antinet I. Residence of each is Sylacauga, Ala.

Albert Crumpler was a member of the House in 1861, and also a delegate to the Secession Convention of 1861, was a Methodist Protestant Minister. He was elected as a co-operationist to the Convention, but when the vote was finally taken on the ordinance of secession, like many others elected as he was, he voted for the ordinance as did his colleagues, Taylor and Leonard, and gave their warm adherence to the Southern cause. In 1836 he moved to the place afterward owned by Maj. J. B. Leonard, and now by John Smith, a son-in-law of Leonard, and son of Alexander Smith. Crumpler opened a good farm, and sunk a good tanyard. In 1845 he sold here and bought on the Turnpike a large farm, three miles below Rockford. He built a large nice residence, and sunk another good tan-yard, and built a mill, both saw and grist, on Swamp Creek. He also kept the poor of the county a number of years. He had two sons, Albert, a clerk for a number of years in the stores and offices at Rockford, now a farmer in Talladega, and Lewis, who was a Major in the Confederate army, now a merchant at Sylacauga; and a daughter, Catherine, who married John P. Oden of Talladega, and who now lives at Sylacauga. Crumpler was deficient in education, but had a strong practical business mind, and possessed some magnetism as a speaker. He made but one set speech in the House, upon an important measure, but it was highly complimented, as the most thoughtful speech of the discussion. After the War Between the States he moved into Talladega near Childersburg, and opened a good farm and tan-yard. He died a vigorous man at a ripe age. He was only a local preacher, but a strong man in the pulpit, and much beloved. The hospitality of his home was unbounded.

T. U. T. McCain was a Georgian who settled early upon the old Georgia road, below Central. He was a good citizen, and much esteemed. He was ambitious for political preferment, and though several times a candidate for the Legislature, was never successful until 1863 and 1865. His wife was a Thornton. He had a family much respected, and some of them continued to live a long while in the old neighborhood. The Thorntons were a good family in the same neighborhood.

Dr. E. S. C. Parker seemed content to live on his farm which he opened early, west of Nixburg, and attended to his mill and practice until 1863, he was induced to go to the House, and after that settle down to the old routine. He married a daughter of Henry Lee, an early settler and hotel keeper at Nixburg. His son, John, became a lawyer both at Rockford and Wetumpka, and was senator, 1888 to 1892, and a delegate to the Convention of 1901. He died at Wetumpka in 1902.

James Vanzandt was a member of the House from 1863 to 1869, leaning in 1863 to the Union side of politics, and squarely so in the later years. He was a Methodist Protestant preacher, a man of only ordinary ability. He had the confidence and esteem of those who knew him.

Dr. John Edwards was tolerably early in the county, living about two miles above Central on the Plank Road. He had a small farm, a tan-yard, and a good practice as a physician. He was a Methodist, and active in his church life. He had a son, Jessee, who became a lawyer, and practiced for some years at Rockford and then went to Clanton. His other children lived not far from the old homestead.

Robert H. Gulledge was a son of Joel Gulledge, an early settler of Coosa, a man of much influence both politically and religiously. Robert was a good Confederate soldier, and after the war married Miss Lizzie, daughter of Stephen Jackson, by whom he reared a good family. He first lived in Traveler's Rest beat where he was raised. He was elected sheriff between 1870 and 1875, and moved to Rockford. He served in the House in 1875-76. He afterward bought the Tuck place above Nixburg. He made a good officer. He had several brothers, all good soldiers, good men and citizens. The family are Methodists. His father died at Rockford, recently, over ninety years of age.

The following, recently obtained from F. A. Gulledge, of Verbena, will be added, as Joel and Jack Gulledge, so long connected with Coosa, needed more notice than the writer was prepared to give. He says: "Joel Gulledge was among the pioneer settlers of Alabama from Anson County, N. C. His first vote was cast in that county for Andrew Jackson for president of the U. S. He was married in 1833 to Elizabeth Mitchell, also of Anson County. Her father was one of the Minute Men near Boston, Mass., during the Revolutionary War. Mr. Mitchell and wife, and Joel Gulledge and wife came to Alabama, reaching old Fort Toulouse, near Wetumpka, December 24th, 1834. Mr. and Mrs. Mitchell both died here and were buried at the old fort in 1835, where their remains still sleep. Gulledge came near dying the same year, and for a more healthy locality moved to Nixburg, in Coosa County. He was a man of grit and aspiration, hence made friends of those worth knowing, viz. Howell Rose, James R. Powell, Solomon Robbins, William Weaver, Alexander Smith, Col. Wm. L. Garrett, and others. He began at the foot of the ladder and climbed not to fame but to success. To him were born nine sons, six of whom reached manhood, and five gave their services to the Confederacy, all in the Virginia army. Two were killed, two wounded, and the other made an invalid, dying later. Gulledge was a Douglas Democrat and opposed secession, but when the State seceded he said to his sons, 'Go, boys, there is only one honorable way out of war. I would rather see you returning in a pine box than going off under guard.' He ever kept faith with the Democratic Party, never voting any other ticket. He died June 17th, 1902, at 91 years of age, with not an enemy on earth of whom he had knowledge.

"He was a farmer all his early and middle life, and made a success of it. He is survived by his sons, Capt. R. H. Gulledge of Patrik, Ark., J. W. E. Gulledge of Clanton, Ala., and F. A. Gulledge of Verbena, Ala. He lived at Rockford for a number of years after the war. After the death of his second wife, he lived with his sons.

"William A. J. Gulledge (commonly known as 'Jack') came to Nixburg from Anson County, N. C., in 1844. His wife was a Miss Mary Rushing, and to them were born ten children. She died in 1858. After this he married Miss Susan Bradbury of South Carolina. By this marriage there were two children. He was small of stature, but fearless. He had a clear head, thought for himself, and had the courage to stand by his convictions. Some few years after settling at Nixburg he and Joel both moved into Traveler's Rest beat, where they both continued to reside until after the war, and Jack to his death, which occurred on March 2nd, 1898, 86 years of age, after a useful pious life.

"He was a successful farmer. Politically he was a Whig while the party existed as such, voting also the Bell and Everett ticket. He was an ardent Southerner, and would have gone to the army, but age and size (being quite small) was not received. He was never really reconstructed. He is survived by only five children, all by the first wife. He was a Methodist."

In 1877 the county elected Dr. John B. Kelly to represent it in the House, which he did well. He was a son of Dr. James Kelly, who settled early in the county, and was one of its most widely known and respected citizens. He was of Scotch descent, and a Presbyterian. Dr. John was a good soldier, and after the war married a daughter of Lennard Marberry, a wealthy planter below Sockapatoy, and now owns the old Marberry farm. Some years back he moved to Anniston where he now resides.

Daniel J. Thompson lived in Hanover beat from a tolerably early time until about 1890, when he moved into Clay County. He was a good farmer, a popular public spirited man, and a very useful member of Poplar Springs Baptist Church. Thompson went as First Lieutenant in Co. A., 46th Ala. Regt. in February 1862. He made a good and gallant officer, and commanded the company during most of the fighting period of the war, as Captain Brewer of the company was in command of the regiment. In 1879 he was a member of the House from Coosa, and made a good member. His wife was Miss Hunt, by whom he had several children. Robert and George lived for years, if not yet living, in Hanover beat. One duaghter, Virginia, was the wife of Samuel Calfee, a son of Evan Calfee, and who was once sheriff of Coosa. His son, George, is still a resident of Hanover.

John A. Suttle, a nephew of Judge Isaac Suttle, and the only son of William and Mary Suttle, was a native Alabamian, and came as a child to Coosa with his father in 1831 from Bibb. He was never robust. He had several sisters, Mary, the wife of Charles Buckner; Ann, the wife of Williamson Spears; Laura, the wife of Rev. Shun Kelly; Rhoda, the wife of Isaac Johnson; and Martha, the wife of Joseph Smart. These sisters have reared good families, and some are among the most honored of the present people of Coosa. John married Rebecca, a daughter of Hiram Bentley, as his first wife, by whom he reared several good children. His second wife was a daughter of Rev. Robert Carlisle, a prominent Primitive Baptist preacher. She was a good wife, looking well to his comfort in his feebleness. Several useful sons and daughters were born to them. John was for a good many years a Missionary Baptist, but changed to the Primitives and became a preacher. Though feeble, he always managed to support his family and educate them. He held minor offices at different times, and sometimes farmed, and at other merchandized. He was treasurer for the county for a good while. He was in the House in 1885. For a good many years he lived at Rockford, and died there a few years since. He and some children are buried there.

J. H. Nabors represented the county in 1887, and made a good member. He married Sarah Mathews of Hanover beat in 1854, by whom there were eight sons and three daughters. For a long time he has been a leading substantial farmer and citizen west of Goodwater. Several of his sons live about Goodwater, Bradford, and Crewsville. He is a Methodist.

William C. Brown, born 1825, when a child came with his father into the lower edge of Talladega (now Clay County) from North Carolina, and settled at the place since called Brownville, just above Goodwater. His father was of Scotch descent, and a Presbyterian, but William and a daughter, Mrs. Susan Willingham, became Baptists. William married Miss Margarett, daughter of George W. Graham, in 1849, and the next year settled the place where he has ever since lived, near Mt. Olive. His children live in Coosa. In 1870 he married a Mrs. Calfee, daughter of Benj. Kimbrough. He was in Company C., 10th Confederate Cavalry. He was for a long while justice of the peace. In 1889 he represented the county in the House. He was a good citizen, a fine neighbor, a worthy Mason, and a valuable church member of Mount Olive.

In 1895, H. R. Robbins was a representative in the Legislature. He had been a sheriff in 1880. He is a good farmer in the neighborhood of Sockapatoy, where his father, Daniel Robbins, settled after leaving Nixburg, of which he was early a citizen. The following sketch of Daniel Robbins was recently obtained from R. H. Robbins.

Sketch of the Robbins Family in Alabama

(Contributed by H. R. Robbins)

Prior to the seventeenth century there was a colony of immigrants from Germany settled in the State of North Carolina, from which the Robbins family, and the name generally spring. During the seventeenth century one Benjamin Robbins married Miss Bostick. The result of their marriage was four sons and one daughter, Solomon, Daniel, Joel, and Benjamin. Eliza was the name of the daughter. In the early part of the eighteenth century the family moved to Alabama and settled in what was known afterwards as Autauga County, which covered a large territory of the State. The family engaged in agriculture and had a great deal of trouble with the Indians. Solomon, the oldest son, married a Miss Sellers who bore two children (Betsy and Solomon, Jr.), and died. Solomon married his second wife, Miss May Wilson, a daughter of Benjamin Wilson who moved from the State of Virginia to Alabama. The result of their marriage was four sons and five daughters. Those were Putnam, John, Thomas, and George, all of whom were killed or died in the late War Between the States, each one leaving widows and children. The daughters by the last marriage were Jane, Martha, Eliza, Adeline, and Kate. All of whom married and died in Alabama except Solomon, the eldest son, and Adeline, next to the youngest daughter, who died in the State of Texas, leaving honored and prominent families. J. W. Robbins (the oldest son of Solomon, Jr.) has been elected State Treasurer twice, and served several terms in the

Texas Legislature.   Kate Robbins Grayson is the only one of the family living.   She lives in the State of Texas.   W. O. Robbins, a grandson of Solomon Robbins, Sr., and son of Thos. Robbins (deceased), is Sheriff of Elmore County, Alabama.   Solomon Robbins, Sr., served in several official positions in the early history of Alabama.   After the death of Benjamin Robbins, Sr., Solomon, Sr., and Daniel moved to Coosa County, Alabama, and their brothers, Benjamin and Joel, moved to Florida and were lost sight of by the others of the family.   Daniel Robbins married Sarah Mitson (the sister of the second wife of Solomon Robbins, Sr.). The result of their marriage was five sons and four daughters, namely, B. W. Robbins, W. J. Robbins, S. E. Robbins, H. R. Robbins, and D. B. Robbins, and the daughters, Emeline, Sarah, Martha, and Casina.   Daniel Robbins, with his brother, Solomon, and other early settlers of Coosa County had many troubles and daring conflicts with the Indians, often being driven back across the Coosa River, as the Indians claimed the territory of Coosa belonged to the Red Men.   In the organization of the first Circuit Court of Coosa County, Daniel Robbins was a member of the Grand Jury of said court which was held in an Indian house about two miles south of the present Court House of said County. The County of Coosa then reached from Montgomery to Talladega.   Solomon Robbins, Sr., and Daniel Robbins served in the War of 1812 for which Solomon drew a pension until his death. Daniel died before the pension law passed.   His widow filed her application for pension but was rejected.   His life was spent on the farm and in performing any public duty he was called to.   He died in about 1850.   His eldest daughter married Isaac Mitchell, who moved to the State of Louisiana about 1855.   B. W. Robbins (the first son of Daniel Robbins) married Miss Marjorie Mitchell, and moved to Louisiana in 1858.   When the war broke out in 1861 he established and served four years as second lieutenant of a company in the 30th Louisiana Regiment.   He filled many responsible places of trust, and died in 1875, a high toned Christian man, though a poor farmer.   W. J. Robbins the second son of Daniel Robbins, moved to Louisiana with his sister and elder brother, and engaged in merchandising on Red River and accumulated considerable property, but in 1861, he volunteered in the company with his older brother and was elected first lieutenant of the company, and served four years. When he returned from the war he found his property destroyed (except lands). After the days of Reconstruction were over, he was elected Tax Collector and Assessor of his Parish, in which position he served with credit to himself, and his constituents. Then he was selected as Parish Surveyor in which he served until he grew feeble, and eyesight failed him. He is almost helpless at this time. S. E. Robbins, the third son of Daniel Robbins, moved to Louisiana in about 1858. In 1861 he volunteered in a company in the 12th Louisiana Regiment and served as a brave soldier in said regiment until 1863 when he obtained a transfer to the 17th Alabama Regiment where he had a younger brother in the service. He served in Company D., 17th Alabama Regiment until the 20th day of June, 1864, near Peach Tree Creek, in a desperate battle was severely wounded, carried to the Oakmulga Hospital, where he died from his wounds, and was buried with thousands of like unfortunates. H. R. Robbins, the four son of Daniel Robbins, was only four years old when his father died and when he became responsible he took charge of the little homestead left by his father and preserved in the name of his mother until her death in 1896. He is a farmer, has spent his time as an agriculturist, except while in the army—teaching school occasionally, and when in an official position. In 1871 he was elected Justice of the Peace of his precinct and at the expiration of his term as Justice of the Peace, in 1880, he was nominated by the Democratic Party for Sheriff of Coosa County, Alabama, and elected by a large majority over his opponent, an independent candidate. He served the full term as Sheriff with credit to himself, and to the wishes of the whole people. In 1894 when the Democrats were divided, the people in mass meeting nominated him for a member of the State Legislature, and he was elected by a good majority. He has been an elder in the Cumberland Presbyterian Church over thirty years. D. B. Robbins, the fifth and youngest son of Daniel Robbins, was as the most of the family, a farmer, married Miss C. F. Rogers in 1882, and died in 1900, leaving a wife with three children. He was a poor hard working man, loved and respected by all who knew him. The religion of the family was mostly Presbyterian, of a liberal disposition in their views on all subjects and principles.

The McKinney family were prominent and influential in the county. It originated here from Harris McKinney, a native of Virginia, but who moved to Georgia, and from there to Jefferson County, Ala. He came to Coosa at an early period, settling in the eastern part. The McKinneys were of Scotch origin, and were Baptists. Harris McKinney was uneducated, but a man of superior mind and judgment, and succeeded in accumulating a good property by farming. He had a son, Patrick McKinney, who lived between Sockapatoy and Bradford,, having a handsome home, a fine orchard and a good farm cultivated by a good negro force. There was another son, Jasper McKinney, who married a daughter of Nathan Bozeman, Sr., who also owned a good farm and slave property in the upper part of Coosa. But he went to Texas about 1852. Patrick McKinney had a son, William, who married a daughter of Reuben Maxwell, and still lives near Alexander City. His two daughters by his first marriage were married, one to Lewis Maxwell, and the other to Richard Slaughter. Harris McKinney had a daughter, Emily, who married Robert McAdory, and was the mother of P. Jasper McAdory, Mary J., widow of Dr. Neil Baker, and Celia, wife of John N. Slaughter, of Goodwater. Dr. Baker and Slaughter have been men of influence, prominence, and property in Coosa. Jasper McAdory is still a citizen of Coosa, and is among the few who have lived longest in the county. He is a very fine citizen, who though never aspiring to office, has been public spirited, and wielded much influence in the county. He owns a fine farm in Hanover, besides large landed possessions elsewhere. He has a remarkably fine memory, is a good judge of human nature, and a good manager of men. His wife was Miss Eliza Saddler of Jefferson. They have had no children of their own, but have taken and raised others.

ROBBINS FAMILY

(Contributed by Mrs. Kate Grayson)

My fahter, Solomon Robbins, was born in Brunswick County, N. C., January 14th, 1791. His parents were Benjamin and Sarah

Robbins (nee Wells). My father served as a private soldier through the War of 1812. With a wife and babe he came to Alabama about the year 1816, settled in Montgomery County, near Judkins Ferry on the Tallapoosa River. While living there his second child, Solomon, Jr., was born. The location proving unhealthy, he moved from there to Autauga County, settled near the Alabama River in the neighborhood of Coosawda. There his wife died, and he afterwards married Mary Wilson, daughter of an old Virginia gentleman, Capt. Benjamin Wilson, who commanded a Company of Virginia troops during the War of 1812. Captain Wilson was born in Isle of Wight County, Va., September 3rd, 1773. His father, James Wilson, was born February 14th, 1747, served as a private soldier through the Revolutionary War, and died April 12th, 1830. My father, Solomon Robbins, was married to his last wife, Mary Wilson, May 27th, 1822. In 1832 he moved with his family to Coosa County among the Creek Indians, and was the first white settler to found a home in that County. As he moved from Autauga County, he opened up his road as he went. With the help of the hands who assisted in driving his wagons and stock, horses, cattle, sheep, hogs, etc., of which he owned vast numbers, they cleared the road heading from Wetumpka to Nixburg, via Central Institute, which road is in use to this day. He bought a large tract of land from the Indians, paying them in silver (they would accept no other kind of money), and having the entire county to select from, of course, he made a judicious selection and bought land unexcelled for fertility of soil, fine timber, most excellent range for stock, and watered by at least a dozen large, bold springs of never failing clear, cold, sparkling freestone water. Wild game was abundant, so plentiful indeed that father could go out any morning before breakfast and kill a deer or bring in as many wild turkeys as he could carry. I have heard my mother say she often had as much as a large wash tub full of turkey breasts alone salted down at a time. I have often heard my father remark—even when 80 years of age—that if he knew of a country as fine as that when he went there, he would go to it even at his advanced age. He bought a great deal of land from the Indians, which he afterwards sold to the white settlers as they came in, and realized from his land speculations, quite a snug little fortune. He kept the first P. O.

ever established at Nixburg, although it was then called Robbins-
ville, as can be seen by referring to maps of that date. The second man who sold goods there was named Nix, hence the change
to Nixburg. The first merchant who sold goods there was murdered in his bed one night by an Indian. His name I have forgotten. An old Indian came to father at a late hour one night,
and being able to speak a little English, succeeded in making him
understand that he feared the merchant was killed, for a drunk
Indian had come to his house with a bottle of whiskey, tobacco,
and a lot of cloth, and there was blood upon his clothes. Father
told him to return home at once and keep the Indian there until
he could go and investigate. On reaching the store, he found the
merchant dead in his bed, having been knocked on the head with
an iron wedge. He arrested the Indian, and started alone with him
to Talladega County to jail (there being no jail nearer), but the
Indian got away from him and a week or more elapsed before he
recaptured him. He finally caught him, however, carried him to
Talladega where he was hung. Just before the rope was adjusted
around his neck, he insisted that another Indian take his place,
proposing to give him two ponies if he would do so. The Indian
refused, and he remarked lightly that he did not care, as he
would be in Arkansas in three days anyway. While en route to
the jail, the Indian told father he saw him several times while he
was searching for him, and came very near killing him one day,
raised his gun, took aim, and had his finger on the trigger, but
happened to think how good and kind he had been to his people
and would not shoot. Father lived surrounded by the "red men"
and their families for three years on the most amicable terms.
By the aid of linguists, he soon learned their languages and they
his, sufficiently to converse with each other quite well. The old
Chiefs would often come to him to learn something of the "white
man's law," as they termed it. On one occasion father was much
amused at the remark a chief made. They had conversed for
some time when the chief said: "Well, Robbins, we have talked
enough, for if people talk too much, are mighty apt to tell some
lies." One of the chiefs had a very pretty daughter, as beautiful
in form and features as any white lady. A white man, a young
lawyer, came into the neighborhood, fell very much in love with
the chief's pretty daughter and asked for her hand in marriage.

The old chief was silent for some minutes, apparently in deep thought, then turned to the lawyer and said, "No, you can't have her; if you were of any account you would not want 'Injun' wife, and if you are no account you can't have her."

The first year after going to Coosa, father had to take all his grain to Autauga to have it ground, a distance of 36 miles, leaving mother with her little ones alone until he returned. Never once were they molested or treated with the slightest disrespect. Those were the days and subsequently when "Capt. Simon Suggs" (Bird Young) figured so conspicuously in that country. If Johnson Hooper could have seen my father before writing the history of "Captain Suggs," father could have given him material for a book twice the size of the one he wrote. He was often a guest at my father's house, as he made that his stopping point to spend the night on his trips to and from Wetumpka. Often have I heard father tell of the tricks and schemes of the "Captain" to swindle not only the Indians but the whites as well. The man who came in contact with him and did not get "taken in," congratulated himself on his extreme good luck. There was one praiseworthy trait in the Indians' character that I must not omit to mention since it deserves recognition and admiration. Father said they, as a whole, were the most truthful people he ever saw in his life, until the white people (to their shame, be it said) came among them and learned them to drink whiskey and otherwise corrupted them.

My father was so fortunate as to witness the exihibition of the "stars falling," as it was called—on the morning of November 13th, 1833. He and a negro man were camped out on the roadside between Central Institute and Wetumpka, on their way to the latter place with cotton for the market. The darkey was very much alarmed, thought "Judgment Day" had come and prayed for deliverance with all his might. Father, who was a very calm, quiet, self-possessed man, experienced not the slightest fear or excitement, but greatly enjoyed the grand spectacle, which was probably the greatest display of celestial fireworks that has ever been seen since the creation of the world, or at least within the annals covered by the pages of history. Father and mother reared a large family, 12 children (11, I should have said, as one died in infancy), on the old home bought of the Indians, both died there and were laid to rest in the old cemetery at the Protestant Methodist church in sight of their loved home. To me that cherished old home is the most sacred spot on earth; endeared to me by ten thousand tender ties and hallowed association. The dear old home is now owned by W. H. Crawford, who married one of father's granddaughters. He (Crawford) is a son of ex-Treasurer Daniel Crawford of Alabama.

The names and ages of my father's children are as follows: Elizabeth was born in Brunswick County, N. C., March 20th, 1814. Married Esqr. R. L. Martin, and together they reared a large family near Equality, Coosa County, Ala., and there both died. She was a member of the Baptist Church. One son, D. S. Martin, is a prominent Baptist Minister, and still lives in the neighborhood of their old home. The next child, Solomon Robbins, Jr., was born in Montgomery County, Ala., April 9th, 1818. Was married to Amanda M. Funderburgh, was a member of the Methodist Protestant Church, died in Texas, October 7th, 1878. His eldest son, John W. Robbins, is serving his second term as State Treasurer of Texas. The next child, Martha Ann, was married to Rev. J. H. Mitchell, a Cumberland Presbyterian Minister. Was a member of the Methodist Protestant Church until after her marriage when she united herself to the C. P. church. She was born in Autauga County, Ala., February 16th, 1823, died September 6th, 1853. The next was John Wells, who was born in Autauga County, Ala., July 29th, 1824. He married Frances Weaver, daughter of Wm. Weaver, one among Coosa's first settlers. He was a member of the Methodist Protestant church, died July 30th, 1863, while in the Confederate service. The next, Mary Jane, was born in Autauga County, December 27th, 1825. She married Alexander Smith, a prominent man of Scotch descent, of which blood he was very proud, was once, perhaps twice, elected to the State Legislature. She was a member of the Methodist Protestant church, but after her marriage affiliated with her husband's church, old school Presbyterian. Died———. The next, Eliza, was born in Autauga County, September 30th, 1828. Married W. D. Walden, a merchant of Nixburg, who was once elected to the State Legislature. He was Captain of a Company during the civil war, and was killed at the Battle of Chickamauga. She was a member of the Methodist Protestant church, and died August 2nd, 1853. The next was Wm. Peyton, who was born in Autauga County, April 18th, 1830. Was a member of the Methodist Protestant church. Married Martha Freeman. Died November 17th, 1862, while in the Confederate service. The next, Thomas Clinton, was born in Autauga County, Ala., January 30th, 1832. Was a member of the Methodist Protestant church. Was first married to Sarah Freeman, who died childless; after her death was married to Tampa E. Ellis. Two sons were born of this marriage, Wm. O. Robbins, the present Sheriff of Elmore County, and his brother, Thos. S. Robbins, of Louisiana.

The next was Sarah Adeline, who was born in Nixburg, Coosa County, Ala., June 10th, 1834. Was a member of the Methodist Protestant church, was married to Samuel Hill. Died in Texas, December 24th, 1903. The next, George Washington, was born in Nixburg, Coosa County, Ala., May 6th, 1836. Was a member of the Methodist Protestant church, married Susan Caroline Jackson, and died July 10th, 1863, while in Confederate service.

The next, W. Kate, was born in Nixburg, Coosa County, Ala., March 18th, 1839. A member of the Methodist Protestant church. Married Charles Oliver Grayson, resides now near Tyler, in Smith County, Texas, the only one of the 12 children now living.

The next was Laura Virginia, born in Nixburg, Coosa County, Ala., March 24th, 1842, died October 13th, 1842.

Now, my dear boy, I have done the best that an old woman with defective memory and nervous hand could be expected to do, with my rambling reminiscences. There were many amusing incidents in connection with the Indians in Coosa's early days, but time and space forbid. Your publishers can accept or reject as best suits them. But before closing I wish to impress upon your mind the character of my father's noble sons, your own dear father being one of them. My father was a very remarkable man in many respects. He was noted far and near for his exemplary piety. His benevolence was such that no one in need ever called upon him for aid whose wants were not liberally supplied from his ever generous hand. His natural mental abilities were of the first order, far above ordinary. His disposition was the sweetest and most lovable I have ever seen in any human being. He was warm hearted, broad minded, gentle, sincere, pure and good, an ideal husband, father, neighbor, friend and master, beloved by all who knew him, both white and black.

His sons were all that such a father could have desired. They were reared in a village where whiskey drinking, gambling, horse racing and other evils common in such places are usually practiced, yet such was their training, and the influence and example of their Christian parents, that of the five sons no one ever heard an oath from the lips of one of them, never saw one enter a saloon, any place of vice or immorality, or be guilty of any act that could cause the hearts of their beloved parents a moment's pain. They were honest, honorable, upright, high minded men, pious, well-to-do prosperous farmers, who had the confidence and esteem of all who knew them, worthy every way the good man who was proud to call them sons. Not a blot or stain ever tarnished the name or character of one of his children, and it is a source of great pride and gratification to me to be able to say the same of his numerous grandchildren. You may feel proud, my dear boy, of the distinction of being a grandson of such a model man, whose equal I have never yet seen. I cannot find language to do justice to his worth.

Affectionately your aunt,
Kate Grayson.

P.S. In glancing over what I have written. I see that I failed to give the dates of the deaths of several of the family which can be inserted in the proper places. Solomon Robbins, Sr., died May 19th, 1879. Mary Robbins, his wife, died June 28th, 1878. They were both members of the Methodist Protestant church. The date of the death of your aunts, Jane Smith and Elizabeth Martin, I have not got. You can get them, however, by writing to your cousins, D. S. Martin at Equality, Ala., and L. K. Smith, Nixburg, Ala. In a short time after my father moved to Coosa County, his brother, Daniel A. Robbins, and family also settled near Nixburg, and there reared a family of nine children. His wife and my father's were sisters, both daughters of Capt. Benj. Wilson. He remained there until most of his children were grown, then moved near the old town of Sockapatoy, where he and his wife died, both at an advanced age. One of his sons, Howell R. Robbins, still lives with his family at the old homestead,, and is a man of upright, unblemished character, enjoying the confidence and esteem of all who knew him. He has been honored with the office of Sheriff of Coosa County, and has served one or two terms in the State Legislature.

B. B. Bonner, Zacharia Powell, Wm. Townsend, Wm. Weaver, Izer Wilson, Mark E. Moore, Wm. Moore, —––— Carrol, Ped Crumpler, Mr. Suttle, and many others whose names I cannot now recall were among the early settlers of Coosa. The latter, Suttle, was shot and killed, they supposed by an Indian, while digging and cleaning out a spring. His wife was with him, but never knew from whence the shot came. Suttle's was the first body ever laid in the old grave-yard at Nixburg, my father making the coffin and superintending the digging of the grave.

John Clisby

The parents of John Clisby were John Paul Clisby, son of Joseph Clisby and his wife, Lois Eaton, of Boston, and later of Medford, Mass., and Martha Butters, daughter of Benjamin Butters and his wife, Elizabeth Stimpson, who lived first at Reading, then Andover, Mass.

John Paul Clisby was commander of the old Medford Light Infantry in 1814, Town Moderator, Town Assessor and Selectman for a number of years.

The Clisbys came from England in 1663 and settled in Boston, Mass. Joseph Clisby served in the Revolutionary War at sea;

first on board the brigantine Tyrannicide and later on a privateer. Benjamin Butters marched from Reading, Mass., on the Lexington alarm April 19th, 1775, as private in Capt. John Walton's company, Col. David Green's regiment. He afterwards served under Colonel Brooks, and Col. Jacob Gerrish.

John Clisby came to Alabama at the age of 17 and began merchandising at Washington Landing. From there he went to Montgomery in 1832. Moved to Coosa County in March, 1842, and farmed.

He was magistrate of Coosa County and postmaster of Weogufka during the Civil War. He was Captain of the old Montgomery True Blues. Served in the Seminole War in Florida in 1836. He was a Democrat, and for many years was a steward in the Methodist Church.

He married Emily Damaris Hughes, February 4th, 1839, at Montgomery, Ala. She was a daughter of John Hughes and his wife, Elizabeth Tillman, who lived in Montgomery. John Hughes came from Virginia and his wife, Elizabeth Tillman, from South Carolina. The ancestors of both served in the Revolutionary Army. John Clisby lived in Coosa County first at Sockapatoy, later at Weogufka, stayed there from 1842 to 1866, when he moved to Wetumpka. In 1875 he moved to Verbena, where he lived until his death, March 16th, 1894. In 1872 he had a stroke of paralysis and never again engaged in any active business.

The following is a list of his children:

John Hughes Clisby, m. Fannie Young Montgomery, died May 15th, 1902.

George Clinton Clisby, m. 1st Mary Mastin, 2nd Fannie Hubbard, Montgomery.

Freling Clay Clisby, died 1852.

Stephen Hughes Clisby, killed at Battle of Peach Tree Creek.

Alfred Angus, m. 1st Fannie Glover, 2nd Emily Irwin.

Mary Eliza died in infancy.

Emma, m. C. L. B. Marsh, Edgefield, S. C.

Elizabeth, m. James Cobb, Edgefield, S. C.

Lorenzo, m. Clara Barrett, West Point, Miss.

Rosa Mayhew, m. S. W. John, Birmingham, Ala.

Harriett, m. J. E. Morris, Birmingham, Ala.

Annie Mae, still living at Verbena, Ala.

J. B. LENNARD

The parents of John B. Lennard were John Bonum, Sr., born near Richmond, Va., and Mary Wood, who lived at Richmond, Va. The father of Mary Wood was killed in the Revolutionary War. Her mother performed several acts of service, carrying dispatches, moulding bullets, etc. She married a second time. Died at the home of her daughter in Washington, Ga., at an extreme old age.

The Lennard family came from France and settled in Virginia. John Bonum Lennard, Jr., was born January 1st, 1807, at Washington, Wilkes County, Ga., and died in Freestone County, Texas, December 6th, 1870. His father died when he was 14 years of age, and he became a clerk in a store. Afterwards was a merchant, and later a planter in Georgia, Alabama, and Texas.

He was a mmeber of the Constitutional Convention in 1861, and voted for the secession of Alabama. Was in the Seminole War in Florida, 1834, was Major of Cavalry. Robt. Toombs was Colonel. He was an old line Whig, a great friend of Robt. Toombs and Alex Stephens. He was a member of the M. E. Church. Was a Mason for many years. He was three times married. First, on December 2nd, 1829, he married Sarah Frances Marshall. She was a daughter of Joseph Marshall and his wife, Anne Grimage Beard, who lived in Columbia County, Ga. She was an orphan, living with her uncle and guardian, Dr. Crawford, a cousin of Governor Crawford, and nephew of W. H. Crawford. Also a cousin to Nathan Crawford Barrett, so many years Secretary of State of Georgia. She was a great-granddaughter of Rev. Daniel Marshall, one of the pioneer Baptist preachers of Georgia. The family claimed to be related to Chief Justice John Marshall, and were very proud of the relationship. The second marriage was to Miss Daniel of Georgia, on the 14th of April, 1835. His first wife died 7th of March, 1833, leaving two sons. His second wife left five children. After her death he moved to Coosa County, Ala., where he married Miss Eliza Townsend. After the war they moved to Freestone County, Texas. Both died, leaving three daughters, the son died at the age of six years befoer leaving Alabama.

The eldest son by first wife, Dr. Joseph M. Lennard, died at Nixburg, Coosa County, Ala. He never married—was a surgeon in the army and prominent in his profession. Was President of the County Medical Board. The second son by first marriage was John B. Lennard, married Miss Smith, daughter of Alexander Smith of Coosa County. Still living at Alexander City, Ala.

Second wife's children:

Mary Ann, wife of Anderson Kendrick (deceased).

Wm. Daniel, died in Virginia during the war.

Eliza J., now living—widow of A. M. Kendrick.

Thomas C., killed at Battle of South Mountain.

Sarah T., wife of Jno. A. Smith (recently died).

Third wife's children:

Kate E., wife of M. H. Harvis, Freestone County, Texas.

Alice I., widow of W. P. Oden, living at Sylacauga, Ala.

Ellen, wife of A. J. Oden, Sylacauga, Ala.

CHARLES MAYES CABOT

Marston Cabot, the father of Chas. M. Cabot, was born at Harland, Vt., July 17th, 1789, and was the son of Marston Cabot, Sr., and Lavina Sabin. He married Mary Rogers, daughter of Jonathan and Polly Mayes Rogers, who lived at Loundonderry, New Hampshire.

The Cabots are of Norman race. Men of that name settled on the Island of Jersey at a very early period and were large land owners there. The American family appeared in New England in the latter half of the Seventeenth Century in the persons of two brothers, George and Jean. George Cabot married Abigail Marston. Their son, the Rev. Marston Cabot, graduated at Harvard in 1724. Married May Dwight, daughter of Rev. Josiah Dwight, and was pastor of the church at Pomfret, Conn., for twenty-six years.

Jonathan Rogers had been a private soldier under his father, who was a Captain, in the Revolutionary War. The Rogers are descendants of John Rogers, the Martyr.

Chas. Cabot removed to Wetumpka, Ala., in 1840, and engaged in mercantile business. Went to California about 1850, returned in 1853 and engaged in mercantile and agricultural pursuits.

He held the office of county commissioner. Was a member of the Constitutional Convention of 1865. Was a Democrat. Not identified with any church.

He married Eliza Judson Holman at Wetumpka, Ala., May 10th, 1853. She was a daughter of Rev. Robert Holman, a Presbyterian minister whose life was devoted to the preaching of the gospel throughout Alabama.

He died at Wetumpka, and in the cemetery there stands a handsome monument, erected by the young men of Wetumpka as a tribute to his memory. The following named were his children:

Marston Cabot, who married Miss Addie Reese, a daughter of Lawrence Reese of Lowndesboro, Ala. Now living at Gate City, Ala.

Janette Cabot Lynch, widow of Clarence M. Lynch, now resides in Birmingham, Ala.

Eliza Judson Cabot, who married Col. Osceola Kyle. After his death she married F. M. Cabot and moved to Florida. Mr. Cabot was killed by a railroad accident at or near Hales Sound where Mrs. Cabot still lives.

Chas. M. Cabot, who died in Birmingham.

Cabot Lull, a nephew of Chas. M. Cabot, has spent the most of his life in Wetumpka, an honored and useful citizen. He has filled several offices with credit to himself and benefit to the community. He has been Mayor of the City, Judge of Probate for the County and largelly interested in merchandising. Has been a prominent and useful member of the Baptist Church and for many years Superintendent of the Sunday Sshool.

East of Nixburg lived Mr. Sellers, a brother-in-law of Solomon Robbins; Paschal Townsend, a son of Wm. Townsend; Milton Russell, the grandfather of J. L. Thompson and also uncle of Rev. James M. and Timothy Russell, so long and well known as Baptist preachers of Coosa churches, each of whom were early settlers and long residents of Coosa County and quite influential.

Near Russell lived John Willis, who was for several years one of the prominent Commissioners of Coosa County and a highly esteemed citizen. He married a daughter of Isaac Jones, long a well known citizen and farmer living west of Rockford on Hatchett Creek. John A. Logan was a brother-in-law of Willis, having married another daughter of Isaac Jones. He was for a some years a teacher and then became a successful planter. He was also a Commissioner for some years and always active in public affairs both of Church and State. He accumulated a good property, built a good home, and was public spirited. Politically became a Republican after the war.

John Chancellor, the Murphys, Alex and James Logan, John Garnett, Darden, Stone, Conoway, and the Russells were all of such usefulness that they ought to be more fully noticed, if facts were known.

John A. Pylant

No man was better known in Coosa who was not long in office than John A. Pylant. He was a native of Tennessee, and moved to Coosa about 1840. He bought the home of James Lindsey, now occupied by Jasper McAdory, and lived there till removed to Central Institute about 1856. From the Institute he went to Wetumpka, engaging in mercantile pursuits until about 1871 or 1872, when he went to Texas where most of his children had preceded him. His wife was a sister or near kinswoman of Mrs. Lindsay, and was long and widely known as "Aunt Mary Pylant," noted for her good table, and especially her fine coffee. Pylant was a successful farmer and had a good orchard. He entertained a great deal of company in such good style, as to invite the people to share it. He and Guy Smith (known as Uncle Guy) were for years staunch pillars in Poplar Springs church, and next to the preachers in usefulness in the Association. He was fond of vocal music, and one of the most read and best choristers of the whole country. He filled the place of chorister for his church, the Association, and of almost all religious gatherings he attended. He was the best missionary colporteur ever employed by the Association. He was charitable to the poor—ready to help anyone in need—and very liberal in the support of all church work. His contributions to the Central Institute were liberal, and he was one of its trustees during its ownership by the denomination. Associated with him as a trustee was W. M. Barnes, a Georgian, of good means, who lived near the Institute during all his years in Coosa. Barnes was a man of fair education, pleasant address, and above the average for intelligent business capacity. In 1857 he was a candidate for the House of Representatives; but was beaten though he made a fine race. In 1860 he moved back to Georgia, settling where Senoia now stands, and there made a success of both his farm and mercantile enterprises. The town of Senoia covers much of his farm. He died there a few years since.

Rev. James W. Jeter was also a trustee of the Central Institute, closely associated with Pylant, Barnes, and Bozeman, the four with Allen Maxwell, constituting the financial nucleus of the Board. Jeter was always an active member of the church and influential in the Association. He was a man of good property, and liberal toward worthy objects. He was not ordained to the ministry until he had reached the meridian of life, and so did not labor much among churches. He died about 1867, and is buried at old Union Church, which was for so long the religious home of the community around Central.

Wm. H. Thomas, whose wife was a Maxwell, bought the Barnes home and he and his family continued the ownership until the recent death of him and his son, Simeon. This was a very fine family, possessing a good property, and were very useful and much loved.

Rev. B. L. Selman, now a retried minister living at Georgiana, was raised in the neighborhood of Sockapatoy, where some of the family have lived from the early settlement of the country. He received much of his schooling at Washington Academy. Soon after reaching manhood he entered the ministry of the M. E. Church, South. His life was earnestly and successfully devoted to winning people for Christ. He stood well with his denomination, and was faithful to every trust reposed in him, until failing health, rather than advanced age, demanded his retirement.

Rev. A. G. Raines

Just before the war, news came into Coosa of a young Baptist preacher of wonderful power, who lived in Tallapoosa County. When the war closed he came into Coosa County in the neighborhood of Concord church. This was A. G. Raines. His antecedents are unknown to the writer. He had, from the first, all the churches he could serve and so continued to have for a number of years. He did not marry for some years, devoting himself to the care of his widowed mother, and an invalid sister. His ability at the time justified his reputation; but he must have sprung full armed into his noble calling, for the promise of his early days was not met by subsequent development. He remained, however, a strong useful preacher, until some fifteen or twenty years ago, when he assumed an attitude of hostility toward some of the organized work of the denomination. In the conflict growing out of it, he became soured, and for years has lived largely in seclusion from the denomination.

Near 1870, he married a daughter of Robert Massey, a prominent farmer in the western part of Coosa. He soon settled on a farm near Providence church, where he has ever since lived. A family of several children were offspring of this marriage.

Robert Massey came to Coosa in the early fifties from Georgia. His wife was of the family of Bazemores who early settled in Coosa, and were always among its best and most useful citiens. Massey was never an officer in the county, but always active in her Masonic, religious, and civil affairs. He had a wife and strong influence. He reared a large and highly respected family of children. The writer regrets not being able to say more of them, and his want of dates. But it would be wrong to close the sketch without mentioning a son, Dr. A. J. Massey, a dentist of extensive practice in various parts of the county and for years an esteemed resident of Rockford. He has been a dentist of good practice for nearly twenty years in Birmingham, but resides in Woodlawn. His wife was Miss Eugenia, daughter of David Lawson and wife. She is noted for her domestic virtues, her fine practical sense, and a mind far above the average for its strength, depth, and quickness of perception. She is a very devoted Christian, always found in the front rank of active church workers. They have raised a large family. Several of the daughters are married to men prominent in life where they live, and likely to be known much more widely. One son is a dentist, associated with his father, and all boys give great promise of great usefulness. Each of these, Raines, Robert Massey, and Dr. Massey, were splendid Confederate soldiers.

GEN. JAMES THADDEUS HOLTZCLAW

James T. Holtzclaw came with his father from Chambers County in the forties, a boy, and lived here until entering the office of Elmore and Yancey. He deserves a place in the history of Coosa, and the county feels honored in recognizing him as one of her sons.

He was born December 17th, 1832, at McDonough, Henry County, Ga. He died in Montgomery, Ala., July 18th 1893. His father was Elijah Holtzclaw, born near Washington, Wilkes County, Ga. In Coosa he owned a farm and mill on Hatchesofka Creek. He was a soldier in the Mexican War. His parents were Timothy Holtzclaw and his wife, Elizabeth, a daughter of John and Martha M. Bledsoe of Wilkes County, Ga.

Jacob Holtzclaw was the first American ancestor, and the great-great-grandfather of the subject of this sketch. Jacob Holtzclaw's native place was Misen, Bavaria, Germany, and he belonged to one of the twelve families who emigrated to America in 1714, through the efforts of Baron Christopher De Graffenried, at the instance of Alexander Spottswood, then governor of the Virginia colony. He and his companions settled near the fork of the Rappahannock River, in what is now a part of Fauquier County, Va., where they obtained large grants of land from Governor Spottswood. They founded a town there which they called Germania. The court of records of Fauquier County contain a copy of the will of Jacob Holtzclaw, probated February 29th, 1760.

James Holtzclaw largely obtained his education at the High School of the Presbyterians, at Lafayette, Ala. He entered the law office of John A. Elmore and William L. Yancey in Montgomery, Alabama, in 1854, as a law student. In 1855 he was admitted to the bar, and began the practice of law which he continued, in Montgomery, until the time of his death, with the exception of the period spent in the military service of his country. He was appointed an Associate Railroad Commissioner in February 1893, serving as such till his death in the following July.

His service as a Confederate soldier began in 1861, when, as first lieutenant of the "True Blues," he went under orders of Gov. Andrew Moore, with his company, to Pensacola, and assisted in the capture of the Navy Yard, Ft. Barrancas, Light House, and other public property. On the organization of the 18th Ala. Regt., in August, 1861, he was made Major of the Regiment. He was promoted to the Lieutenant Colonelcy in the following December. He was in command of the Regiment at Shiloh, and led it gallantly in that battle, until severely wounded. On recovering from his wounds he returned to the command of his regiment as Colonel, having been promoted, and his commission bearing date from the battle. Most of the time, from the latter part of 1862 to the close of 1863, he was in command of a brigade at Spanish Fort, near Mobile. Early in 1864 he received his commission as Brigadier General, which rank he held until the surrender of his Brigade at Meridian, Miss., in May 1865. He was actively engaged in the Battle of Shiloh, Chickamauga, Lookout Mountain, Missionary Ridge, Nashville, Franklin, and Spanish Fort. He was very brave and had confidence of his men so they were ready to go or follow wherever ordered. The writer remembers more than once, his handling of men in battle with such coolness and bravery as to add greatly to the admiration and love of one whom he had long loved and admired.

Politically he was a Democrat. He took a warm interest in the campaigns of 1857-59, in Coosa, and the writer is under obligation to him for very efficient support in those campaigns. He was chairman of the Democratic Executive Committee of Montgomery County from the days of "Reconstruction" to the return of power to the hands of Alabamians, under Geo. Houston, as governor. He was delegate to the National Democratic Convention in 1868; District Presidential Elector in 1876; and Presidential Elector in 1888.

He was not a member of any church, but his sympathies and contributions were to the M. E. Church, South, though his father and family were Baptists.

He was made a Master Mason in 1863, at Mobile, but removed his membership in 1865, to Montgomery; became a R. A. M. in 1867 and a Knight Templar in 1869. He was Grand Commander of the Knights Templar in Alabama from 1885 to 1886. He was buried with Masonic honors in Oakwood Cemetery, where his remains await the resurrection of the dead.

He married Miss Mary Billingslea Cowles in Montgomery, April 10th, 1856. She was the daughter of Dr. John A. and Mrs. Lucy White Cowles, who was the daughter of David White, of Mobile.

He left only one child, Miss Carrie Whiting Holtzclaw, who married John A. Kirkpatrick, a lawyer, January 6th, 1881. They now live in Montgomery, having an only daughter, a most estimable and highly esteemed young lady who is a great favorite with the "Old Confederates." Mrs. Kirkpatrick takes an unflagging interest in whatever promotes the honor of the old Confederate cause and its soldiers.

CAPT. REUBEN JORDAN

Among the early settlers of Coosa and one of its public spirit·ed men was Capt. Reuben Jordan. If not himself born in Virginia his family were Virginians and claimed descent from Pocahontas, the princess daughter of Powhatan, who did so much for Virginia in the preservation of the life of Capt. John Smith, who alone seemed capable of protecting and planting the colony of early settlers. The given names of Reuben's father and grandfather are not known to the writer. The grandfather Jordan married a Miss Maurice of Virginia, by whom he had only one son, the father of Reuben. The grandfathers on both sides of the house were Revolutionary soldiers.

Reuben's father married Miss Bettie Elmore, a sister of General Elmore, the progenitor of the illustrious family of Elmores whose lives are so closely interwoven into the history of Alabama. Reuben with his father moved to South Carolina where Reuben grew up to manhod and became captain of a company of South Carolinians, in the War of 1812.

In 1818, Reuben moved from South Carolina to Montgomery County, Ala., just below Wetumpka, bringing his wife, a Miss Dillard, with the children, negroes and a good many negroes of his uncle Elmore for whom he was to make a crop preparatory to the future coming of the uncle to Alabama. Where he settled on the river was so malarial that after some years he moved to Autauga. Here he remained until the Spring of 1835, when he moved to and settled the place afterward owned by Reuben Maxwell.

By his first wife, Miss Dillard, he had five children, John A., James A., Lucinda P. Mary E. and Pocahontas. John A. became a prominent physician in Alabama, and moved to Texas before the Civil War, where he added to his medical reputation. He left a son and two daughters.

James A. married a daughter of Nathan Bozeman, by whom he had three sons, Reuben, James, and Thomas. His wife dying, he married in 1851 as a second wife, Miss Ann H. Brewer, daughter of Rev. A. G. Brewer, by whom there were six sons, Brewer, William, Charles, Samuel, Archibald, and John, and three daughters, Kate, Sallie, and Ora.

Dr. John's son was a Confederate soldier, and lost by wounds the use of one arm. James Jordan and his eldest son were Confederate soldiers and the son, Reuben, died just at the close of the war, of sickness contracted while in service.

Of the daughters of Mr. Jordan, Miss Lucinda first married a Mr. Archer Cain of Wetumpka, two sons of whom, Elisha M.

and McDuffee, with their children, are still residents of Wetumpka and Montgomery.   After the death of Mr. Cain she married
Dr. F. B. Benson, long known and loved in Autauga and Wetumpka as a physician.   By this marriage there were two daughters,
one became the wife of John Fitzpatrick, son of Gov. Benj. Fitzpatrick, who recently died at Elmore Station; and the other married Mr. Wm. Zeigler.   Miss Mary E. married Judge Benson, a
brother of the doctor, and he was for years Judge of Probate of
Autauga County.   From this marriage there is now one son in
Chicago, a daughter that married Hon. A. W. Rucker of Elmore
County, another that married D. B. Booth of Prattville, another
D. C. Campbell, and another E. A. Stevens.

The other daughter, Pocahontas, did not live to maturity.
She, as was the case with some others in the family, showed the
Indian descent plainly, and her name was given accordingly.
While the Indians were neighbors to Mr. Jordan they used to
claim the child as theirs and teased Mrs. Jordan by taking it up
and starting off with it, saying they were going to take it home
where it belonged.

A brother of Mr. Jordan once lived in the county, who looked
more like an Indian than a white man and possessed Indian traits
as well.

Mr. Jordan's first wife died and he married a second time in
1830, Miss Ann, a daughter of Aaron Spivey, near Rocky Mount
in Autauga County.   By this marriage there were three children,
Reuben E., Alabama R., and a daughter who married Dr. John A.
Mitchell, a distinguished physician both in Alabama and Georgia.
His son, Reuben A. Mitchell, has long been prominent in commercial manufacturing, and other business circles in Alabama.
Though never seeking office, he has been prominent in political
circles as well.   His wife is a daughter of Judge Fern Wood, one
of Alabama's prominent lawyers and codifiers.

Dr. Mitchell also had a son, John, who bore a commission in
the Army of the United States.

There was a daughter, Miss Lizzie, who never married.

Reuben E. Jordan became a good physician, but died too early to make the name he doubtless would have done.

Miss Alabama became the second wife of Mr. Frank Maxwell, by whom she had several sons and one daughter. Among the sons, two, Wm. and Cecil, are physicians who are doing well in the county where they were reared. Meigs is a capitalist in Seattle, Washington; and Eugene is a citizen of Texas. The location and pursuits of the others are not known to the writer.

When hostilities were threatened between the Indians and whites in 1836, Mr. Jordan moved his family to the fort prepared at Sockapatoy; but not feeling that safety was assured here he soon carried them to Wetumpka. When quiet was restored he came back to Coosa, and settled at the place near the Camp Ground, where he continued to live until his death in 1840, and where the family lived, until one by one they had scattered, finding other homes of their own.

The family are thus shown to have participated largely in the wars of the country, furnishing several soldiers of the Revolution, some of the War of 1812, and a number in the War Between the States.

The widow of Mr. Jordan died in Coosa County in 1888. The family were Methodists.

AARON AND EPHRIAM SPIVEY

These two men may well be associated with Jordan, for much of their lives were blended with the same scenes in the early settlement of Alabama and Coosa County.

Both of the Spiveys were born in Virginia (date unknown). Their father, Aaron Spivey, was a soldier in the Revolutionary Army, and so was his son, Aaron Spivey, Jr., of this sketch, who carried the marks of a wound inflicted by a British officer to his grave.

The Spiveys moved from Virginia to North Carolina, and from there came to Autauga County in 1818, settling between Robinson Springs and Rocky Mount. The writer has been to the old home where for years the elder Aaron Spivey lived and where he died in 1835. The same year, 1835, Aaron, Jr., and Ephriam together with Mr. Jordan moved to Coosa and settled a few miles above Nixburg. They and the Jordans soon had a Methodist Church, and it was here the Camp Meetings were held. As this was a good section of the country, and the Indian town of Fish Pond not far off, they had quite a number of Indian neighbors with whom they lived in peace and pleasantness, except for the brief period of alarm arising from the killing of Mr. Suttle.

They were good and substantial citizens, never seeking office, but doing well their duty, extending and receiving the generous hospitality so characterizing that period.

The old home still stands, a land mark of the past. Aaron Spivey died here in 1840, a Revolutionary pensioner. There was another Revolutionary pensioner at this time. Mr. Wm. Casey, who died in the fifties in what is now Elmore, then Autauga County, at the home of his son-in-law, Mr. Richardson. He left one son, Micajah Casey, who dwelt among the Indians of Coosa until he became somewhat expert in the Indian language, acting as interpreter and who was a useful citizen. He married Miss Elizabeth, a daughter of Dr. John S. McDonald, by whom he had one son, Robert Casey, and two daughters, Priscilla and Florence. His widow afterward married a Mr. Benjamin Manning. They settled several miles east of Rockford, and there reared a large family of useful men and women. He died soon after the war, but Mrs. Manning lived till quite a recent period.

JOHN D. LETCHER

While never seeking nor filling any offices except minor ones such as road reviewer, road overseer, magistrate's office and perhaps commissioner, John D. Letcher was yet widely known throughout the county as a man of public spirit active in whatever was promotive of the public good, and a most worthy citizen.

His family were Virginians, but emigrated to Edgefield, S. C., where John D. was born. His grandfather was Joseph Letcher, who was killed by the Tories during the Revolutionary War. Giles Letcher was the father of John D. He came to Coosa County and settled in the country between Nixburg and Sockapatoy as early as 1833 or 1834. He married Miss Ann Matilda, daughter of Nathan Bozeman, about 1836. Letcher moved from the Sockapatoy country down to the neighborhood afterwards called Central Institute, perhaps in 1840. They lived here until long after the War Between the States and until after all their children had established homes of their own. They had ten children, the eldest of whom was Dr. Francis Marion Letcher, who has been a practicing physician near Cross Keys, Alabama, most of the time since the late war. He married a widow Clanton whose maiden name was Howard. They have raised six children who are still in Macon or Montgomery counties. The doctor had a fine practice and accumulated a good property. His family are all Baptists.

Several of Mr. Letcher's family went to Texas. One son did a fine practice as a physician in Dallas. One daughter married Mr. Davis who was a gunsmith and did good work in that line during the war.

Several of Mr. Letcher's sons were in the Confederate army and did good service.

Mr. Letcher was one of the Trustees of the Central Institute as long as it belonged to the Baptists. The old couple, Mr. and Mrs. Letcher, were always beloved by all who knew them. They retained their freshness and vigor longer than most who live to their age. Both lived to be ninety or more, and when seen by the writer since the 20th century began, they were both sprightly in body and mind for those approaching centenarianism. Both have at last passed over the river, full of years and good works.

Henry, or Harry, Macon

In the early settlement of Coosa came Henry Macon from Georgia and settled on the Jackson Trace road, above George Taylor and Howell Rose, about five miles north of Wetumpka. His father was a soldier in the Revolutionary War, and Henry was one in the War of 1812. He was a native of North Carolina, and his wife was a Miss McDaniel of Georgia and an aunt of the McDaniel who afterwards became governor of the State.

He had two sons, John Awsley, and Pleasant Awsley, as he was called, opened a farm in the Turnpike road, six miles above Wetumpka, where he spent his life in successful farming and stock raising. He reared a large family, and one son still owns the old farm, and lives there with his large and highly respected family. Some of the other children are still in Elmore and at Wetumpka. Pleasant was a well known citizen, and a good soldier in the 46th Regt. for some time, and then transferred to the cavalry service under Gen. Joseph Wheeler. Soon after the war he went west. The father and sons were well known in the county and took active interest in its affairs.

John Moon

Though not one of the early settlers of the county, John Moon became a citizen aboot 1855, coming from Georgia into Alabama, and settled about seven miles above Wetumpka. His father, John P. Moon, was a native of South Carolina, but moved to Harris County, Georgia, before the War of 1812, of which he was a soldier. He was a Baptist, and in the split, went with the Primitives. John was a Missionary Baptist, and in Coosa, a member of Antioch church. He was a true Confederate soldier. His wife was a daughter of John J. Burkhalter, a native of South Carolina who became one of the early settlers of Coosa, where he spent most of his life, and sleeps in her soil. John Moon died in 1871, fifty-four years of age.

T. P. Moon, a son of John Moon, grew to manhood in Coosa, and married a daughter of H. Mourning Holly, who was a son of

John Holly, a native of North Carolina. Mourning Holly was a native Georgian, but came early to Coosa, settling near Buyckville, and raised a large and highly respected family, most of whom are still around in Elmore and Wetumpka. T. P. Moon lived till a few years past in the vicinity of Lebanon church of which he and his wife were both members. He was a successful farmer; accumulated a good property by industry and economy. Some years back he was ordained to the ministry by his church. He has not devoted much of his time to the pastorate. He now lives at Wetumpka, and he and his family are much esteemed for their religious worth and sterling characters. His oldest son, John P., succeeding to the name of the first born son of the Moon family, is a successful and highly esteemed physician and druggist at Wetumpka, where most of the family now live. He and the rest are Baptists.

WILLIAM H. JOHNSON

William H. Johnson, who lived for many years an upright and honorable life in the neighborhood of the Providence Methodist church, north of Buyckville, was a son of James G. Johnson, who was born and raised in Autauga County. He was the son of William Johnson, a soldier of the Revolutionary War. He came from Tennessee to what afterward became Autauga County about the beginning of the nineteenth century. The family were the same to which Gen. Albert Sidney Johnson belonged, the celebrated Confederate soldier who lost his life so inauspiciously at the Battle of Shiloh. W. H. Johnson married a daughter of Vine Smith, a very early settler of Coosa, who established the well known Smith's Ferry across the Coosa River before Coosa was organized as a county. The ferry still remains in the family, being owned by Mr. Higgins, a son-in-law of Smith.

Wm. Johnson was raised about Wetumpka, where his father died in 1856. His mother and sisters still lived in the old home until one by one they died after the close of the Confederate war. William was a soldier in the 46th Ala. Regt., where he was faithful to every duty. Andrew Collins, a sergeant in the same regiment, and a brother to the gallant Lieut. John H. Collins, married a daughter of Wm. Johnson, from which union has sprung a family of most excellent citizens of Elmore County. One son, Lafayette Johnson, married the youngest daughter of David Lawson, Mary Fannie. He has for many years been in mercantile life in Montgomery. He has been a useful citizen, and has raised an estimable family of sons and daughters. Another son, J. H. Johnson, is a resident of Equality, and County Superintendent of Coosa.

William Johnson, Andrew and John Collins are always associated in the mind of the writer, because they were substantial citizens of the same community, gallant soldiers of the same regiment, and each high minded and honorable. Religiously they were Baptists. Lieut. John Collins was a gallant and most efficient officer, and because of his fitness was often detached from his company to other commands. After Adjutant Brooks was disabled by wounds, and acting Adjutant McFarland was killed at Jonesboro, Lieutenant Collins was made acting adjutant of the 46th Regiment. They are now all dead, but have left the heritage of a good name as soldiers and citizens to their children and country.

MISCELLANEOUS

The following names are of families that deserve a more extended notice than can be given for want of information. There are a number of other families whose names do not appear in these pages because the memory of the writer does not recall them except in a shadowy way.

In the Traveler's Rest beat, on the Trace, lived James Lykes, in a pretty and comfortable home. He owned the Lykes Mill on Big Wewoka, where the Trace crosses it. It has long stood, doing the grinding for several generations of people. It is now owned by James Willett, a son-in-law of Calvin Humphries. Willett was an excellent soldier of Co. A., 46th Ala. Regt., who by industry and attention to business has accumulated a good property, and been a most excellent citizen. He has a brother, William Willett, now near Shreveport, La., who was also a fine soldier in the same command, who has the most wonderful memory of anyone known to the writer. He could, just a few years since, call from memory the name of every man in the compnay, and tell in what battle each member of the company was killed or wounded—where each one died—and who and where any deserted. At last information, he was preparing a history of the company. Lykes was of Dutch descent from the early settlers of Alabama. He was a nice, cultured gentleman, a good Christian, member of the Methodist E. Church. He was very hospitable. He had several children. His son, John, was for a time a merchant at Wetumpka.

Living in the same section was James Willis, a man of good property, fine address, and in every way a most estimable gentleman and citizen. He raised a company for Confederate service from Coosa, and carried it out as captain. It was not long, however, until he resigned and came home. He was soon ordained to the ministry by his church. He was a Baptist.

Dr. Davie of Buyckville was an excellent physician, a gentleman of fine address and large influence. He was a native of South Carolina. His wife was a daughter of Captain McKenzie, Scotchman of fine physique, a strong and cultivated mind. In the opinion of the writer, he bore a commission in the British Army before coming to America. He was also the father of the wife of Judge A. A. McMillan. Dr. Davie's eldest son, Willie, was a brave and efficient captain in the Confederate service.

Captain Cox, Sr., was a man of substantial property, living near Buyikville, and also was an owner of a mill on Wewoka. He earned his title as captain in the Indian war. He was a Georgian who came early into southeast Alabama where he taught, and was also a surveyor. He had sons and daughters who ranked in the community among the best for years. One son, Charles Cox, Jr., was a good soldier and a captain in the Confederate army. One daughter, Miss Fannie, married Dr. Ed. Wall, another Mr. Deloney, and another Mr. Watts, who died some years since at Rockford.

William Moore and William Dunlap lived near each other for years on the Turnpike, about a mile east of Buyckville, and were both good substantial citizens. But few men in this section live so long on one place as did Dunlap. For more than half a century he knew no other home than the one on the Pike. They were both Methodists.

Still further east of them, near Rogers' Mill lived Mr. Rawles, a substantial and useful citizen. He was an uncle of the wife of Col. W. H. Barnes, so long prominent in the State. One son, John, was a successful farmer on Hatchesofka Creek, and married a daughter of Robert Rogers, the owner of the mill known then as Rogers' and later as Williams'. Another son was Dr. Jabez, who settled at Buyckville, and who was killed there since the war. He was rather a brilliant man.

In the vicinity of Eclectic, during the fifties, there lived a very substantial farmer, Owen Swindall, who afterward lived close to Lebanon church, near Buyckville. He had several sons, the older of whom was educated at Central Institute in its palmy days, but whose history is unknown to the writer except that of Calvin, who married a daughter of that fine old citizen, Charles Gregory. He, Calvin, was a member of Company B. of the 46th Alabama Regiment. He was a brave soldier, and was made a sergeant by the commander of the regiment for conspicuous gallantry. After the war when somewhat advancing in life he was ordained to the ministry by his church, which was Baptist. He was more profound than brilliant, and being owner of a good farm, he gave himself more to that, so did not rise to prominence in the ministry. He was highly esteemed for his solid worth. He once represented Elmore in the House. He has a son, Osee Swindall, who is a minister of much power in the pulpit, and of such attractive characteristics as to bind those who know him very closely to him. He has attained to a good position in the Baptist ministry of the State. His history belongs to Elmore rather than Coosa, but the father and grandfather belonged to Coosa, and their relation was severed by the formation of Elmore from so much of Coosa.

Another good substantial farmer about the same vicinity as Swindall, was Uriah Williams, who was a fine citizen, a good Christian of the Baptist faith. He had a family who were highly esteemed. One of his sons, Milton Williams, was a fine soldier of Company B., 46th Alabama Regiment, who was also promoted for gallantry, and made a fine officer. Since the war, he and his excellent wife have prospered, and raised a fine family of children, most of whom with the parents live about in Elmore County. Another son, Ed. Williams, succeeded well as a farmer and owned a good body of land about Central. Of late years he does not seem to have prospered so well.

Abram Calloway and wife lived just below Central and were for a long while among the leading spirits of the country for good. His oldest boys finished their schooling at Central Institute, and were very promising young men. They had not time to develop into what was expected of them before the exigencies of the Confederacy called them to the army, where they did well their duty. After the war was over, like the rest of the noble sons of the South, they set in to build up the ruins of the land. Slow progress was made, during the days of "Reconstruction" (better called "Destruction"); and while these days were pending, the family went west, and more of their history is not known. He was a Baptist and a trustee of Central Institute.

Major Pevy lived between Central and Eclectic from an early period, and continued there until his death which did not occur until a good while after the war. The writer is sorry that he does not know more of him for he was a man of fine reputation, beloved of his neighbors. His title was perhaps obtained by rank in the militia. He was a pious member of the Methodist church. One of his sons has taken good rank in the Methodist ministry of the State.

Among those prominent in the history of Coosa is Hon. Thomas Williams, the son of the Rev. J. D. and his wife, Mary (Johnson) Williams. Rev. John D. Williams was born in Granville County, N. C., in 1800, and Mrs. Williams was born in Greenville County, Va., in 1796. They settled in Wetumpka in 1834, having a good property, but the bulk of which was lost in the strenuous times commencing in 1837. Mr. Williams died in 1871, Mrs. Williams died in 1880, aged 93. Thomas Williams' great-grandfather was Thomas Williams, a sturdy Welshman, and a Revolutionary soldier who was killed at the Battle of King's Mountain.

Owing to loss of property on the part of his father, the educational advantages of Mr. Williams were interrupted by the need of his work on the farm, after the removal of his father to the Elkahatchee neighborhood. But after growing up he made money enough to pay his way through the East Tennessee University, and at twenty-seven years of age was admitted to the bar where he made a success, for 22 years. He was a regular attendant at all the courts at Rockford until some years after the formation of Elmore County, and to almost the time of abandoning the profession to look after his large farming interest.

He married Miss Rebecca Judkins, the daughter of John C. Judkins, and sister of James Judkins, for some years a law partner. They had six sons, Robert, William Yancey, Sampson Harris, Harry L., Thomas J., and Seth Storrs, and two daughters, Jennie, the wife of Peter Buyck, and Mary Johnson. He had a roomy and quite attractive home at New Georgia, about two miles north of east Wetumpka. His home was a large, roomy, and attractive one, which was burned in 1891 with nearly all its valuable and useful contents.

He held no office, nor sought one while connected with Coosa, nor did he ever seem to desire office. But in 1878, without his knowledge or consent he was nominated and elected to Congress, and was twice re-elected.

He did not unite with any church until one summer, while a member of Congress, and taking summer rest at Biloxi, Miss., he was converted at the Methodist camp-meeting, and became a member of that denomination.

He was a large hearted and very liberal man in his controbutions to any worthy cause, and very genial in his nature. He died a few years since (1913) in Wetumpka, loved by all those who knew him. He was at one time the largest landholder in Elmore, and one of its most extensive planters.

Neil Smith Graham was another prominent man of Coosa for a number of years. He was of that considerable number of North Carolina Scotch Presbyterian settlers who, from an early period, had much to do with the formation and development of Coosa. His father was John G. Graham, who came to Alabama from North Carolina in 1819, settling first in Autauga County, but moving to Coosa soon after its organization. He bought a large farm a few miles north of Nixburg, and built a large and beautiful home. This home was, after him, occupied by his son-in-law, Boling Hall, once a member of the House from Autauga; and still later by the wealthy John Goldthwaite, a brother to Judge George Goldthwaite. Smith Graham, as he was usually called, was born in North Carolina in 1818, and the next year, with his father, was moved to Alabama. His mother was a sister of Malcom Smith, who came to Autauga about the same time that Graham came; and moved to Coosa about the same time with him. Smith G. was educated at Princeton College, N. J., and began the practice of law in 1841. He soon had a good practice, and was a regular attendant upon the courts held at Rockford, having a part in many of the cases tried, both civil and criminal.

In 1851, he and Henry W. Cox were the chosen representatives to the House of what was known then as the "Fire-Eating" party, growing out of the intense feeling of the South at what it esteemed the unjust course of the majority in Congress in the management of the California question, together with its attitude toward the other territory secured from Mexico. The race was exciting, and Graham and Cox won by a very small majority over George Johnson and A. B. Nicholson, a prominent man for years living in the valley of Hatchett Creek, above Goodwater. Graham was again elected to the House in 1855, with George Taylor, defeating Col. Joseph Braford and George Johnson. In 1856 he moved to Tuskegee, associated with Mr. Abercrombie in practice.

He was later made Chancellor of the Middle Division, holding the position for a number of years, until removed by death.

William Graham, a brother of John G., came to Alabama about the same time, 1819, and settled in Montgomery County, of which he was County Judge for some years. In 1841 he moved to Coosa, thus adding to the number of those already numerous staunch Scotch citizens, so useful and respected for long series of years. But most of their descenants are now in other parts of the U. S.

In 1847, the year of the first session of the Legislature of Alabama at Montgomery, Judge Graham was elected State Treasurer, continuing to hold the office for ten years, loved and trusted by all. After his election as treasurer he bought a farm in Autauga, near Prattville, where he spent the remainder of his days, leaving behind him a noble set of sons and daughters.

Malcom D. Graham was another prominent son of John G. Graham and a brother of Neil Smith Graham. He was born in Autauga County in 1826, and with his father moved to Coosa in the thirties, where he grew to manhood. He was educated at the Transylvania University, and there also took the legal course. He began the practice at Wetumpka, and like the other lawyers of Wetumpka was a regular attendant at the courts at Rockford. He was a good lawyer with good capacity as a speaker. Like most of the Grahams, he was handsome, graceful, and manly in appearance and manner. The writer, who knew personally more than a dozen of the Grahams, does not remember to have seen so many finely finished, courtly, and handsome men out of any other family. The daughters were beautiful and cultured.

In 1853, he was elected Clerk of the House of Representatives over A. B. Clitherall. But the next year, 1854, he went to Texas. There, in 1858, he was elected Attorney General of the State. In 1860 he was on the Breckenridge electoral ticket for the state at large. He became a colonel of a regiment in the Confederate army early in the war, but he did not see much service, for, in 1862, he was elected to the Confederate Congress. He was captured and carried to Johnson Island in 1864, where he was kept a prisoner until the close of the war.   In 1866 he came back to Montgomery and entered upon a lucrative practice, because he was debarred from practice in Teaxs by the Federal authority then in control there.   He continued at Montgomery until his death.   One of his sons afterward became mayor of Montgomery.

Thus it appears that Coosa has furnished several eminent orators, one the peer of any; three members of Congress, Harris, Yancey, and Williams; two Secretaries of State, Garrett and Weaver; three State Treasurers, Graham, L. P. Saxon, and Crawford; seven Clerks and Assistant Clerks of the House, and Secretaries of the Senate, Wm. Garrett, Joseph Phelan, Angernon Cook, and W. F. Couch of Wetumpka, 1841, Malcolm Graham, Samuel B. Brewer, and Elmore Garrett. two Speakers of the House, Garrett and Mason, besides a galaxy of men shining in other spheres.

Many of its people are plain, and know but little of the style that governs in cultured society, but as a rule they are warm hearted and hospitable, and give a hearty welcome to the visitor at the home, whether known or unknown.   Up to the time the writer's intimate acquaintance ceased there was better church discipline maintained, and a better moral bearing among church members, as a general rule, than prevails in many other parts of the country.

The population of Coosa in 1860, the last census before the war, was 14,044 white and 5,223 blacks.   The census of 1870, the first after Elmore was cut off, was 8,544 whites, and 3,394 blacks.   By the census of 1890 there were whites 10,552, blacks 5,353.   The total population in 1900 was 16,144.   The assessed value of property in 1870 was $943,875.   In 1900 it was $1,194,-801.

NEWSPAPERS PUBLISHED IN COOSA COUNTY

NEWSPAPERS PUBLISHED AT WETUMPKA

A History of Coosa would not be complete without something about the papers published at Wetumpka, for these had much to do in bringing the place to the attention of the public, and in moulding public opinion. Some connected with these papers left their impress deeply upon the memory of those times, and had much to do in making Coosa take rank among the leading counties of the State. In the introduction of this matter it is proper to copy an editorial notice from a leading paper of the leading city of the State.

The Commercial Register of Mobile, under date of March 20th, 1835, says: "We have received two numbers of a new paper published at Wetumpka, a village which has sprung into existence within the last few months. The paper is called *The Times* and is published by Henry Lyon." A further quotation is taken from the same editorial which shows the condition of Wetumpka at the time, and will be interesting reading to those who have only known the place since it became one of the prominent business points of the State. The writer would say in this connection, that the prediction contained in the quotation, that "in a very few years it (Wetumpka) will be second in importance to no town on the Alabama except Montgomery," was more than fulfilled before the close of 1838. For Wetumpka was not then second to Montgomery, but more than her peer in business and population.

It was a number of years before Selma overtook it. The editor further says: "The village of Wetumpka is another of those wonderful creations which are the results of American enterprise, and with which our country abounds. Its history is briefly told. Two years ago its site was a wilderness. The attention of a few individuals was attracted by its favorable location for business, and it now numbers 1,200 inhabitants—has an academy, two churches, three public houses, twenty-two respectable stores, and a printing office. We are not informed of the quantity of cotton it sends to market, but it already amounts to several thousand bales, and in a very few years it will be second in importance to no town on the Alabama except Montgomery."

This paper, *The Times,* was commenced the first of March 1835, by Henry Lyon. While there are no old files of the paper to be found, and sources of information are meagre, it is believed to have had a continued existence, and for sometime was partly owned and edited by Mr. M. B. Simpson. He was a Scotchman, a good writer, and a popular man. He was prominent in Wetumpka, taking part in every affair of interest to the public. He was a partner in the marble works of the place. For some months, owing to paralysis, he edited the paper from home. The name had been changed from *The Times,* to *The Wetumpka Argus and Sentinel.* Soon after the sale of the paper to the Yanceys, Mr. Simpson died at Wetumpka, at the age of 33. James M. Simpson, his son, has been a bookkeeper at Tallassee and Montgomery for more than thirty years; and now is commandant of soldiers' home of Mountain Creek.

Just after the paper entered its fourth volume it was bought by William L. and B. C. Yancey, who continued its publication from May 15th, 1839, under the name of *The Wetumpka Argus and Commercial Advertiser.* The first issue by them was Vol. 4, No. 8. They dropped the latter part of the name and called it *The Wetumpka Argus,* February 19th, 1840.

About a year from that time Yancey offered the paper for sale by advertisement. Many protests against his retirement from the press came from the people and the press. They felt it would be a calamity to democratic interests of the section to withdraw his strong and lucid editorials and able correspondence from the public. Yancey's wish was to give himself entirely to the profession of law upon which he had entered. As illustrative of the feeling in reference to his severence from the press, the following from *The Democratic Herald* is a sample: "We hope that a sale of *The Argus* will not be effected. We have no desire to lose Mr. Yancey from the 'Corps editorial.' He fills the post too well, his services are too important to the Democratic party, he is too good and efficient a soldier to be parted with without regret."

March 23rd, 1842, he succeeded in leasing the paper to James W. Martin, who conducted it successfully until March 20th, 1844, when Mr. Yancey sold it to B. B. Moore. Moore also made a success of it, until in the early part of 1847, when he sold it to John Hardy and Mr. Stephens. They soon changed the name from *The Argus* to *The State Guard*. It continued to be published by Hardy with considerable ability. He was sometimes caustic in handling an opponent. When Samuel Beman, a half brother of Yancey, was elector for the district in behalf of Zachary Taylor, Hardy frequently assailed him in his paper. Beman stood it patiently until he made a fling at his personal deformity. Beman met him at the post office and gave him a caning, telling him he might attack him in his paper about matters that he was responsible for, but he would not suffer him or any other man to taunt him about a physical deformity for which not he, but God, was responsible.

Hardy published *The State Guard* as a daily from January 1st, 1849, to the close of the year. The file of that year is among the Archives in Dr. Owen's charge. It was changed to a tri-weekly the first of 1850, and published as such for sometime.

September 10th, 1852, Hardy sold to D. W. Dorsey and a Mr. Knight, who did not continue long with the paper. After his withdrawal the name was changed to *Dorsey's Dispatch*. Dorsey had before become pretty widely known as the keeper of the bar-room of the Montgomery Hall, the leading hotel of the city, by the uniqueness of his advertisements. He sold the paper to W. H. Benson, son of Nimrod E. Benson, so long land agent at Montgomery, July 17th, 1857. He called it *The Dispatch*. Later Samuel Dixon, and then James Porter edited it. Sometime during the war Willis Roberts bought it. While it existed it was a staunch supporter of the Democratic party. In the "fire-eating" period of 1851 it inclined to what was called the "Union Side."

Sometime in 1836, Rev. John D. Williams commencing the publication of a family and religious paper called *The Family Visitor*. This was bought by the Yanceys about the same time they purchased *The Argus and Sentinel*, and it was merged into *The Argus*.

Prior to 1839 a paper called *The Courier* had been started, but its founder is unknown. In 1839 it was under the control of Charles Yancey, a Virginian, who was for years in the publishing business at Wetumpka. *The Courier* and *Argus* were usually on opposite sides of most questions. Though thus opposed to each other, once the two papers agreed to insert the advertisements of both in each paper. But party feeling was so intense that those advertising objected to their advertisements appearing in the paper of the opposite party, so the two papers had to cancel their agreement.

In the spring of 1840 *The Argus* bought from Charles Yancey *The Courier*, and for a little while there was but one paper. But in May 1840, J. C. Bates and Charles Yancey started another paper called *The Alabama Times*, which represented the interests of the Whigs, whose candidate for president at that time was William Henry Harrison. *The Argus* was an ardent supporter of Martin Van Buren. Some sharp criticism of Charles Yancey appeared in the editorials of *The Argus*, because he was said to have violated the agreement when *The Courier* was purchased from him. The understanding was that Charles Yancey was not again to go into the paper business at Wetumpka. By December 1840, Bates had retired from *The Alabama Times*, and came to Montgomery, ably conducting, for a number of years, *The Montgomery Journal*, a leading Whig paper. Charles Yancey continued *The Alabama Times*, with a Mr. Randall as editor. Col. Thomas Williams says this Randall was a relative of Samuel J. Randall, once so prominent as a Democratic leader from Pennsylvania, and that he was an able writer. While no direct evidence is at hand, after Bates' retirement, the name of the paper must have been changed to *The Courier*, for *The Argus* in its issue of May 11th, 1842, said that D. C. Neal had become proprietor of *The Courier*, with H. A. Kidd as editor, and there is nothing indicating a third paper. The name and possession was evidently again changed to *The Wetumpka Whig*, and Charles Yancey again proprietor. This opinion is formed because the writer has seen copies of *The Wetumpka Whig*, the first seen of which bears date November 13th, 1846, numbered Vol. 3, No. 20, and owned by Charles Yancey and edited by W. Wilkins. Wilkins' name, as editor, disappears in January 1847. What finally became of this paper is not known.

About January 1st, 1843, Rev. S. J. McMorris, a Universalist minister, who was long a resident of, and who died in Wetumpka, started a paper in Wetumpka advocating the doctrines of the Universalists. The paper was printed by Charles Yancey. The only copy of the paper seen by the writer was dated January 17th, 1845, and was Vol. 3, No. 3. How long the paper continued here is unknown, but it probably became *The Universalist Herald*, so long published and edited by Dr. John C. Burrus, at Notasulga.

July 1st, 1855, J. H. Martin of Columbus, Ga., started a paper in Wetumpka called *The Wetumpka Spectator*. *The Independent* of Gainsville, June 23rd, 1855, had this to say: "We-tumpka Spectator—A newspaper with this title is soon to be started at Wetumpka by J. H. Martin of Columbus. The paper will be devoted to the news of the day, will advocate liberal and impartial State Aid, and in politics, we believe, plants itself on the Georgia Union Platform. Mr. M. stands high among his brethren of the press, and we doubt not will make an excellent paper." It says, September 1st, 1855: "We have received several numbers of *The Wetumpka Spectator*, a new paper lately started by John H. Martin. The appearance is neat, and the editorials evince spirit. Mr. Martin seems to be in a fog as regards politics, but we classify him as a Know-Nothing. We wish him abundance of pecuniary success." In the latter part of 1855, Willis Roberts bought *The Spectator* from Martin, who returned to Columbus, Ga., and became editor of *The Columbus Enquirer*. Roberts continued the paper, with George L. Mason as editor most of the time. For awhile Sidney McWhorter and Osceola Kyle were editors. Roberts edited it himself awhile. In April 1866, Elmore County having been formed, the name was changed to *The Elmore Standard*, with George Mason as editor. He died May 2nd, 1867, regretted by a very large circle of admiring friends. Roberts sold the paper, October 25th, 1867, to Benjamin Trice, a practical printer who had been connected with the paper. The early part of 1868, Roberts went to Columbiana, and started *The Shelby Guide*. From there he went to Birmingham and established a publishing house, which he continued to his death, a few years since, and which is still continued by his son.

This is the best history of the papers published at Wetumpka before it became a part of Elmore that the writer has been able to get up after much research. Since the formation of Elmore, when Wetumpka lost its identity with Coosa, it is not incumbent to continue a history of its papers. But it may be briefly said that E. W. B. Bazer published for awhile a paper called *The People's Banner*. Mrs. Luckey, one called *The Wetumpka Videt*, with Mr. Wynn for editor. Screws and Oliver published *The Wetumpka Gazette*; R. T. Goodwyn, *The Reform Advocate*; G. A. B. Smith, *The Wetumpka Times*; and William Hunter, *The Wetumpka Herald*, which is now owned and published by H. R. Gholson.

There was no other paper published in Coosa until after the war of 1861-65.

The following are the papers published in Coosa since that time:

The first paper published at Rockford was *The Sentinel*, by A. L. and J. L. Watts. It was continued for two years, 1870-71.

In 1876 to 1878, *The Coosa News* was published at Goodwater, by Thomas Jordan and sons.

The Enterprise was launched in 1876 by S. J. Darby and J. H. Parker, lawyers of Rockford. Darby was afterwards solicitor for the Circuit of which Coosa was a part, for several terms. Parker became a prominent member of the bar at Rockford, and later of Wetumpka. He was a member of both the House and Senate and also of the Constitutional Convention of 1901. This paper had a continued existence for about thirteen years, extending to 1888. In 1880, Parker became sole owner. In April 1881, Wash L. Smith became owner. In January 1886, G. R. S. Smith, his son, became associated with his father. September 15th, 1887, J. H. Parker bought the interest of Wash L. Smith, and the paper continued until August 30th, 1888.

In November 1888 began the publication of *The Advocate*, without name of proprietor or editor, but on October 1st, 1891, the name of G. R. S. Smith appears as proprietor and editor. In January 1892, James O. Smith, son of Wash L. Smith, and later son-in-law of Gov. Wm. Samford, became both proprietor and editor. August 15th, 1895, James W. Batson became proprietor and editor, associating, as assistant editor, John J. Thornton. September 19th, 1895, O. P. Bentley, a son of Judge J. S. Bentley, and a lawyer of Goodwater, became proprietor and editor, and removed the paper to Goodwater. With the first issue of 1896, the paper appears under the auspices of a Printing Company with L .M. Bruce and William Chapman as editors. A change was made in January 1897, in which Henry M. Burns was editor, and Capt. C. M. Simpson was general manager, and the name was changed to *The Coosa County Advocate*. The issue of January 20th, 1898, shows a change in name to *Goodwater Advocate*, and Simpson and P. A. Jackson managers, and P. A. Jackson editor; this seems to have continued through to 1904.

The Goodwater Enterprise was started in 1904, with B. B. and W. H. Bridges as proprietors and editors, and has had a continued existence to the present, 1908.

A paper was started in the interest of the People's Party called *The People's Courier* at Rockford, in January 1900, by Henry Pond and sons; and was continued until 1907. Pond was a son of Judge Ebenezer Pond, and his wife was a daughter of Wm. A. Wilson, Miss Mattie. Pond is much better known by the name of "Dick" than "Henry." He and S. M. Suttle are the oldest residents of Rockford now living, each having spent their whole lives as citizens here. Both were good Confederate soldiers.

The End.

314

William 89,241
KARMINSKY 74
KEITH 62
  F.M. 146
KELLEY, James 91
  John B. 123
KELLY, 92
  Archibald 92
  C.A. 146
  Elias 103
  J.D. 156
  James 137,204,255
  John 44,103
  John B. 255
  Moses 50
  Shun 256
  T.A. 113
KENDRICK, 179,230
  (Miss) 220,221
  A. 77
  A.H. 123,178,203,270
  Anderson 242,270
  Anderson H. 123,242
  Julius 220,242
  Julius H. 147
KENDRICKS, 88
KENNEDY, Lewis 177
  Nancy 31,57
  Samuel 51,57
  Thomas 99
KIBBLER, 31,41,93
KIDD, 175
  H.A. 297
  Irby Q. 64
  Seaborn 86
KIGGKAH, James 52
KILPATRICK, Joshua 116
KIMBALL, Archibald 42
KIMBREL, Archibald 50
KIMBRELL, Archibald 87
KIMBROUGH, Benj. 256
  Benjamin 97
KING, 156
  Clinton 127
  F .M. 159
  Robert 102
  Thomas 98
  Thomas J. 155
  Wm.R. 16,69
KINNEY, Benjamin 139
  Bynum J. 138
KIRKLAND, Sion 139
KIRKPATRICK, 163
  (Mrs.) 9,278
  James 139
  John A. 278

Sanford L. 158
KNIGHT 29,35,174,296
  William 105,138,139,179
KYLE, 150,151,177
  O. 147
  Osceola 146,148,150,155,210,
  272,298
  Osee 54
  W.S. 195,198
  William 54
  William S. 62
  Wm. S. 179
LACEY, O.E. 62
LACKEY, William C. 126
LACY, 61,62
LAMBERT, M. 154
  Thomas 99,122
LAMB, Isaac 42,50,51,53
LANCASTER, 85
  W.L. 122
LANE, John 111
LANEY, Wm. F. 147
LARMA, Jimmy 51
LATTIKER 111
LAUDERDALE 31
  D.C. 161
  D.L. 161
  David 41
  John T. 152
  Joseph 94
  Josephus 41,42,94
  Robert 50,53,94
LAW, F.M. 229
LAWBY, Ellender 55
LAWLER, L.R. 58
LAWSON, 37,112,169
  David 111,112,231,244,275,286
  Eugenia 275
  Mary Fannie 286
  Matt 103,111
  Matt. 235
  William 111
LEAK, 62,228
LECROY, 95
LEDBETTER, 117
  J.W. 119
LEE, 121,157,158
  Frances (Pond) 116
  Henry 88,241,253
  Isom 117,191
  Isom L. 158
  James E. 139
  John 157
  John M. 158
  John N. 101
  Robert 116

William T. 157
MASTIN, Mary 268
   Wm. 63,85
MATHEWS, 97
MATHEWS, Sarah 256
MAURICE, (Miss) 278
MAXWELL, 274
   A.T. 246
   Allen 92,123,137,231,245,274
   Allen L. 245
   Allen Leonidas 247
   Allen T. 245
   Anna B. 245,248
   Annie E. 249
   Benjamin F. 245,248
   Cecil 281
   Cecil K. 249
   Charles M. 249
   Clarey A. 245
   Eugene 249,281
   Eugenus 245,250
   Francis M. 245,248
   Francis M., Jr. 249
   Frank 92,137,231,281
   J.C. 9,112,114,117,124,245
   Jacob C. 245,247
   Jessie M. 249
   Joel 245
   Julius P. 249,250
   L.P. 246
   Leila 245
   Lela 248
   Lewis 260
   Lovick P. 245
   Martha L. 249,250
   Mary V. 245,248
   Meigs 281
   Minnie E. 249,250
   Mittie L. 245,248
   Nancy E. 245,246,249
   Otis A. 249
   Perryman 156
   Reuben 92,137,231,245,248,249,
   250,260,279
   Reuben J. 249
   Reuben M. 249,250
   Sarah 245
   Sidney 249
   Susan Emma 249
   Susan M. 245
   Thomas 245
   Virginia 245
   William 245
   William E. 249
   Willis 137,231
   Willis M. 245,249,250

   Willis M., Jr. 249
   Wm. 281
MAYNARD, C.M. 149
MAY, W.F. 161
McADORY, 172
   Celia 93
   Jasper 9,96,164,260,273
   Mary Jane (BAKER) 93
   P. Jasper 260
   Robert 260
McALISTER, 230
   D.L. 120,159
   Lewis 117
McALPINE, 165
   Robert E. 220
McARNS, John 62
   M. 62
McBRAYER, W.A. 99
McCAIN, 175
   Henry 46
   T.U. 86
   T.U.T. 123,183,243,252
   Thomas U. T. 123
McCARY, Louisa 210
McCASSAIL, John D. 127
McCLAIN 191
McCLELLAND, 228
McCLOUD, 93
McCLUNG, H.C. 140
McCLURE, 110
McCOLLERS 107
McCONNEGHA, 62
McDONNELL, Felix G. 46
McCORD, Andrew 104
McCOY, Henry 154,207
McDANIEL, 284
   (Miss) 284
   (Mrs.) 117
   Daniel 115
   G.A. 42
   George A. 42,53
McDONALD, 109,237
   (Mrs.) 119
   Albert 115
   Carrie 118
   David 115
   Elizabeth 282
   George 115,116,117,
   119,192,240
   George B. 119
   J.S. 119
   James 115
   James L. 158
   Jno. S. 108,120
   John S. 43,47,115,127,282
   John S., (Mrs.) 108

Reuben A. 139,280
Thomas J. 153,158
MITSON, Sarah 258
MONK, 93
Joshua 41,43,50,51
MONTGOMERY, 70
Fannie Young 268
Jas. P. 139
MOODY, Theophilus 175
MOON, 105,231
John 284
John P. 284,285
T.P. 284,285
Tandy 105
MOONEY, 169
MOORE, 42,74,75,95,243
(Mrs.) 9,221
A.B. 83
Andrew 277
Andrew B. 147
B.B. 80,296
Eliza 244
M.G. 74,139
Mark E. 47,58,86,87,224,267
Mathew 217
Matthew 127
Obidiah 167
S.D.J. 189
William 105,138,288
William R. 126
Wm. 267
Wm. E.D. 224
Wm. M. 44
Wm. R. 44
MORGAN, Augustus, 242
Frank 112
Gus 88,113
John T. 54
Mary 8
Thomas 139
MORRE, B.B. 179
MORRIS, 189
J.E. 269
James 50
James B. 42,53,140
Jas. B. 50
Jessee 101
Nimrod 127
W.W. 45,54,61,62,70,77,115,123,
177,178,188,190,195
William 101
MORRISON, William 140
MOSELY, Thomas 113
MOSS, 94
MODD, William S. 189
MOLDER, 85

MURCHISON, 112,137,175
Rora 112,138
Rora, Jr. 113
William 112
MORPHY, 273
Joel 97
Mark 97
Virgil S. 152
William 97
MURRAY, Charles 95
MOSCOGEES, 16
MOSKOGEES, 14
MYERS, John J. 89
NABORS, J.H. 256
J.N. 123
Prior 93
NAPOLEON, 28
NARRAMORE, George W. 147
NASH, Geo. B. 93
Zachariah 139
NEAL, 68
D.C. 62,63,297
Elias H. 141
NESBITT, 115
NEWMAN, Larkin 98
NICHOL 85
NICHOLS, Joel 169
NICHOLSON, A.B. 31,93,178,179,291
NIX, 163,262
Absolom 50,51,53,58,88
Ambrose 50,88
Charles 41,42,50,53, 88
J.M.N.B. 58
William 52,53,88,139
NOGOCHEE, 58
NOLAN 175
William 176
Abner 242
Jack 242
R.S. 124,242
Richard S. 122,123,241
Stephen 242
W.J. 242
W.L. 242
William 176
NORRED, Henry 117
NORREL, Henry 104
NORTHROP, A. B . 63,64
NORTON, 168
Joseph 85,167
NORWOOD, 97
NUNNERY, Samuel 154
OCHUSYOHOLO , 58
ODEN, A.J. 271
Alice 9
John 252

REYNOLDS, Michael 42
RICE, 82
   S.F. 54
   William 205
RICHARDS 88,98
   W.A. 98
   William 53,89,126
   Wm. 42,44,53
RICHARDSON, 282
RIDGE, 13
RIGGS, 155,156
RIPETOE, A.H. 44
   Albert H. 58
   Harrison 46
ROACH, 68
ROBBINS, 217,260,262
   Adeline 257
   B.W. 258
   Benjamin 257,258,260
   Benjamin, Sr. 258
   Betsy 257
   Casina 258
   D.B. 258, 259
   Daniel 42,52,89,257,258,259
   Daneil A. 267
   Eliza 257,264
   Elizabeth 59,264
   Emeline 258
   George 88, 257
   George Washington 265
   H.R. 9,124,126,257, 258,259
   Howell R. 267
   J.W. 257
   Jane 221,257
   Joel 257,258
   John 257
   John W.- 264
   Kate 257
   Laura Virginia 265
   Martha 257,258
   Martha Ann 264
   Mary 266
   Mary Jane 264
   Peyton 88
   Putnam 257
   R.H. 257
   S.E. 258,259
   Sarah 258
   Sarah (WELLS) 260
   Sarah Adeline 265
   Solomon 31,40,41,44,52,58,87,88,
   90,126,217,232,244,254,257,258,
   260,261,272
ROBBINS, Solomon, Jr. 88,257,261,264
   Solomon, Sr. 258,266
   Thomas 88, 257

Thomas Clinton 265
Thos. 258
Thos. S. 265
W.J. 258
W.Kate 265
W.O. 258
Wm.O. 265
Wm. Peyton 265
ROBERTS, 299
   (Mrs.) 68
   W. 140
   William L. 159
   Willis 296,298
ROBERTSON, F.M. 154
   William T. 54
   Wm. 43,44
   Wm. F. 53
ROBINSON,32,37,88,97
   Benjamin 126
   G.T.L. 149
   H.H. 147
   Horatio 9
   Horiatio 147
   Leon 147
   Peter 92
   William E. 139
ROGERS, 35,46,87,165,169
   C.F. (Miss) 259
   David 188,231
   John 271
   Jonathan 271
   Joseph 108,140,231
   Mary 271
   Polly Mayes 271
   Robert 108,109,231,288
   Washington 87
   William 92,173
ROLLIN, Silas 139
ROPE, A.D. 157
ROSE, 32,187,188
   Howel 85
   Howell 27,123,178,186,200,254,
   284
ROSS, 13
   Geo. 99
   Howell 81
ROSSEAU, 100
ROWE, Daniel 44
   W.L. 245
RUCKER, A.W. 280
RUFFIN, 105
RUSH, Warren R. 152
RUSHING, Mary 254
RUSSELL 273
   James, 168
   James M. 272

James 50
James W. 58
Jas. B. 62
Jeremy 209
John 100
Joseph 125,214,236
Robert 100
Walter 151
Walter J. 147,150
Zachary 296
TEKELL, John 161
TEMPLE, Epps 88
        Henry 88
TEPEL, John 117
        Nipper 117
TERRELL, A.J. 62,122
THAXTON, Dixon S. 152
THOMAS 85,113
        Albert 95
        Allen 89
        Calvin 96
        Carney 96
        Dred 92
        E.W. 249
        John 41,94,95
        John H. 177
        McKinney 62,81
        Obed 99
        Patrick 150
        S.H., (Mrs.) 221
        Simeon 274
        Stephen 96
        W.H. 62,72
        William 86,231
        William H. 161
        Wm. H. 274
THOMPSON,63,93,169,187
        C.W. 242
        Daniel 97
        Daniel J. 99,123,155,239,255
        George 97,255
        J.L. 232,272
        J. T. 126
        J.W. 159
        James 99
        James L. 229
        John 85
        Robert 99,255
        Victory 50,53
        Virginia 255
        William 99
        William L. 159
THORNHILL, 88
        Edward C. 147
THORNTON, 175,252,253
        Elizabeth 245

John J. 300
Jordan 46,86
THRASHER 47,85
TILLMAN, Elizabeth 268
TIMMERMAN 168
        Benj. 167
        Benjamin 85
        Frederick 85
TINER, Charles H. 147
TIPPET, T.J. 126
TIPTON, John 16
TOMMY, C.C. 146
TOOMBS, Robt. 269
TOONEY, 38
TOPPONG, 140
TOWLES, James 175
TOWNS, 91
TOWNSEND, Annie 224
        Eliza 224,270 223
TOWNSEND, Hiram 224
        James 64
        Jared 53,85
        Jared B, 40,42
        Jarnett 53
        John 223
        John H. 46,110,219
        John H., (Mrs.) 234
        K.A. 140
        Kinchen A. 224
        Leonard F. 224
        Mary E. 224
        Paschal 223,272
        Philip A. 224
        Samuel 223
        William 85,140,223
        Wm. 223,267,272
        Wm. T. 224
TOWNS, Henry C. 138
TRAYLOR, Robert 139
TRICE, Benjamin 299
        Elisha 46
TRIMBLE, Benjamin 188
        James 62
        William 62
TUCK, 29,253
        Joseph 45,89
TULANE, 62
TURNER, (Miss) 220
        B. 53
        Simeon 53
TUSKALOOSA 13
UFALLA, 58
UNDERWOOD, John 31
UPSHAW, John 101
        W.J.D. 229,232
URQUIZA, 194

Sarah 261
WEST, 172
  J. T. 86
WHATLEY, W. V. 248
WHEELER, Joseph 284
WHETSTONE, 29,32,86,105,174,175
WHITE,   14
  Gabriel 94
  Richard 139
  William 85,91,94
WHITEHEAD, Absolom 52
WHITING, J.W. 147
WIDEMAN, 86
WIGGINS, 95
WILKERSON, 92
  James R. 156
WILKIE, Ollie 8
WILKINS, W. 298
  Wm. 16
WILKINSON 89
WILLBANKS 157
  J .H. 87
  James H. 156
WILLETT, 26,27,28,29,104
  J.E. 104
  J.L. 104
  James 244,286
  William 286
  Wm. 104,244
WILLIAM, 113
WILLIAMS, 42,288,290,293
  (Mrs.) 290
  Charles 41,42,50,126,139
  D. 46
  Ed. 289
  Eli 86,175
  Fletcher 86,175
  George M. 153
  Hillary 50,126
  J.D. 61,64,83,92,289
  James 41,43,50
  John D. 60,64,207,289,297
  Lamkin 50
  Larkin 50
  Mary 223
  Mary (JOHNSON) 289
  Milton 289
  N.B. 147
  R.C. 233
  Robert 63,207
  Thomas 9,52,54,62,68,206,207,
  289,290,297
  Uriah 86,289
WILLINGHAM, Isaac 97
  Robert 95
  Susan 256

WILLIS, 173
  James 287
  James M. 154
  John 272,273
  John, (Mrs.) 103
  Laura Ann 8
WILSON, 101,182
  Adolphus 151,238
  Benj. 267
  Benj. H. 166
  Benjamin 257,261
  E.E. 58
  Hugh 238
  Isacah 139
  Izer 267
  James 261
  Jessee 52,101,238
  Jessee M. 41,126
  Jno. D. 52
  John 238
  John D. 42,45,52,126,138,139
  L.M. 229
  Locuis M. 151
  Lucien 238
  Mary 261
  Mattie 238,300
  May 257
  W.A. 100
  Washington 116
  William 50
  William A. 50,101,103,124,126,
  158,238
  William B. 151
  Wm. A. 31,41,42,43,45,70,100,
  119,300
WILTON, 89,230,234
WINGATE, Seaborn 85
WINSLETT, William 42,92
WINSTON, Jno. A. 198
  John Anthony 149
WINTER, John G. 48,49
WITHERS, Jones M. 144,148
WOMBLE, John 233
  Judson 233
  Susie 233
  W.H. 117,233
  William 119
  Wm. 233
  Wm. H. 233
WOOD, 99, 100,121
  Allen 43,102
  Eason 154
  Eason B. 154
  Fern 280
  Mary 269
  Solomon 85,126

WOODRUFF, 62
      (Mrs.) 228
      C.J. 62,108
      Lorenzo 139,141
      L. 139
WOODS, M.L. 155
WOODY, 98
WORD, John J. 142
WORKS, 98
WORRELL, Kenchen 139
WRAY 196
WRIGHT, Elizabeth 251
      John 138
WYNN, 299
YANCEY, 80,141,187,196,197,198,276,293,
      295,296,297
      B.C. 141,193,194,195,199,295
      Benj. C. 68
      Benjamin C. 193
      Charles 69,297,298,
      W.L. 64,178,194,195,199
      William L. 48,54,62,68,76,122,123,
      177,189,277 ,295
      William Lowndes 195
      Wm. L. 77,80
YATES, Aaron 46
YOUNG, Bird 263
      W.E. 154
ZEIGLER, 32,62,113
      Ca tharine 251
      Maria 251
      Nicholas 251
      Wm. 280
ZIMMERMAN, Sarah 223

www.ingramcontent.com/pod-product-compliance
Lightning Source LLC
Chambersburg PA
CBHW031117020426
42333CB00012B/114